P9-DKD-758

BLAIRSVILLE SENIOR HIGH SCHOOL
BLAIRSVILLE, PENNA.

Time-Life   98-99

14024

WORLD WAR II

THE AMERICAN STORY

WORLD WAR II

by the editors of Time-Life Books, Alexandria, Virginia

CONTENTS

PACIFIC THEATER

A decade of Japanese expansion and aggression would eventually bring the island nation into conflict with the United States. The chronology below outlines the steps by which the two Pacific powers went to war.

SEPTEMBER 18, 1931 Japan begins occupation of Manchuria.

MARCH 27, 1933 Japan announces withdrawal from the League of Nations.

NOVEMBER 25, 1936 Anti-Comintern Pact signed by Japan and Germany.

JANUARY 19, 1937 Japan ends Washington Conference Treaty limiting the size of its navy.

JULY 7, 1937 Undeclared war between China and Japan begins.

DECEMBER 12, 1937 Japanese bomb the U.S. gunboat *Panay* on the Yangtze River.

JULY 25, 1940 United States puts a trade embargo on Japan.

DECEMBER 27, 1940 Japan joins Germany and Italy in the Axis alliance.

APRIL 13, 1941 Soviet Union and Japan sign neutrality treaty.

JULY 27, 1941 Japan occupies French Indochina.

NOVEMBER 17, 1941 Japan demands United States lift trade embargo.

DECEMBER 7, 1941 Japanese planes attack Pearl Harbor, Hawaii, base of the U.S. Pacific Fleet.

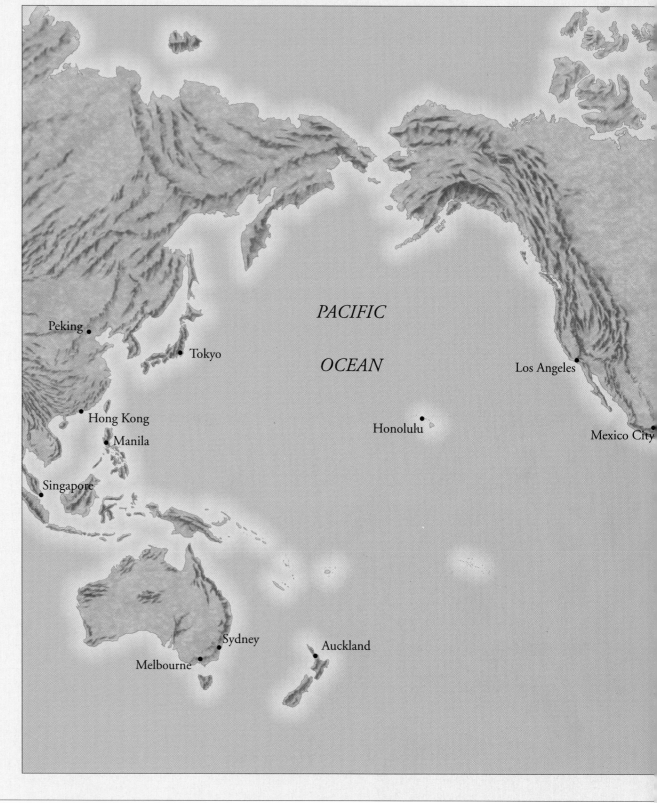

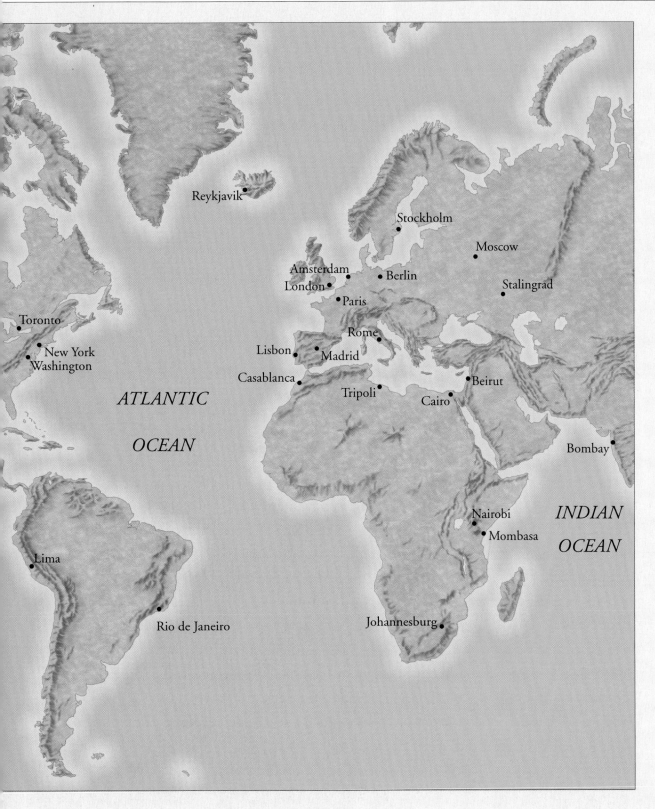

EUROPEAN THEATER

As shown below, in just eight years Germany would overrun much of Europe, from the Mediterranean to the Arctic Circle, and from the English Channel to the borders of Soviet Russia. By 1941 the Nazis were ready to take on the world.

JANUARY 30, 1933 Hitler becomes chancellor of Germany.

OCTOBER 14, 1933 Germany withdraws from the League of Nations.

MARCH 11, 1938 Germany annexes Austria.

SEPTEMBER 29, 1938 Munich Agreement cedes Czechoslovakia's Sudetenland to Germany.

MAY 22, 1939 Germany and Italy sign Pact of Steel.

AUGUST 23, 1939 Soviet Union and Germany sign nonaggression pact.

SEPTEMBER 1, 1939 Germany invades Poland.

SEPTEMBER 3, 1939 Britain and France declare war against Germany.

APRIL 9, 1940 Germany invades Denmark and Norway.

JUNE 22, 1940 France surrenders to Germany.

JULY 10, 1940 Battle of Britain begins.

MARCH 24, 1941 Germans attack the British in North Africa.

JUNE 22, 1941 Germany invades the Soviet Union.

DECEMBER 11, 1941 Hitler declares war on the United States.

ENCOUNTER IN THE ATLANTIC

When the presidential yacht *Potomac* motored north through the Cape Cod Canal on August 5, 1941, an official banner flying from its mast, vacationers on the banks of the waterway were delighted to catch sight of a convivial group gathered on the afterdeck. To all appearances, their 59-year-old president, Franklin D. Roosevelt, was enjoying a respite from the strains of dealing with the global aggression of the Axis powers—Nazi Germany, Fascist Italy, and Imperial Japan.

But the onlookers were the object of a deception: The president was not among the holidaymakers aboard the *Potomac*. Late the previous night, after a day in which he had constantly been on display while fishing and dining, the yacht had slipped away to the western end of Martha's Vineyard. There Roosevelt had boarded the cruiser *Augusta,* where he joined the principal officers of the armed forces of the United States. While the *Potomac* made its leisurely way through Cape Cod, the *Augusta* got under way eastward, into the open Atlantic, then headed north for a top-secret meeting.

On the morning of August 9, in a remote Newfoundland bay, the *Augusta* met up with the battleship HMS *Prince of Wales,* which dispatched a party to come aboard the American vessel. Roosevelt waited, braced on the arm of his son Elliott to conceal the fact that polio had left him unable to stand unassisted. As the navy band struck up the British national anthem, a stout figure clambered aboard and regarded the American leader. The visitor was clad, as always when he was at sea, in a plain blue naval uniform devoid of insignia—looking, *Life* magazine reported, "rather like a well-to-do tugboat captain."

Thus did the president of the United States and Winston Churchill, prime minister of Great Britain, lay eyes on each other for the first time. "At last, we've gotten together," said FDR, a radiant smile spreading across his face. "Yes," responded Churchill, "we have."

Aides to these two leaders of the free world had worried for months about this meeting, afraid that the two towering egos would not be able to accommodate each other. But their friendship blossomed immediately. That warm personal relationship was evident the next morning, a sunlit Sunday, when Roosevelt joined Churchill and hundreds of British and American sailors for a religious service on the quarterdeck of the *Prince of Wales (opposite).* They sang "Onward, Christian Soldiers" and a dozen other well-known hymns and listened as chaplains read prayers. "The same language, the same hymns, and more or less the same ideals," Churchill reflected that evening.

But despite their shared values and a common goal—the defeat of armed totalitarianism—the two men were operating in acutely different circumstances. The 66-year-old Churchill represented a country that had been at war for two years and desperately needed U.S. help. Roosevelt, on the other hand, was the leader of a resource-rich country that shunned entanglement in any foreign war.

An isolationist Congress had been sufficiently alarmed by Germany's defeat of France in 1940 to pass the president's lend-lease legislation allowing him to help Great Britain with shipments of war matériel, but it would not permit armed intervention. The hamstrung Roosevelt could offer Churchill little more than his continuing personal support and his commitment to the just signed Atlantic Charter, in which they agreed to seek "the final destruction of Nazi tyranny."

Although American eyes were at the moment turned on Europe, events in Asia would soon seize their attention. Even as Roosevelt and Churchill were meeting, the Japanese were preparing a military blow that would shock the world and in a single day put an end to American isolationism and bring the U.S. wholeheartedly into World War II.

"My spine tingled when I saw billowing black smoke....I looked way up and saw the formations of silver bombers riding in. Something detached itself from an airplane and came glistening down. My eyes followed it down, down and even with knowledge pounding in my mind, my heart turned convulsively when the bomb exploded in the middle of the harbor."

CORNELIA CLARK FORT, FLIGHT INSTRUCTOR FLYING NEAR PEARL HARBOR, DECEMBER 7, 1941

The *Arizona* slips beneath the water *(right)*, taking with her 1,000 men trapped belowdecks. Clockwise from top left, a sailor runs for cover past burning planes; crewmen swarm over the sides of the capsizing *California*; a victim of the Japanese attack lies dead at the shoreline; and smoke from an explosion rises over a destroyed airfield.

CHAPTER 1

TRAGEDY AND TRIUMPH IN THE PACIFIC

"Yesterday, December 7, 1941—a date which will live in infamy—
the United States of America was suddenly and deliberately attacked by
naval and air forces of the Empire of Japan."

FRANKLIN DELANO ROOSEVELT

They were two old friends, aged and wearied beyond their years by illness and the burdens of political power. Sitting together on a quiet Sunday afternoon, they were determined to let the world burn unattended for a while, to avoid all the subjects that depressed them—the relentless advance of war and the fragility of democracy and of their own bodies.

Only very old friends could chat so long without touching on unwelcome topics. Harry Hopkins had for years been Franklin Roosevelt's favorite companion, one who shared his private enjoyment of cigarettes, cocktails, bawdy jokes, and political stratagems. Hopkins was able to read his friend's mood and respond exactly as the president desired. Thus he would not mention the president's mother, who had died three months before, or the president's longtime secretary, Missy LeHand, who had suffered a physical and mental decline that had left her unable to speak or walk.

For his part, Roosevelt refused to talk about health, on both his own and his friend's account. He never referred to the polio that had left his legs paralyzed, and he required the same reticence of everyone else. Hopkins had been told in the fall of 1937, after drastic surgery that removed a malignant tumor along with three-quarters of his stomach, that he had four weeks to live. Yet with frequent transfusions and daily injections he had confounded the doctors for four years and would, in fact, outlive his friend the president.

There was also no talk of the Japanese strike force that, American intelligence officers knew, had sailed from its home islands on November 26 and disappeared somewhere in the Pacific Ocean. But Japanese aggression was on both their minds.

For a decade Japan had been expanding its influence in South Asia. The country had gone to war with China in 1937, joined Nazi Germany and Fascist Italy as an Axis partner in 1938, and invaded French Indochina in July 1941. In the face of such aggression, Roosevelt felt that the United States must send a strong signal of disapproval. He hurt the Japanese in the way they would feel it most, by freezing Japanese assets in the United States and cutting off vital shipments of iron, steel, and oil to the small, resource-poor island nation. And though U.S. and Japanese negotiators had been attempting to resolve the differences between the two nations, it was impossible to ignore the potential military threat to the United States itself. The Pacific Fleet, which had been moved from its home base in San

President Franklin Roosevelt delivers a call for a declaration of war to a joint session of Congress on December 8, 1941, the day after the Japanese attacked Pearl Harbor. Seated behind the president are Vice President Henry Wallace *(left)* and Speaker of the House Sam Rayburn.

DRAFT No. 1   December 7, 1941.

PROPOSED MESSAGE TO THE CONGRESS

Yesterday, December 7, 1941, a date which will live in ~~world history~~ *infamy*

the United States of America was ~~simultaneously~~ *suddenly* and deliberately attacked

by naval and air forces of the Empire of Japan.

The United States was at the moment at peace with that nation and was

still in ~~continuing the~~ conversation with its Government and its Emperor looking

toward the maintenance of peace in the Pacific. Indeed, one hour after

Japanese air squadrons had commenced bombing in *Oahu* ~~the American island of~~

the Japanese Ambassador to the United States and his colleague delivered

to the Secretary of State a formal reply to a ~~former~~ *recent American* message.

~~While~~ This reply ~~contained a statement~~ *stated* that diplomatic negotiations *it seemed useless*

~~must be considered at an end,~~ *it* contained no threat ~~and~~ *or* hint of *war or*

armed attack.

It will be recorded that the distance ~~of Hawaii and especially~~ of

Hawaii from Japan make *s* it obvious that the attack ~~was~~ *was* deliberately

on past weeks planned many days ago. During the intervening time the Japanese Govern-

ment has deliberately sought to deceive the United States by false

statements and expressions of hope for continued peace.

Roosevelt dictated to his personal secretary, Grace Tully, the speech that he delivered to Congress and then made handwritten revisions to the original draft *(above)* that included changing the phrase "a date which will live in world history" to "a date which will live in infamy."

Diego to Pearl Harbor on the Hawaiian island of Oahu in 1940, would be the first line of defense against Japanese aggression.

At about 1:40 p.m. on that Sunday—December 7, 1941—Roosevelt and Hopkins were interrupted by a telephone call from Secretary of the Navy Frank Knox. He relayed a message just received from the commander of the U.S. Pacific Fleet. "AIR RAID PEARL HARBOR," it read. "This is no drill."

Hopkins was incredulous: "There must be some mistake." But Roosevelt wasted no time on denial. It was, he remarked, "just the kind of unexpected thing the Japanese would do" while negotiating peace in the Pacific.

Twenty-five minutes after the president learned of the attack, the Japanese ambassador to the United States and a special envoy arrived at the office of Secretary of State Cordell Hull. Ambassador Kichisaburo Nomura had requested an appointment on Sunday—a very unusual day for diplomats to meet—to present his government's response to the latest U.S. proposals. He had further breached protocol by specifying the time—1:00 p.m. The ambassador was an hour late for the appointment, and while he waited in Hull's outer office to be received, the secretary was on the telephone with Roosevelt discussing the attack on Pearl Harbor. The president told Hull to receive the Japanese, listen to what they had to say, and "bow them out." Furious but controlled, Hull had the emissaries shown into his office, where he simply stared at them and waited, not even asking them to sit down.

Ambassador Nomura began by apologizing for being late. Hull curtly demanded why he had specified that particular day and hour to meet, but Nomura could say only that he was following the instructions that Tokyo had given him. In fact, the unfortunate diplomat did not know that his country had already launched the conflict he had worked so vigorously to avoid. Nor did he and his superiors in Tokyo know that U.S. intelligence had broken the Japanese diplomatic code.

Hull read through the document that Nomura handed to him, but he was already familiar with its contents. It had been intercepted during transmission from Tokyo, decoded, and delivered to him hours before Nomura's arrival. A provocative rejection of the American position on Asian affairs, it began with a long digest of complaints and concluded that it was "impossible to reach an agreement through further negotiations." There was no declaration of war or even a formal breaking off of diplomatic relations, but Washington had read it as a chilling warning that war was close at hand.

"In all my 50 years of public service," Hull told Nomura with icy contempt, "I have never seen a document that was more crowded with infamous falsehoods and distortions—on a scale so huge that I never imagined until today that any government on this planet was capable of uttering them." Without giving the emissaries an opportunity to respond, Hull showed them the door.

Hull then rushed to the White House, where Roosevelt and his advisers were receiving reports as they came into the Navy Department on the extent of the damage done to the Pacific Fleet. "Within the first hour," recalled Roosevelt's personal secretary, Grace Tully, whose duty it was to take the reports over the phone and relay them to the president, "it was evident that the navy was dangerously crippled." She saw that Roosevelt "maintained greater outward calm than anybody else, but there was rage in his very calmness. With each new message he shook his head grimly and tightened the expression of his mouth." When Eleanor Roosevelt came into the room, she noted that her husband looked strained and tired, but as always reacted to bad news by becoming "almost like an iceberg." No

one knew what might be coming next, and at one point during the afternoon the president's butler overheard Roosevelt and Hopkins speculating that the Japanese might invade the West Coast and drive inland as far as Chicago. At that point, the president thought, overextended lines of Japanese supply and communication would allow the Americans to start driving them back.

As the late autumn twilight descended on Washington, hundreds of anxious people who had learned about the attack by word of mouth and from reports on the radio gathered outside the White House fence. Meanwhile, Roosevelt summoned Grace Tully into his study. "Sit down, Grace. I'm going before Congress tomorrow. I'd like to dictate my message. It will be short."

That evening at 8:00 the cabinet gathered to hear from Roosevelt firsthand what had happened at Pearl Harbor. With a "gray, drawn look," as Labor Secretary Frances Perkins described it, Roosevelt told them that this was "the most serious meeting of

In his White House study with a three-masted frigate from his collection of model ships behind him, President Roosevelt confers with his long-time friend and trusted adviser on foreign affairs Harry Hopkins. Hopkins lived in a suite on the second floor of the White House from May 1940 until December 1944.

the cabinet that had taken place since the outbreak of the Civil War." He reported that Japanese planes had bombed not only Pearl Harbor but all of the airfields on Oahu, and casualties were extremely heavy. The Pacific Fleet had been taken completely by surprise; no air patrols had detected the presence of Japanese aircraft carriers within range of Oahu, and more than half the ships had been caught at dockside in the harbor.

The leaders of Congress then joined the meeting. "The principal defense of the whole west coast of this country has been very seriously damaged today," the president told them. The congressmen listened to his recital in dead silence, and even when it was over they had to collect themselves before reacting. At length, however, the chairman of the Senate Foreign Relations Committee, Thomas Connally, found his tongue. "Hell's fire," he blurted, "didn't we do anything?" Turning to navy secretary Knox he demanded again, "What did we *do?*"

Knox could only mumble unhappily while Connally worked himself into a rage. "Didn't you say last month that we could lick the Japs in two weeks? Didn't you say that our navy was so well prepared and located that the Japanese couldn't hope to hurt us at all?" As surprised as he was by the attack, Connally said, "I am still more astounded at what happened to our navy. They were all asleep. Where were our patrols? They knew these negotiations were going on."

While the nation reeled in shock, the grim task of counting the dead and tallying the destruction at Pearl Harbor went on. More than 2,300 American servicemen had been killed. Eight battleships, three destroyers, and three cruisers had been sunk or heavily damaged. Luckily, the Pacific Fleet's four aircraft carriers had been away from port on maneuvers and had not been caught in the attack.

The army's air strength on Oahu had suffered as grievously as the Pacific Fleet. The standard precaution against air attack was to park the planes in individual revetments separated by earthen banks. But the army commander in Hawaii had been more concerned about possible sabotage by the island's Japa-

nese population and had parked the aircraft wing tip to wing tip so they would be easier to guard. One hundred eighty-eight planes had been destroyed.

On Monday, December 8, Roosevelt addressed a joint session of Congress and, via the radio networks, the nation as a whole. "The American people in their righteous might," he vowed, "will win through to absolute victory." His outrage, defiance, and resolve summed up the mood of the nation, which had been galvanized and united by the attack on Pearl Harbor, perhaps as never before. The following day the Congress voted to declare war as young men were pouring into recruitment offices eager to enlist. By December 12 the United States was formally at war with Japan's partners in the Axis, Germany and Italy.

One-half hour after the last Japanese planes disappeared through the clouds of smoke over Pearl Harbor, the telephone rang in General Douglas MacArthur's penthouse atop the Manila Hotel. It was 3:40 a.m. on December 8 in Manila; lying on the other side of the International Date Line, the city was 19 hours ahead of Honolulu. MacArthur took the call in his bedroom. "Pearl Harbor!" he exclaimed when he heard the news. "It should be our strongest point!" MacArthur hurriedly donned his first uniform of the day—he always changed at noon and again at dinnertime, to maintain his immaculate appearance in the wilting tropical heat—and spent a few minutes reading his Bible, then strode to his headquarters on Victoria Street.

It was almost inevitable that the flash point of World War II should find MacArthur in the Philippines. His father, Arthur, a Medal of Honor winner in the American Civil War and veteran of the

At dawn on December 7 crewmen on the flight deck of a Japanese aircraft carrier prepare a Zero fighter *(foreground at right)* for takeoff. Launched first, the nimble Zeros ran interference for the dive bombers and torpedo planes that devastated Pearl Harbor. Next morning's headlines like the one in the *New York Herald Tribune* shown here stunned the American public and prompted panic on the West Coast.

Spanish-American War, had served as military governor of the Philippines at the turn of the century. The elder MacArthur had played a key role in putting down the revolution with which Filipino patriots greeted the news that with the end of Spanish rule their country had not gained the independence they had fought for but had instead become a U.S. territory.

Following in the illustrious footsteps of his father, Douglas enjoyed a brilliant army career spanning three decades. He had been a decorated hero in World War I, superintendent of the military academy at West Point, and army chief of staff. In 1935, during this last assignment, he had been appointed military adviser to the Philippines, responsible for training the fledgling Filipino army as the country prepared for independence from the United States. He resigned from the U.S. Army two years later but remained the head of the American mission in the Philippines, now with a Philippine rather than an American military title. That same year he married his second wife, a pretty, vivacious heiress from Tennessee named Jean Faircloth who had been on a world cruise when they met. In 1938 the aging general welcomed the birth of Arthur, his first son. He proved to be a doting father.

The Philippines consist of several thousand volcanic, jungle-clad islands bracketed by the two largest, Luzon in the north and Mindanao in the south. Situated on the west coast of Luzon, Manila Bay was flanked by the city of Manila and a naval base at Cavite. Clark Field, a major U.S. air facility,

AN AMERICAN FIRST

In a May 27, 1942, ceremony aboard the carrier *Enterprise* presided over by Admiral Chester W. Nimitz *(above, left),* mess attendant Doris Miller became the first African American to receive the Navy Cross, the service's highest award. On the morning of December 7, 1941, Miller was gathering laundry on the battleship *West Virginia* when he heard the roar of explosions and low-flying planes. He raced topside to find Captain Mervyn Bennion sprawled on the deck bleeding heavily. After helping drag the mortally wounded skipper to cover, Miller rushed back into the open to an unmanned machine gun and, although he had no experience in aerial gunnery, began firing. He was credited with downing four Japanese planes.

His lack of experience was a product of the navy's discriminatory policy, which restricted African American seamen to menial noncombat duties. The navy brass was loath even to recognize Miller's courage and initiative in combat, and he received the Navy Cross only after a direct order from the White House. Still serving as a mess attendant, Miller died when his ship was sunk by a Japanese submarine in November 1943.

lay northwest of Manila. The strategic value of the archipelago to both Japan and the United States was undeniable, but MacArthur, for all his experience in the region, was ambivalent about the role the Philippines would play in a conflict with Japan. At times he described the territory as a critical barrier to Japan's aggression because of its position on the flank of vital sea lanes between Japan and Southeast Asia, India, and Europe. Yet on other occasions he discounted the Philippines' importance to Japan. So sprawling a territory would, MacArthur suggested, be impossible to govern and not worth the costly amphibious assault that would be required to conquer it.

MacArthur and the U.S. military establishment were in profound disagreement about the best defense for the Philippines. In the 1920s the army had formulated a plan for dealing with an invasion of the Philippines that called for all units to withdraw into prepared positions on the Bataan Peninsula, which stuck down like a 40-mile-long thumb on Luzon's west coast between the South China Sea and Manila Bay. Bataan's rugged terrain would work to the defenders' advantage, and large supply depots established on the peninsula would permit the army to hold out until the navy could bring relief. But MacArthur modified the plan: He boldly asserted that he could stop a Japanese invasion on the beaches and drive the enemy back into the sea. Consequently, he had ordered the supply depots to be moved from Bataan to Luzon's central plain, closer to likely landing sites.

By late 1941 the Philippines were surrounded. The Japanese had occupied the east coast of China and the island of Formosa and then had moved into French Indochina to the west across the South China Sea. They held island outposts to the east, and their navy plied the waters to the south undisturbed. One of the measures President Roosevelt had taken earlier that year to counter Japanese expansion was to recall Douglas MacArthur to active service. He was appointed commanding general of Philippine forces, and $10 million was appropriated for the territory's defenses.

In all, MacArthur had 25,000 American troops and more than 110,000 Filipino troops. But despite his efforts of the past six years, they were desperately short of equipment and ammunition. Nevertheless, he told everyone who would listen that "the Philippines could be defended and, by God, they would be defended." He managed to wheedle 6,000 more American soldiers by December 7, and his naval support consisted of 16 warships, 18 submarines, and a half-dozen PT boats.

Air power was Washington's trump card in case of attack. Two weeks after the Atlantic Conference in August 1941 between Roosevelt and Churchill, at which the British had enthusiastically praised the effectiveness of the Boeing B-17 Flying Fortress heavy bomber, the Army Air Corps ordered that all available B-17s be sent to the Philippines. By December, MacArthur had parked on his three main airfields, under the command of Major General Lewis H. Brereton, a fleet of more than 200 aircraft, 74 of them heavy bombers. It was, boasted War Department chief of staff George C. Marshall, "the greatest concentration of heavy bomber strength anywhere in the world."

At the end of November MacArthur would write, "I prepared my meager forces, to counter as best I might, the attack that I knew would come from the north, swiftly, fiercely, and without warning." By December 7 warnings of impending hostilities had been frequent and unmistakable, including a Japanese expeditionary force that was known

to be at sea; frequent sightings of Japanese aircraft; heavy Japanese convoy activity throughout the area. War was coming, MacArthur confided to some reporters, off the record, but probably not until January. At 3:40 a.m. on December 8, he found out that war had already arrived.

MacArthur was told at his Victoria Street headquarters that General Brereton was on his way and had already alerted his aircrewmen, 1,200 of whom had just returned to their bases after having attended an all-night party in Brereton's honor at the Manila Hotel. Philippine president Manuel Quezon arrived at headquarters to plead, as he had been doing for some time, that MacArthur do nothing to antagonize the Japanese.

At 5:30 a.m., two hours after MacArthur learned of the Japanese attack on Pearl Harbor, Washington informed him that a state of war existed and ordered him to implement the previously drawn plans for the defense of the Philippines. Yet at sunrise, shortly after 6:00 a.m., MacArthur's ships were still anchored, his aircraft were on the ground, and his troops were without orders.

It was after 7:00 a.m. when radar operators at Iba Field, a small air base on the west coast of Luzon 40 miles from Clark Field, reported aircraft over the South China Sea headed toward Manila. Brereton had just received orders from Washington to disperse his aircraft to prevent a repetition of what had happened at Pearl Harbor. He had already sent half of his B-17s to Mindanao, out of range of the Formosa-based Japanese fighters, and he now ordered the remaining B-17s at Clark Field to take off and fly patterns over Luzon, out of harm's way. He also sent up his P-40 fighters to engage the approaching enemy aircraft, which veered away and avoided contact.

To a query from the War Department about any indications of an attack, MacArthur responded that "our tails are up in the air," meaning that everyone was fully alert. But the colorful metaphor notwithstanding, MacArthur had still not acted on the

7:00 a.m. radar warning. At about 9:30 a.m., Brereton reported that the Japanese had bombed three locations in northern Luzon and asked MacArthur's permission to launch a counterattack against Japanese airfields on Formosa. The first response from headquarters was negative, but a little while later, MacArthur's chief of staff called Brereton back and gave him the go-ahead to fly a photo reconnaissance mission over the Japanese bases on Formosa, as a preliminary to a bombing raid on them, and to ready his B-17s for an offensive strike. At 11:00 a.m., Brereton recalled the circling B-17s to Clark so that three of them could be fitted with cameras and the rest loaded with bombs. At noon the P-40 fighters came in for refueling.

But it was too little too late, for nearly 200 bombers and Zero fighters from Formosa were now entering Philippine air space. They were quickly

naval assistance for what he called "the locus of victory or defeat."

Japan now controlled Philippine air space and the surrounding waters, but MacArthur did not make an immediate move when Japanese troops landed at three widely separated spots on the Luzon coast. The main invasion, he thought, would come at Lingayen Gulf 100 miles north of Manila across Luzon's central plain, and he judged these landings to be no more than diversions. Having declared that he would stop a Japanese invasion on the beaches, MacArthur deployed his troops at Lingayen within easy reach of the supply caches that had been moved from Bataan Peninsula and set up on the plain.

At dawn on December 22, Japanese troops came ashore on three Lingayen Gulf beaches, swept aside the American and Filipino defenders with surpris-

"I prepared my meager forces, to counter as best I might, the attack that I knew would come from the north, swiftly, fiercely, and without warning."

GENERAL DOUGLAS MACARTHUR

spotted by a radar operator and by Filipino coastal watchers, but the warnings that they sent by teletype to Manila languished in an office while the lone teletype operator was having lunch. At about 12:15 p.m., as the three B-17s with reconnaissance cameras aboard were rolling toward their takeoff position on the runway, aircrews on Clark Field looked up in astonishment at the first arrowhead formation of Japanese planes. In the space of one hour every aircraft caught on the ground and every structure at Clark, and those at Iba Field as well, was reduced to fiery ruins.

Having smashed MacArthur's air power, Japanese bombers returned two days later in order to wipe out the naval base at Cavite on Manila Bay. As a result of this action his naval counterpart in the Philippines, along with the chief of naval operations in Washington, decided the Philippines were beyond saving, even while MacArthur was calling for, and assuming he would get, massive air and

ing ease, and started south on the highway leading to Manila. MacArthur was on his way north from Manila to assess the situation when he received word that another Japanese force, 7,000 strong, had landed at Lamon Bay, 70 miles southeast of Manila. The city was now the focus of a pincers movement from the north and from the south, and MacArthur was forced to abandon his defensive strategy and invoke the army's 1920s plan, which consisted of a retreat into the Bataan Peninsula. The logistics of disengaging from these advancing enemy spearheads were daunting. MacArthur had to unite his force making a fighting retreat from the north with another doing the same against the Japanese who had landed at Lamon Bay.

With MacArthur orchestrating from Manila, each force had to hold fast in the face of the enemy with a small portion of its men while the rest fell back some distance to prepare a new defensive position. Then the remaining men would make a dash for the new line. The bridges along both routes of retreat had to be blown up at the last possible moment; usually the last defenders crossed just ahead of the Japanese, who followed in quick pursuit. It was a matter, recalled MacArthur, of "stand and fight, slip back and dynamite. It was savage and bloody, but it won time."

It was imperative that the timing be precise. The northern force had to hold back the Japanese long enough for the Americans and Filipinos in the south to get into Manila, then march 20 miles northwest of the city to a pair of bridges across the Pampanga River. These provided the only way for both forces to reach Bataan, because the river was unfordable along much of its length and all roads leading from the north and the south in central Luzon converged at these bridges. It would be a very close thing.

For as long as he could, MacArthur directed operations from his Victoria Street headquarters, laboring long into the night, sleeping only in snatches, and maintaining close contact with his hard-pressed troops. But he knew that the enemy advancing on Manila posed increasing peril to him and his family. Knowing the city would fall very soon, Jean MacArthur and the general celebrated Christmas early so that three-year-old Arthur could open his presents and have a few hours to play with them. The parents opened their gifts as well and promised each other they would use them later.

His gold-braided Filipino field marshal's cap set squarely on his head and his hands folded over a walnut cane that had belonged to his mother, General MacArthur *(left)* confers with Philippine president Manuel Quezon on Corregidor, the island stronghold at the entrance to Manila Bay.

On Christmas Eve it was time to get out. With the Japanese closing in, the navy dispatched its remaining ships south to the island of Java. General Brereton departed for Australia. MacArthur, accompanied by his family, staff, and Philippine president Quezon, took refuge on the tiny island of Corregidor—known as the Rock—lying off the southern end of the Bataan Peninsula squarely in the mouth of Manila Bay.

Corregidor was pocked and scored with numerous foxholes and entrenchments, and its shoreline was laced with barbed wire. Behind the beaches the island rose in three jungle-clad terraces, called Topside, Middleside, and Bottomside, all of which bristled with guns. Now the 10,000-man garrison and the 2,000 resident civilians awaited the inevitable Japanese onslaught.

MacArthur refused the opportunity to take shelter in one of the island's tunnels. Instead, he and his family moved into the commanding officer's cottage, which was prominently perched on the Topside plateau. MacArthur said it had a great view; his aides thought it was entirely too exposed. "That's fine," responded MacArthur. "Just the thing."

Back on Luzon, the defenders retreating from the south had cleared Manila and reached the bridges over the Pampanga River, which for two days in late December was the site of a 10-mile backup of refugees, supply trucks, mobile guns, and demoralized troops trying to get to Bataan. The northern Japanese invasion force had driven to within 10 miles of the Pampanga when, early on New Year's Day, the last American tanks raced across the two bridges and engineers blew them up.

The move stunned the Japanese commanders, who had expected MacArthur to fight for Manila. But his successful retreat into mountainous Bataan did little more than delay the inevitable. His forces were bottled up and there was no chance of reinforcement or rescue.

When the Japanese occupied Manila on January 2 and found out where MacArthur had gone, they sent 18 bombers to pound Topside for four hours.

Jean and Arthur huddled in an air-raid shelter while MacArthur stood in the open, smoking a cigarette, counting the enemy planes, and watching the bombs fall. One of them smashed into the bedroom of their cottage, and shrapnel from another slightly wounded an aide standing at his side. When Jean emerged from the shelter after the raid, he said to her, "Look what they've done to the garden."

Not only his cottage but every other building on Topside had been destroyed. From then on, daily artillery barrages and frequent bombing missions—more than 300 over the course of the next three months—pounded the Rock, but MacArthur refused to sleep underground. He appropriated a small cottage on Bottomside, a few hundred yards from the entrance to the Malinta tunnel, the island's main air-raid shelter and communications center, which would now serve as MacArthur's headquarters in the battle for Bataan.

Jean MacArthur worked out a routine that met her obligations to both Arthur and her husband. When the air-raid sirens wailed, she would bundle Arthur into a car, dash to the tunnel, and deposit him in the care of the MacArthur household's staff. Then she would return to her husband's side and stand with him in the open so that she could share whatever fate awaited him.

Prior to December 7 Allied strategists who were preparing for the possibility of war had pondered where the Japanese might hit first: Malaya, Hong Kong, the Netherlands East Indies, the Philippines, or perhaps even Hawaii. The air raid on Pearl Harbor had answered that question, but in the three-month period following that attack, the Japanese astonished the world by striking all the other targets in addition. They drove down the Malay Peninsula to capture 90,000 British troops and the supposedly impregnable fortress of Singapore. The Imperial Navy wiped out an Allied fleet in the Battle of the Java Sea and seized the Indonesian archipelago from the Dutch, thus gaining huge new sources of rubber and oil.

Raising their hands overhead and displaying a white flag of surrender, Americans exit from the Malinta tunnel on Corregidor under the watchful eye of Japanese soldiers. More than five months of daily bombing and shelling forced the troops to surrender at noon on May 6, 1942. Moments before, a radio operator typed out the last message from Corregidor: "We are waiting for God knows what. Damage terrible. Too much for the guys to take. Going off air now. Good-bye and good luck."

Only MacArthur held out. He sent off a blizzard of dispatches to Washington. Some proclaimed defiance, others claimed successes, and almost all asked for help. His men on the Bataan Peninsula were fighting under terrible conditions. They had little food or ammunition—most of the supplies that MacArthur had cached on the central plain had been destroyed to prevent their capture by the Japanese. Much of the ammunition that remained on Bataan was old prewar stock, and up to 80 percent of the grenades and shells were duds. The troops had to subsist in thick jungle, in nearly constant rain and beset by snakes and insects. They succumbed not only to enemy fire but to a wide array of fevers and parasites. Yet they fought stubbornly, yielding ground slowly and at one point driving the enemy back far enough that MacArthur briefly considered trying to retake Manila.

Although MacArthur referred constantly to being outnumbered, he actually had twice as many soldiers on Luzon as did the Japanese. But the Americans were desperately short of the sinews of war—and no additional supplies were reaching them. MacArthur kept telling his troops that help was on the way, and he believed this to be the case. President Roosevelt, in a special broadcast, also assured the people of the Philippines that they could count on U.S. support. He then wired President Quezon his "solemn pledge" that his people's "freedom will be retained and their independence established and redeemed. The entire resources in men and materials of the United States stand behind that pledge."

But depite his promises, Roosevelt had in fact written off the Philippines even before the fall of Manila. Along with Chief of Staff Marshall and Dwight Eisenhower, the new deputy chief of the army's War Plans Division and MacArthur's former aide, he reluctantly agreed that MacArthur and his command had to be sacrificed. Roosevelt's strategy

In a luxurious private railcar, General MacArthur and his wife, Jean, share a relaxed breakfast on their way to Melbourne, two days after their arrival in Australia.

was to focus the preponderance of the Allied war effort against Germany and to make Australia the center of resistance to the Japanese. On both these counts, diverting men and supplies to the Philippines did not make any sense. Not one American supply ship, airplane, or reinforcement reached Luzon from outside the Philippines after the siege had begun. "It was Japan's ability to continually bring in fresh forces and America's inability to do so," MacArthur wrote with some bitterness, "that finally settled the issue."

By January 24 the defenders on Bataan had been driven back to their last line of defense. When it became obvious that they were to get no help, the men were bitter and disillusioned. They believed that MacArthur had intentionally deceived them. His reputation among American troops on Bataan was also hurt by the fact that during the 77 days MacArthur spent on Corregidor, he paid only one brief visit to the battlefront on Bataan. Some of

the Americans began to refer contemptuously to their commander as Dugout Doug, an epithet that dogged him for years.

When it began to dawn on MacArthur that the Philippines were on their own, he cabled Roosevelt to expect "the complete extinction of this command." The president urged him to hold out "so long as there remains any possibility of resistance." MacArthur replied that his plans were already made— he would fight on to destruction. "I have not the slightest intention in the world," he said, "of surrendering or capitulating."

President Quezon, after raging at the betrayal of his country and threatening to surrender it to the Japanese, subsided into depression and accepted his evacuation to Australia. In the third week of February, MacArthur helped the sickly old man to board an American submarine that would take him to safety. Quezon took off his presidential signet ring and slipped it onto MacArthur's finger. "When

A crowd of 5,000 hails General MacArthur's triumphant arrival in Melbourne on March 21, 1942 *(left)*. To quell Axis propaganda claiming the general had deserted his troops in the Philippines, he was awarded the Medal of Honor five days later.

they find your body," Quezon told him in a faltering voice, "I want them to know that you fought for my country."

When Jean was offered passage out on the same submarine, she responded without consulting MacArthur that "we have drunk from the same cup, we three shall stay together." MacArthur and his wife had a long talk in private, during which he apparently tried without success to persuade her to leave. Afterward he said with satisfaction, "Jean is my finest soldier." When an incredulous aide asked what was to be done about young Arthur, the general snapped, "He is a soldier's son."

On the home front, MacArthur was getting headlines because he was offering the only organized resistance to the Japanese tide rolling over the Pacific, and his growing reputation prompted the politically sensitive Roosevelt to have second thoughts about leaving the general to his fate. Shortly after noon on February 23, MacArthur received a presidential order to leave Corregidor and proceed to Melbourne, Australia, where he was to assume command of all U.S. troops in the Southwest Pacific. MacArthur appeared shaken by the order to abandon his men. Ashen faced, he consulted with Jean, then told his aides he would resign his commission rather than leave. The staff argued vigorously that obeying the order and then leading a relief expedition from Australia back to the Philippines constituted the only hope for the men on Bataan. At length MacArthur allowed himself to be persuaded, but he put off his departure for two weeks.

The Japanese naval force in the area took MacArthur's capture as their primary goal and intensified sea and air patrols around the Philippines. It took a dangerous two-day run in a PT boat through heavy seas to get MacArthur, his family, and his staff nearly 500 miles to the north coast of Mindanao. From there he made his way by air and rail to Melbourne. During the last leg of his journey he learned the real state of affairs: There was no massive buildup of Allied forces in Australia to relieve the Philippines; in fact, there was grave doubt about

A MARATHON OF AGONY

When the 76,000 American and Filipino troops defending the Bataan Peninsula surrendered to the Japanese in April 1942, they were in terrible condition for the week-long march up the peninsula to Camp O'Donnell, an army barracks in central Luzon that had been hastily converted into a prison camp. The men had been on short rations during the three-month siege, and many were seriously ill with malaria, dysentery, and beriberi.

Japanese soldiers beat their prisoners and robbed them of their blankets, food, and personal possessions, then herded them together to start the march. Stragglers who could not keep up the pace were clubbed, shot, bayoneted, beheaded, or buried alive. One officer later recounted a heinous act he was forced to perform: "I was taken out of the line and escorted to where the Japs had placed this unconscious man in the ditch. One of them handed me a shovel. Another jabbed a bayonet into my side and gave me an order in Japanese. A Jap grabbed the shovel out of my hands and demonstrated by throwing a few shovelsful of earth on the unconscious soldier. Then he handed me the shovel. God! . . . It doesn't help to tell myself that the soldiers, and others later, were already more dead than alive." Only 54,000 emaciated survivors reached Camp O'Donnell.

Starvation, disease, torture, and executions claimed up to 400 Americans and Filipinos a day at the camp. In a secret diary, an American colonel described his fellow prisoners: "Aged incredibly beyond their years. Remnants of ragged gunny sacks as loin cloths. Bloodshot eyes and cracked lips. Smeared with excreta from their bowels." For many prisoners the suffering would last more than three years; they were later moved from the Philippines to Japan and remained captive until war's end.

Nearing the end of the Bataan death march, prisoners carry their sick and weakened comrades in makeshift litters *(above)*. At right, three thin, exhausted American prisoners rest briefly during an infrequent pause on the road to Camp O'Donnell.

whether Australia could be defended successfully if the Japanese attacked. Gaunt, ill, and exhausted, MacArthur blanched at the news. "God have mercy on us" was all he could say. It was, he said later, the "greatest shock and surprise of the whole war."

On Friday, March 20, nine days after his departure from the Rock, MacArthur stepped off the train to face members of the press, who had been alerted to his escape by President Roosevelt. The general had scrawled two sentences on the back of an envelope. "The President of the United States ordered me to break through the Japanese lines . . . ," he said, "for the purpose, as I understand it, of organizing the American offensive against Japan, a primary object of which is the relief of the Philippines." His next sentence was to become one of the most celebrated promises of World War II: "I came through," he declared, "and I shall return."

B-25 bombers from the deck of the USS *Hornet* to bomb Tokyo. Although it boosted American morale, the raid did nothing to slow down the Japanese advance across the Pacific. Then, on May 7, Rear Admiral Frank Jack Fletcher fought the Japanese to a standstill in the Coral Sea off Australia's east coast, severely damaging two of their aircraft carriers and stopping their thrust toward New Guinea and Australia. But in the process, the aircraft carrier *Lexington* was sunk and the *Yorktown* badly damaged.

The Battle of the Coral Sea was a harbinger of the new kind of warfare that would dominate the Pacific theater. For the first time in naval history the opposing combatants' ships never came within sight of each other. All the damage was wrought by carrier-based dive bombers and torpedo planes. The lesson was not lost on Nimitz and his subordinates: They could prosecute the war against Japan without the wrecked bat-

"The President of the United States ordered me to break through the Japanese lines... for the purpose, as I understand it, of organizing the American offensive against Japan, a primary object of which is the relief of the Philippines. I came through and I shall return."

GENERAL DOUGLAS MACARTHUR, ON HIS ARRIVAL IN MELBOURNE, AUSTRALIA

The American and Filipino troops on Bataan surrendered on April 9; Corregidor held out until May 6. Now the only remaining force in the Pacific to oppose the Japanese juggernaut was the aircraft carriers of the U.S. Pacific Fleet.

While the Japanese Imperial Fleet ran riot in the Far East in the months after Pearl Harbor, the U.S. Navy struggled to rebuild its decimated battleships and husband its precious carriers. On December 17 Admiral Chester W. Nimitz had taken over as commander in chief of the U.S. Pacific Fleet. "I will be lucky to last six months," Nimitz wrote to his wife. "The public may demand action and results faster than I can produce."

During the next five months Nimitz gave the public plenty of action, with mixed results. In April Lieutenant Colonel James H. Doolittle led 16 army

tleships lying in the mud of Pearl Harbor, but if such a catastrophe befell the carriers, Hawaii might very well fall, and the Japanese could threaten American shipping throughout the entire Pacific.

While Fletcher's task force shepherded the battered, limping *Yorktown* back to Pearl Harbor, Nimitz worried about where the Japanese would strike next. He received conflicting advice from his staff. Some expected an all-out attack on Hawaii, whereas others predicted an invasion of Alaska by way of the Aleutian Islands. George Marshall thought there might be a full-scale invasion of the U.S. West Coast targeted on San Diego.

The truth about Japan's immediate intentions came from a windowless basement room at the Pearl Harbor station where a team of navy cryptographers, who were led by Lieutenant Commander Joseph Rochefort, had cracked the Japanese navy's

PRISONERS IN THEIR OWN COUNTRY

After Pearl Harbor, the 120,000 West Coast Japanese Americans were looked on with mistrust and hostility. They were viewed as potential saboteurs and spies, and unfounded rumors spread rapidly. On February 19, 1942, President Roosevelt signed Executive Order 9066, which paved the way for the mass relocation and confinement of people of Japanese ancestry, 77,000 of whom were U.S. citizens. Japanese Americans in Hawaii were exempt because they were essential to the defense industry's labor force there.

Residents of communities like Bainbridge Island, Washington (left), were given as little as two weeks to sell homes, farms, businesses, and possessions before leaving under an escort of military police. Among the first of the 15,000 who were banished from Washington State were Fumiko Hayashida and her one-year-old daughter, Natalie, with identity tags hanging from their coats (inset). The few who resisted evacuation were arrested and jailed.

For the next three years, detainees were housed in converted chicken coops, horse stalls, and makeshift tarpaper barracks ringed with barbed wire and guard towers in one of 10 concentration camps scattered across the West and in Arkansas. Life in these "relocation centers" was harsh. A family of seven might share a 20-by-25-foot space, and overcrowded communal washrooms and mess halls made life smelly and unsanitary.

The War Department closed the camps on December 17, 1944, the day before the U.S. Supreme Court ruled that the government could not detain a citizen based on suspicion of disloyalty. Not until 1988 did Congress vote to make amends in the form of more than $38 million in property claims—an estimated 10 percent of the actual value—and a formal apology for its ignoble treatment of Japanese Americans.

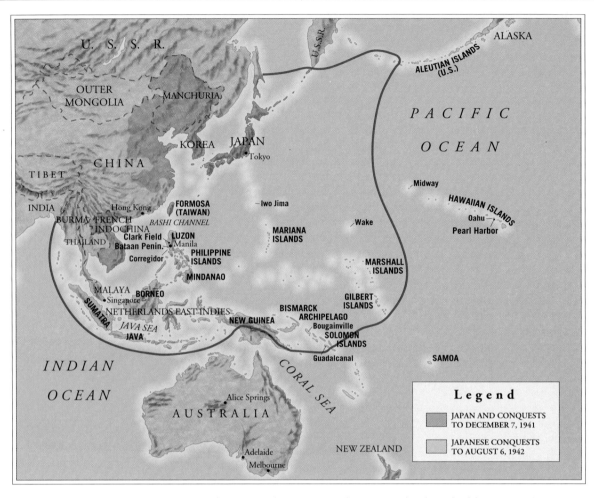

On the map at right the red line marks the extent of Japan's imperialist expansion in August 1942. The reach for empire began in 1931 with the occupation of Manchuria. In 1937 Japanese troops overran large tracts of China. The Nazi victory over France in 1940 allowed Japan to seize French Indochina. When war with the United States came in December 1941, Japanese forces were well positioned to invade Malaya, Burma, the Netherlands East Indies, the Philippines, and island groups in the South Pacific.

operational code. From the middle of May, Rochefort had been reading a flood of messages crackling across the Pacific. These messages indicated that the Japanese were mounting a major invasion of a place that they designated AF.

Rochefort surmised that AF was the tiny atoll called Midway. Located near the midpoint of the Pacific at the far northwest end of the 1,100-mile-long chain of the Hawaiian Islands, Midway consisted of two islands of volcanic rock, coral, and sand totaling less than three square miles in area. A narrow channel separated the little islands, which were ringed by a coral reef enclosing a small lagoon. A three-runway airfield had been constructed on Eastern Island, and across a narrow channel on Sand Island were barracks for several hundred marines, a seaplane base, and a large fuel dump.

Midway was clearly valuable as a midocean refueling station and intelligence outpost, and thus a likely target, but Nimitz could not risk committing his forces to its defense without proof that the atoll was indeed AF. Rochefort knew that the Japanese were monitoring American radio traffic, so he laid a trap in hopes of tricking enemy cryptographers into revealing AF's identity. Using the secure undersea cable linking Hawaii and Midway, he directed the commander of the garrison to send an uncoded radio message to Pearl Harbor stating that his water distillation plant had broken down.

Two days later Rochefort intercepted a Japanese report of a freshwater shortage on AF. Nimitz had gotten the break he needed, and on May 28 Task Force 16, consisting of the carriers *Enterprise* and *Hornet* along with their escorts, sailed from Pearl

Harbor to intercept the Japanese fleet in the vicinity of Midway.

As the navy prepared for battle, Task Force 16's commander, Vice Admiral William F. "Bull" Halsey, lay in a shoreside hospital bed, disabled by an excruciating skin rash. His replacement, Rear Admiral Raymond A. Spruance, was an unknown quantity to the officers and sailors on board the ships headed for Midway. Many of them—as well as Spruance himself—had been surprised by his promotion to command a carrier striking force, because he had no experience in naval aviation. He was not widely known, nor did he have a spectacular record. But he had Halsey's total confidence; Halsey had recommended him, and that was good enough for Nimitz.

A month away from his fifty-sixth birthday, Spruance was a quiet and unassuming officer with a technical background—he had specialized in shipboard electrical systems during World War I—and a reputation for caution. But the caution was balanced with an ability to take sudden, bold action. "He was the type who thought things through very carefully, and then, when he decided to strike, struck hard," Nimitz observed. "I sorely needed commanders of that type."

Spruance had one advantage few naval commanders enjoy on the eve of battle—he knew what he was up against in the coming fight for Midway. Rochefort's cryptographers had intercepted and decoded the entire order of battle and the timetable of Admiral Isoroku Yamamoto, commander of the Japanese combined fleet. Comprising 86 surface warships, the fleet was headed for Midway in three groups. An invasion force of 5,000 troops aboard transport ships protected by two battleships, eight cruisers, and many destroyers was approaching Midway from the southwest. Yamamoto was following the invasion force with a separate support and command group, a powerful assemblage of seven battleships that included his flagship, the *Yamato*, the largest warship in the world. This armada of big guns was formidable, but the real offensive punch was provided by the strike force of four aircraft carriers with 325 fighters, bombers, and torpedo planes

under Vice Admiral Chiuchi Nagumo, who had commanded the attack on Pearl Harbor. This force was to approach Midway from the northwest, knock out the islands' defending aircraft and gun emplacements, then pounce on the U.S. carriers if they came to Midway's relief.

Wiping out the carriers was, in fact, Yamamoto's principal mission; occupying Midway was secondary. Luring the crippled U.S. Pacific Fleet into an all-out battle at this point would, he believed, provide Japan's best hope for victory. The American warships were outnumbered nearly 3 to 1 by his own battle-tested forces. But in the crucial component—aircraft carriers—his advantage was not as big as he believed. Japanese pilots had reported sinking two American carriers in the Coral Sea, the *Lexington* and the *Yorktown*. The *Lexington* had indeed been sunk, but unbeknown to Yamamoto the *Yorktown* had been repaired and was steaming toward Midway. The two Japanese carriers damaged in the Battle of the Coral Sea, on the other hand, were still in port. Yamamoto's actual edge was thus four carriers to three.

Nimitz also had the aircraft based on Midway to augment his carrier forces; all told, he actually had 23 more planes than Yamamoto. But his biggest advantage was knowing his enemy's strength and plans in detail, thanks to Rochefort. It gave the American forces the opening to surprise the Japanese, to catch them unawares and unprepared. The admiral directed Spruance's Task Force 16 and Fletcher's Task Force 17 to rendezvous on June 2 at a spot 325 miles northeast of Midway that Nimitz optimistically christened Point Luck. There, Fletcher, as the more senior of the two, assumed overall command of the combined force of 27 surface ships, including the three carriers bearing 233 aircraft. Fletcher and Spruance would lie in wait at Point Luck for the Japanese strike force coming from the northwest.

The orders from Nimitz were to hold Midway, but not at all costs. He directed that the operation be governed by the principle of calculated risk, which he defined as "avoidance of exposure of your force to attack by superior enemy forces without good prospect of inflicting, as a result of such exposure, greater damage on the enemy." The task force commanders had to be ready to move aggressively, yet in order to put their three precious carriers in a position to strike the Japanese, they would have to move them within range of enemy planes. The battle, it seemed, would hinge on who discovered the other side first.

Midway had been in a state of high alert since May 21, and from then on 30 patrol planes had flown continual 700-mile search patterns in an effort to find the Japanese fleet. At 9:25 a.m. on Wednesday, June 3, a message that everyone had been waiting for came back from a U.S. scout plane 700 miles out to the southwest, in the vicinity of Japanese-occupied Wake Island: "Sighted main body."

Nimitz immediately radioed Admiral Fletcher: "That is not, repeat not, the enemy striking force—stop—that is the landing force. The striking force will hit from the northwest at daylight tomorrow." Fletcher and Spruance eased a little closer to Midway, until they were about 200 miles northeast of it, and listened to the radio traffic as B-17s from the atoll attacked the Japanese invasion transport ships during the afternoon of June 3. But, because they were bombing from a high altitude, the B-17s failed to score any hits on their moving targets.

These attacks on the troop ships did not worry Admiral Nagumo, commanding the strike force northwest of Midway. He reported confidently to Yamamoto that "the enemy is not aware of our plans." The Americans, he added, had no "powerful unit, with carriers" in the vicinity.

As dawn brightened the sky over the central Pacific Ocean on June 4, Spruance was still in the dark as to the exact whereabouts of the Japanese striking force. Nothing but empty ocean was visible from his vantage point on the bridge perched atop a structure called the island. Towering high above the *Enterprise's* 800-foot-long flight deck, the island functioned as the control tower for the aircraft

taking off and landing. So far none of Spruance's or Fletcher's scout planes had reported any sign of the strike force coming from the northwest. And Spruance was well aware that the Japanese carriers steaming toward Midway had their scouts out looking for American ships.

Midway was already a hive of activity at dawn. Thirty minutes earlier, 16 B-17 bombers had taken off to attack the Japanese transport group again. Precisely at sunrise—4:37 a.m.—fighter pilots started their aircraft engines and antiaircraft gunners took their stations, in anticipation of attack from carrier-borne aircraft; they did not yet know where the carriers were.

A half-hour passed. The fighter pilots shut down their engines. Another half-hour, and then the word came from a patrol plane: An enemy carrier was in sight. Now there could be no doubt that the blow would fall very soon. The fighters started up again, and the antiaircraft crews prepared to open fire. At 5:45 a.m. another scout pilot, too excited to encode his message, yelled, "Many planes headed Midway!" They were 150 miles out, to the northwest.

Every airworthy fighter aircraft on the island— 20 old, clumsy F2A-3 Buffaloes, called flying coffins by their pilots, and six F4F-3 Wildcats, newer and better but still far inferior to the enemy's fast, highly maneuverable Zeros—took off and headed northwest. Midway's radar now showed the first attack wave 90 miles out. The 16 B-17s on their way to bomb the troop transports were ordered to change course and head toward the Japanese carriers.

Spruance and Fletcher had to bide their time until their scout planes gave them the information they needed to pinpoint the location and distance of the Japanese fleet. They could not launch their dive bombers, torpedo planes, and fighter escorts without being reasonably confident that the aircraft would have enough fuel to reach their target, attack, and get back to the carriers. While they waited for this information, every minute was another chance for enemy patrols to find the *Enterprise, Hornet,* or *Yorktown* and ruin the Americans' principal advantage—surprise.

Spruance, with his two-carrier force, would provide most of the strike aircraft, with Fletcher contributing some torpedo planes and dive bombers. As Spruance waited for more information he edged closer to Midway and prepared to launch every plane he had. Fletcher, with the patched-together *Yorktown,* hung back, launching patrol planes and holding some of his fighters in readiness to defend the American fleet in case it was discovered.

At 6:03 a.m., Spruance received the report he needed: An American pilot had sighted the Japanese carriers 180 miles northwest of Midway and 175 miles from the U.S. fleet. That was the maximum range of the task force's aircraft, but with the threat of discovery constantly preying on Spruance, he decided that he could not wait any longer. As Fletcher put it, the Americans had to "strike first, strike swiftly, strike in great force."

Spruance turned his carriers into the wind—the planes needed the added boost of the wind over their wings to get airborne from the short flight deck—and at 7:00 a.m. began launching his aircraft: 67 dive bombers, 29 torpedo planes, and 20 fighters. It took an hour to get them all in the air, formed up in attack formations, and on their way. An hour later, Fletcher launched a small second wave of 25 fighters and bombers.

Now it was back to waiting for Spruance. While his planes made the two-hour flight to the enemy's location, he kept track of Midway's defense by radio-telephone in the flag shelter, a windowless room adjacent to the bridge that served as his command post.

Since launching its bombers against the Japanese fleet, Midway itself had become a target of attack. At 6:12 a.m., the leader of the six Wildcat fighters from Midway had spotted enemy planes at 12,000 feet. Along with the Buffaloes, the Wildcats attacked the incoming Japanese bombers 40 miles out. The Americans managed to shoot down three, but the swifter

Thanks to cryptographer Lieutenant Commander Joseph Rochefort *(above),* naval intelligence learned in advance of Japan's offensive against Midway atoll, the westernmost point in the Pacific still flying the Stars and Stripes in spring 1942. Over a period of years, Rochefort and his team had gradually deciphered the Japanese navy's operational code, which consisted of some 45,000 five-digit numbers representing words and phrases and a larger pool of random numbers thrown in to confuse code breakers.

Zero fighters, swooping protectively around the bombers, shot down 17 American planes, killing 14 pilots. Seven other fighters were disabled; two remained in condition to fly.

Having punched through the airborne defenses, the Japanese bombers now flew into the teeth of the American antiaircraft fire to begin bombing and strafing Midway. The guns were no more effective at stopping the bombers than the fighters had been. Midway took a tremendous pounding, and when it was over its seaplane hangar, fuel dump, dispensary, power station, and water distillation plant were reduced to smoking ruins. Remarkably, the runways and gun batteries were still in operation, and only 24 of the 3,000 men on the ground had been killed.

To the northwest, the attack squadron that had departed Midway before dawn reached its target and made five passes over the Japanese carrier fleet. Fifteen American planes were lost without scoring a hit. Although his fleet had escaped damage this time, Admiral Nagumo—still unaware that American carriers were in the vicinity and had launched planes now headed in his direction—decided to strike Midway a second time to eliminate the threat of aerial attack on his fleet.

Nagumo's decision caused a flurry of activity on his carriers, because the planes already on deck for a second attack wave had been armed with torpedoes in case they encountered any American ships. Since these weapons were useless against a land target, the ordnance on every plane had to be changed to bombs. This was a time-consuming process that involved lowering the planes from the flight deck to the hangar deck, removing the torpedoes, loading the bombs, and raising the aircraft to the flight deck again.

The job was halfway completed when, at about 7:30 in the morning Nagumo received a report from a scout plane pilot who had just spotted what he believed to be 10 American ships about 200 miles east

of him. Thirty minutes later, the pilot had flown close enough to the enemy ships to add a disconcerting detail to a follow-up report: One of them appeared to be a carrier.

Nagumo's confidence that the enemy was ignorant of his plans and did not have any carriers within range crumbled. With all of his fighters engaged in the attack on Midway and his bombers in the process of being equipped with land bombs, he realized that he might be attacked at any moment by carrier-based aircraft. He did not have any choice but to order his sweating and disconcerted crews to immediately begin removing the bombs they had just loaded and put the torpedoes back, so he could go after the carriers. In their haste, the loading crews left the bombs stacked on the hangar deck amid the aircraft.

The crews were still changing ordnance when planes that were returning from the attack on Midway began circling the carriers waiting for clearance to land. Nagumo had to interrupt the rearming in order to clear the flight decks for the returning aircraft. All the planes had landed by a little after 9:00 a.m., and Nagumo changed course and headed toward the American fleet.

At that moment, Spruance's Task Force 16 attack aircraft were flying toward a spot in the ocean where, based on the American scout plane's report, they should find the Japanese fleet. But because of Nagumo's course change, the sea was empty when the planes arrived over the spot. The pilots did not have enough gas to make a long search for the enemy ships. The first 35 bombers from the *Hornet,* along with 10 fighters, turned southeast, found nothing, and landed on Midway. Lieutenant Commander Wade McClusky, with two squadrons from the *Enterprise,* turned northwest away from Midway to look for the enemy.

On the morning of June 4 the USS *Yorktown,* fire blazing on its flight deck, lumbers beneath a sky splattered with black smoke from antiaircraft flak. After a second Japanese attack, the ship was abandoned. On June 6 the carrier suffered a torpedo hit from a Japanese submarine and capsized the next day.

Gregarious and playful, 35-year-old Isoroku Yamamoto poses with smiling schoolgirls in 1919 in Waltham, Massachusetts, during his stint as a fellow at Harvard University, where he studied English and mastered bridge and poker. He was posted to Washington in 1925 as naval attaché, and his two years there left him enamored of American culture and deeply impressed by the nation's industrial strength.

JAPAN'S NAVAL GENIUS

Isoroku Yamamoto, commander in chief of the Japanese fleet and the mastermind of naval strategy in the Pacific, had opposed war with the United States. "Japan cannot beat America," he told a group of Japanese schoolchildren in 1940. "Therefore, Japan should not fight America." But when war came, Yamamoto the patriot gave himself completely to his country's cause. His audacious long shot gamble at Pearl Harbor paid off, and Yamamoto became an overnight hero in Japan.

Yamamoto could not repeat his success at Midway, and as he had predicted, Japan's fortunes began to decline. In April 1943 Yamamoto was in the Solomon Islands trying to stem the relentless American advance. To boost morale among his men, he set out to visit his forward bases. But the U.S. Navy's cryptographers, who had helped foil his plans at Midway, decoded his itinerary: On April 18 Yamamoto would arrive on Bougainville in one of two twin-engine bombers escorted by six Zero fighters.

Major John W. Mitchell, commander of Fighter Squadron 339 on Guadalcanal, 400 miles southeast of Bougainville, received orders to "at all costs reach and destroy Yamamoto and his staff." Sixteen P-38 Lightning fighter planes took off on the morning of April 18. A little over two hours later, one of the pilots spotted the two bombers at low altitude preparing to land on Bougainville. While 14 of the P-38s held off the Zeros, the remaining two dived on their quarry and opened fire. One bomber plunged into the sea; the other, carrying Yamamoto, burst into flames and crashed in jungle, where searchers later found his charred body. Japan's great naval tactician was dead.

Listening tensely to the pilots' radiofrequencies, Spruance heard one of McClusky's pilots report just after 10:00 a.m. that he was running dangerously low on fuel. Moments later the pilot sighted the enemy—two carriers, two battleships, and eight destroyers. Spruance's chief of staff impulsively grabbed a microphone and yelled, "Attack! Attack!" There was a moment of silence, and then McClusky's dry response: "Wilco, as soon as I find the bastards." Then, at 10:20 a.m., came McClusky's shout of "Tallyho!"

While McClusky's dive bombers were preparing to pounce from high above the Japanese carriers, two squadrons of torpedo planes that had been following McClusky came in at low level. They ran into a swarm of defending Zeros that reminded one American pilot of "the inside of a beehive." To launch their torpedoes, the planes had to fly slow, straight, and level, just above the tops of the waves. It was like target practice for the Zero pilots. One after another the American planes went in, and one after another they were shot out of the sky.

Most of the planes plunged into the ocean before the pilots could even release their torpedoes; the few who managed to fire missed their targets. All 15 planes of Torpedo Squadron 8 from the *Hornet* went down, and only one man survived. Ensign George Gay managed to extricate himself from his sinking plane, then trod water and hid under his seat cushion while the Japanese fleet sailed around him. Gay would be spotted and rescued by a navy seaplane the next day.

Not one Japanese ship had been damaged so far, and American losses in aircraft and pilots were high. Admiral Nagumo was now poised to launch his counterattack on the American carriers, but his strike force was not yet airborne when McClusky's bombers came screaming down out of the sun in near-vertical dives. The sacrifice of the torpedo plane crews had not been in vain, for they had drawn the Japanese fighter cover down to sea level. For the moment the Zeros could do nothing to stop

McClusky's planes as they drew a bead on the two largest carriers, *Akagi* and *Kaga.*

The first bombs fell with triphammer effect on the *Kaga.* One exploded among the fighters on the flight deck, igniting gasoline and ordnance; another smashed through to the hangar deck; a third blew up a gasoline truck, killing everyone on the bridge; a fourth hit near the left side of the flight deck. Fires erupted along her entire length, and most of the crew was trapped belowdecks. Looking like "a skull smashed open," as one sailor put it later, the *Kaga* would explode and sink seven hours later.

Admiral Nagumo's flagship, the *Akagi,* fared no better. The first fighter of the Japanese counterattack force was on its takeoff roll when the carrier took two direct hits that blew 200 men overboard, destroyed the radio room, disabled the engines and the helm, and wreaked havoc among the densely parked planes. The bombs stacked on the hangar deck began to go up in a chain reaction that turned the carrier into what Nagumo's chief of staff described as "a burning hell." Nagumo and his staff had to slide down a rope to abandon ship.

A group of dive bombers from the *Yorktown* found a third carrier, the *Soryu,* off to the northeast of the two burning Japanese carriers. Sighting on the rising sun emblazoned on her flight deck, the bombers scored three direct hits in three minutes. The *Soryu* burned out in little more than 30 minutes and sank a few hours later.

In the space of less than half an hour the tide of the battle had been reversed. Now it was three American carriers against the one remaining Japanese carrier, the *Hiryu,* which had managed to escape attack. At 10:40 a.m., in an effort to avenge the morning's stunning losses, the *Hiryu* launched 18 dive bombers and six fighters, which followed the *Yorktown's* dive bombers back to their ship.

Smoke billows from the *Hiryu,* the last of four Japanese carriers hit by American planes during the Battle of Midway. Rear Admiral Tamon Yamaguchi, the commanding officer on board, had himself lashed to the bridge and went down with his ship.

U.S. fighters shot down 10 of the bombers before they could release their payloads, but others got through to score three direct hits. The first crashed through the flight deck to the hangar deck, killing 17 men and setting three planes on fire. Another blaze was started by a bomb that penetrated to the fourth deck, threatening the ammunition stores. A third hit punched through several steel decks to the central smokestack before exploding and extinguishing the boilers. The returning Japanese pilots reported that the ship was burning and dead in the water. But thanks to quick firefighting and damage control, the *Yorktown* was under way again in slightly more than two hours.

The *Hiryu* launched a second attack to deliver the *coup de grâce* to the *Yorktown*. When her pilots found their presumed target steaming under her own power with no sign of fire, they thought they must have stumbled across a different carrier. Five Japanese torpedo planes managed to get through the defending fighters and launch their projectiles. The *Yorktown* evaded two torpedoes but then took hits from a third and a fourth.

Badly damaged below the water line, her fuel tanks ruptured, and her power and communications systems down, the *Yorktown* began to list, and in 10 minutes one edge of the flight deck was nearly touching the surface of the ocean. The condition of the ship was such that it was beyond saving, and the *Yorktown*'s 3,000-man crew was ordered to abandon it; Admiral Fletcher and his staff had already transferred to a nearby cruiser.

Scout planes had been out searching for the *Hiryu,* and in the midst of the assault on the *Yorktown* Spruance got word from a Task Force 17 pilot that the Japanese carrier and a number of support vessels had been sighted. Spruance immediately ordered dive bombers to take off in pursuit, then sent a message to Fletcher: "TF 16 air groups are now striking the carrier which your search planes reported." In deference to the senior commander, he added, "Have you any instructions for me?" Fletcher knew that it was impossible for him to di-rect a carrier battle from a cruiser, and he replied: "None. Will conform to your movements." Spruance was now in charge.

The *Hiryu* was about to launch another wave of bombers and torpedo planes when Spruance's dive bombers found her at 5:00 p.m. They dealt with her as swiftly and effectively as they had the other Japanese carriers, delivering four direct hits on her bow within seconds. In an attempt to dodge the bombers, the *Hiryu* began maneuvering at high speed, but the fire that had erupted spread quickly and enveloped the entire ship. She went to the bottom the next morning.

Mindful of Nimitz's principle of calculated risk, Spruance resisted the temptation to chase the rest of the Japanese fleet and headed toward Midway, where American carrier- and land-based aircraft could support each other. Then he went to bed at his regular time and slept soundly until breakfast. Of his decision on the eve of battle to give Halsey's command to the unknown Spruance, Nimitz later said, "It was a choice I never regretted. Spruance had excellent judgment."

At 2:55 a.m., a profoundly depressed Admiral Yamamoto sent his fleet a message that began, "The Midway operation is canceled." He had lost four aircraft carriers and one cruiser, and 3,500 men had been killed. Most ominous of all for Yamamoto's future prospects, the cream of Japanese naval aviation—275 aircraft and their irreplaceable crews, veterans of Pearl Harbor and Coral Sea—had gone down with their ships. The outnumbered Americans had lost one carrier, one destroyer, 132 aircraft, and only 307 lives.

No one yet realized that Midway signaled the turning point in the Pacific war, but Americans could rejoice that, after six months of disaster, defeat, and surrender, their country had trounced Japan in battle. "Pearl Harbor has now been partially avenged," declared Admiral Nimitz. "Vengeance will not be complete until Japanese sea power is reduced to impotence. Perhaps we will be forgiven if we claim we are about midway to that objective." ◆

The Home Front Goes to War

In December 1941 the full might of the United States' armed forces—army, navy, and Marine Corps—responded to the military challenge presented by World War II. But America's commander in chief, President Franklin Roosevelt, was convinced that victory was possible only if the energies of all the American people, military and civilian alike, were unleashed. In the second fireside chat he broadcast after the war began, he declared that there is "one front and one battle where everyone in the United States—every man, woman, and child—is in action. That front is right here at home." A receptive country heard and responded to the president's message: Civilians were mobilized, industry geared up, and the home front went to war.

During the course of that war, activities such as rationing, recycling, carpooling, and queuing became part of daily life for most Americans. Many also faced the prospect of relocating to another part of the country. For America was a nation on the move: In addi-

tion to the 16 million people who left home for military service, nearly as many civilians changed their residences, most of them moving to cities to take new jobs. As a result, urban centers suffered acute housing shortages, and in some places landlords rented so-called hot beds to shift workers—eight hours of rest for 25¢.

In spite of such hardships, these were years of hope and optimism, a time when Americans—who were caught up in the greatest collective experience of their lives—felt more united than at any other time in their history. Everyone was able to play a role in the war effort, from the women who joined the work force in record numbers to the children who collected scrap materials for their use by industry and the Hollywood stars who entertained the troops. "That was one of the best times of my life, even though there was a war on," recalled one young woman whose father and boyfriend were fighting overseas. "Everybody was so kind. We all had somebody over there. So everybody understood."

Looking strong, serious, and competent, Rosie the Riveter symbolized the vital importance of women workers to the defense industry.

Industry Gets in Gear

While war was being waged overseas, another great struggle was launched at home: industry's battle to outproduce the enemy. New factories sprouted all over the United States, and existing plants quickly converted to defense production. Grenade belts replaced corsets on one assembly line. Workers produced munitions in plants that had previously made Cokes and Kodaks. And a factory that at one time made merry-go-rounds began producing gun mounts.

By the spring of 1944 American industry was operating at full pitch: 202,000 planes, 59,000 boats and ships, and 380,000 big guns had rolled off the country's assembly lines. Plants grew so efficient that they could churn out a merchant ship every 10 hours and a B-24 bomber in little more than one hour. Smaller planes took five minutes, jeeps just two.

To be able to make such a huge leap in production, the country had to turn for help to groups of people who had been largely excluded from factories in the prewar days, even to convicts who were

serving time. At San Quentin prison in California, for example, inmates made everything from antisubmarine nets to night sticks for the National Guard.

The most visible change in American manufacturing was the sudden arrival of women in factories all over the country. By 1943 two million women were working in war industries. They soldered steel and loaded munitions, welded troop carriers, and riveted bombers. Factory managers who had at one time spurned women as workers were suddenly eager to recruit them. "If I had my way now," confessed one executive impressed with his patient and detail-oriented female work force, "I'd say, 'to hell with the men. Give me women.'" The experience proved to be an equally momentous one for the workers. "Those years changed our lives," said a mother of three children who was employed as a welder in a California shipyard. "All of a sudden I was making money. I was head of a household and it made a different person of me."

Channeling his strength into the war effort, the worker in this patriotic poster epitomized America's formidable industrial muscle and efficiency.

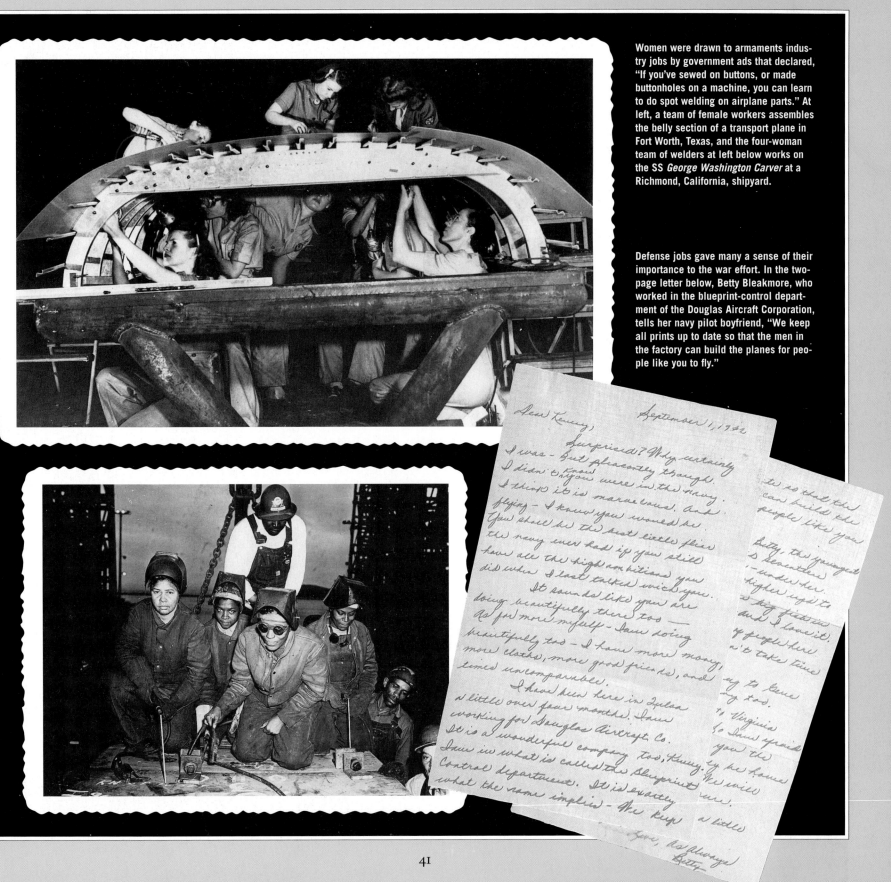

Women were drawn to armaments industry jobs by government ads that declared, "If you've sewed on buttons, or made buttonholes on a machine, you can learn to do spot welding on airplane parts." At left, a team of female workers assembles the belly section of a transport plane in Fort Worth, Texas, and the four-woman team of welders at left below works on the SS *George Washington Carver* at a Richmond, California, shipyard.

Defense jobs gave many a sense of their importance to the war effort. In the two-page letter below, Betty Bleakmore, who worked in the blueprint-control department of the Douglas Aircraft Corporation, tells her navy pilot boyfriend, "We keep all prints up to date so that the men in the factory can build the planes for people like you to fly."

"Here's Our Answer, Mr. Roosevelt"

The amazing growth of U.S. industrial production demanded huge quantities of critical materials. A B-17 bomber, for instance, required half a ton of rubber, and an army tank used a ton. The Southeast Asia plantations that supplied most of the world's natural rubber were now in Japanese hands, and to meet the demand President Roosevelt ordered large-scale synthesizing of rubber from petroleum. But he also recognized that another potential source was reclaimed scrap rubber—and that the only way he could tap this source was to rely on the public at large.

In June 1942 Roosevelt called on Americans to turn in "old tires, old raincoats, old garden hose, rubber shoes, bathing caps, gloves." Recycling became a patriotic duty, and within four weeks the president's appeal brought in some 450,000 tons of scrap rubber. Among the rubber items contributed to the war effort was a girdle that arrived at the White House with a note that read, "I hope I may claim the privilege of being the first to donate personal wearing apparel for the cause."

Other shortages met similar responses from the public. Nationwide drives collected aluminum for airplane production, cooking fats, which yielded glycerin for high explosives, and paper, which was used in the manufacture of cartridge belts. "Junk ain't junk no more," crooned Bing Crosby, " 'cause junk can win the war."

But the war effort also needed plain old money. In addition to instituting the federal "pay-as-you-go" withholding tax, the government issued war bonds, which were priced at $18.75 and worth $25 after 10 years. Bonds were amazingly popular: In a war that would cost the country $304 billion, bond sales met one-sixth of the expense. Students in particular became enthusiastic supporters of the program, honing their math skills as they calculated exactly what their bonds purchased. One Kansas class figured their $331 bought one machine gun, five helmets, a tent, and nine tools.

Don't Let That Shadow Touch Them
Buy **WAR BONDS**

Bringing the threat of Nazi domination close to home, this poster urges
Americans to protect their children by supporting the drive for war bonds.

Home-front scrap drives gave children all over the country a way to share in the war effort. Above, Boy Scouts from Stevens Point, Wisconsin, lead a parade of trucks loaded with old auto tires, while New York kids *(left)* collect aluminum from their neighbors on the Lower East Side.

A crowd gathers in Times Square in front of a huge cash register recording war bond sales in the nation's fifth loan drive. Children bought 25¢ stamps and pasted them in albums like the one shown above, right. When the last space in an album was filled, it was exchanged for a bond.

"Doncha Know There's a War On?"

The major personal sacrifice that was required of most civilians during World War II was involuntary: the rationing of essential items by the federal government. The rationing system was designed to ensure the equitable distribution of what remained after military needs had been filled. A household was issued pocket-sized ration books containing coupons that represented its weekly or monthly allotment of meat, butter, cooking fat, shoes, gasoline, and so on. A shopper had to have both money and the proper number of coupons in order to close a sale.

In all, some 20 major items were affected by rationing, and for the most part Americans could understand why. Sugar, for example, was rationed because sugarcane was converted into gunpowder; canned foods because tin was needed for the production of armaments; and coffee because the military had other uses for the ships that once brought coffee beans from South America. But why was ketchup on the ration list? The most likely

response to this—or any other question about rationing—was a simple one: "Doncha know there's a war on?"

The scarcity of goods forced people to exercise creativity in their domestic affairs. Housewives who were limited to a pound of coffee beans every five weeks saved the grounds and reused them to produce a watery brew dubbed Roosevelt coffee. "It was," said to one woman, "sort of brown, sort of tasted like coffee, and didn't keep us up at night."

Wartime shortages also caused a transformation of fashions. In order to save cloth for military use, skirt hems were shortened, and men began to wear "Victory" suits that featured cuffless trousers and narrow lapels. When nylon stockings disappeared from the shelves in stores, women wore leg makeup and carefully drew a line up the back of each leg to simulate stocking seams. The ersatz seams, however, were not weatherproof. "If it rained," one woman noted wryly, "you'd have stripes down your legs."

HAVE YOU REALLY TRIED TO SAVE GAS BY GETTING INTO A CAR CLUB?

A wounded GI exhorts citizens to conserve gasoline. By imposing driving limits, gas rationing cut down wear and tear on tires and reduced rubber consumption.

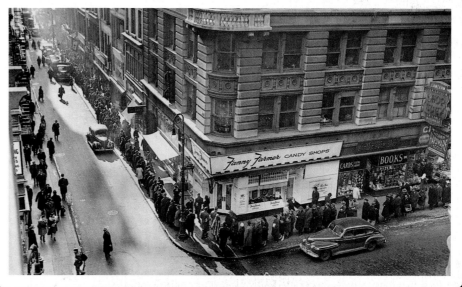

"Friendly but firm" is how *Life* magazine described the members of the Ration Board of Bristol, Connecticut. The nation's 5,500 local boards oversaw rationing, which involved the exchange of some three billion ration coupons every month.

While Americans would wait in line for many items, like the scarce cigarettes responsible for this queue of nicotine-starved New Yorkers, the unrationed horse meat for sale at a Newark, New Jersey, meat market named for a champion racehorse *(left)* rarely drew a crowd.

Showtime Stateside

Americans craved diversions during the war, and the Hollywood movie industry gave them exactly what they wanted: more war. Movies such as *Casablanca, Guadalcanal Diary, Crash Dive,* and *Commandos Strike at Dawn* packed theaters across the country. Many movie theaters were open 24 hours a day for the benefit of those workers who were coming off the night shift, and they were often crowded despite the hour. Americans in the war years were enthusiastic moviegoers, with the majority seeing at least one film a week.

For tourists and servicemen alike, one of the best places to get away from it all was New York City. Broadway theaters offered free or discount tickets to members of the armed forces and packed them in— more than 11 million people attended shows in 1943. War was as popular on stage as it was on film, featuring plays like *Winged Victory,* with an all Army Air Force cast, and *Doughgirls,* about housing shortages in wartime Washington, D.C. So great was the demand for entertainment that even second-rate productions did well at the box

office, prompting the *New York Times* drama critic to write, "It was a public so anxious to attend the theater that for a time it would attend anything playing in the theater."

Another magnet for off-duty servicemen who were visiting New York City was the Stage Door Canteen, where celebrity volunteers danced with GIs and dispensed doughnuts and milk. Soldiers lined up outside the canteen's famous red door each night for a chance to hobnob with stars like Milton Berle or Ethel Merman. Clubs run by the United Service Organizations (USO) also provided relaxing off-duty hangouts for soldiers who were new to town. Over coffee they could bend the ear of a patient USO hostess or cut loose on the dance floor with tireless volunteers. But for some members of the USO staff the clubs sometimes more closely resembled combat zones. "The small dance floor was so crowded we couldn't help getting kicked in the shins and ankles," recalled one bruised hostess. "We'd silently count to ten and say, 'I'm due for my purple heart any day now.'"

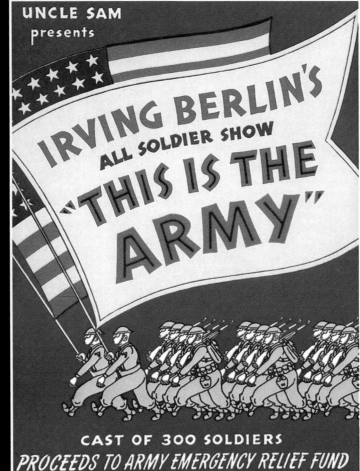

Complete with a cast of 300 soldiers, Irving Berlin's Broadway show *This Is the Army* was a rousing depiction of military life set to music.

Entertaining the troops was a patriotic duty for everyone from the volunteer serving punch to a soldier at a Washington, D.C., USO to the Andrews Sisters, who brightened spirits with their cheery three-part harmony.

A lucky GI gets to blow out the candles on a birthday cake served up by actress Bette Davis at New York's Stage Door Canteen. The canteen provided entertainment for U.S. and foreign servicemen, most alone and in New York City for the first time.

From her piano-top perch, actress Lauren Bacall listens appreciatively as Vice President Harry Truman displays his talent at the keyboard with a rendition of the "Missouri Waltz" at Washington's National Press Club.

A Back Door into Europe

When the Anglo-American Allies landed in western North Africa in November 1942, Germany and Italy controlled Tunisia; Morocco and Algeria were colonies of Vichy France; and Spain and Spanish Morocco, although officially neutral, were sympathetic to the Axis.

Eleven months after the attack on Pearl Harbor, the U.S. Army embarked on its first major offensive of the war. Despite the public's wish for revenge against Japan, it was not a strike against the Japanese empire. Nor was it an assault against Adolf Hitler's Fortress Europe, even though President Franklin Roosevelt was committed to a Germany First policy. In the spring of 1942 the western Allies did not as yet have the men and supplies needed for such an operation. Nevertheless, having promised Soviet leader Joseph Stalin that the United States would open a second front that year, Roosevelt agreed to a British proposal that would take some of the pressure off the Russians: an invasion of German-dominated North Africa.

Under the command of U.S. Lieutenant General Dwight Eisenhower, more than 100,000 American and British troops landed at nine sites in North Africa on the morning of November 8, 1942. They quickly overwhelmed the forces of the Vichy government, which had been collaborating with the Germans since the fall of France in June 1940, and seized the key French colonial ports of Casablanca in Morocco and Oran and Algiers in Algeria. Eisenhower hoped it would take only two weeks to complete the final stage of the mission—a 450-mile race to the coastal cities of Tunis and Bizerte,

Tunisia—before the Axis could bring in reinforcements. Hitler responded quickly to the invasion, however, and a day after the Anglo-American landings Axis troops began to pour into Tunisia from Sicily. The Allies had lost the race to Tunis and Bizerte, and after sparring with enemy forces throughout December, halted temporarily at Eisenhower's command because of the winter rains.

When fighting resumed in the new year it was the Germans who took the offensive. In February General Erwin Rommel, who had been driven from Egypt into Tunisia by Britain's General Bernard Law Montgomery, attacked the Allies in western Tunisia. Green American troops faltered and retreated before Rommel's experienced army and fell back 50 miles to the Kasserine Pass, where Allied reinforcements eventually halted the German thrust.

Bloodied but not beaten, U.S. forces regrouped under new leadership from General George Patton and Major General Omar Bradley, and in the following month American, British, and anti-Vichy French troops began a slow, determined advance against Rommel. On May 7 the Americans took Bizerte and the British entered Tunis. The last of the Axis forces in Tunisia, more than 250,000 men, surrendered a week later. The war in North Africa was over.

Gathered around their half-track personnel carrier, the troops of a U.S. armored unit pause in the Tunisian desert to plan their next move against the Germans. For most American servicemen, their first encounter with the enemy was a horrifying experience. The grim-faced Army Air Corps sergeant at right was wounded after a German bombing raid on his airfield near the Tunisian-Algerian border in December 1942.

American infantrymen pick their way through the rubble of the coastal road between Palermo and Messina that Axis troops had destroyed during their retreat from Sicily. "With railroads wrecked, bridges destroyed, and many sections of roads blown out," General Dwight Eisenhower observed, "the advance was difficult enough even without opposition from the enemy."

INVADING THE AXIS

After their victory in the desert the Allies had several choices of where next to strike the Axis. Southern France was a possibility, as was the mainland of Italy. Adolf Hitler himself was certain that the targets would be German-occupied Greece and the Italian island of Sardinia. But for months Dwight Eisenhower and the Allies had set their sights on another Italian island: Sicily.

On July 10, 1943, a British army under General Montgomery landed on the southern tip of the island and started to drive toward the northeastern port city of Messina, which lay within sight of the toe of Italy's boot. On the same day a U.S. Army led by General Patton came ashore on the southwestern coast with orders to protect Montgomery's flank. But Patton chafed at what he considered this subordinate role. After rebuffing a German attack on his beachhead he dashed north across Sicily to take the lightly defended capital, Palermo, on July 22. Three days later Italian dictator Benito Mussolini resigned.

Both Allied armies reached Messina on August 17 to find that the Axis forces were gone. A week earlier Germany's Field Marshal Albert Kesselring had begun ferrying his troops and equipment across to the mainland of Italy. The Allies would meet these soldiers again, on the other side of the Strait of Messina.

Leading victorious GIs through Messina's streets in a horse-drawn cart, jubilant Sicilians celebrate the departure of the Germans on August 17, 1943. The fall of the city marked the end of the Sicily campaign and the start of negotiations between the Allies and the Italian government.

THE ROCKY UNDERBELLY

Winston Churchill had called Italy "the soft underbelly of the Axis." Politically speaking, the British prime minister may have been right, for on September 3, 1943, the government in Rome signed an armistice with the Allies. But in trying to move up the mountainous Italian peninsula against a still determined German foe, the Allies would find that the soft underbelly had turned rock hard.

Less than a week after Italy withdrew from the war, the main Allied force landed at Salerno Bay, just south of Naples. The Germans were waiting for them. Only after nine days of bitter fighting did the defenders fall back. But the Germans continued to resist as they retreated, and only on October 1 were the Allies able to enter Naples.

But between the Allies and the Italian capital lay a maze of mountains and streams in which the Germans, under Kesselring, had set up a strong defensive position called the Gustav Line. Repeated Allied attempts to break the line failed, and in an effort to end the deadlock the Allies decided on an end run around the enemy positions. On January 22, 1944, an amphibious force of 36,000 U.S. and British troops landed at the resort town of Anzio, just 25 miles south of Rome and 60 miles behind the main battle line. The landing came as a total surprise to the Germans, but once ashore the Allies moved too slowly and lost their advantage, giving the enemy time to mount an assault that bottled up the invaders on the beach. By early March the two fought-out armies had settled down to a stalemate.

Not until May would the Anzio troops join up with other Allied units advancing from the south toward Rome, which fell on June 4. But by then the Allies' main efforts were directed toward another front. From bases in Britain an Anglo-American force was about to launch the long-awaited invasion of France. Eisenhower, Montgomery, Bradley, and Patton had moved to England to direct the operation, and in Normandy Erwin Rommel was preparing to meet them.

In the mountains east of Cassino, GIs drive donkeys bearing an 81mm mortar and its ammunition. Some parts of the rugged region were too steep for the animals, however, and the loads had to be taken over by soldiers, who carried them in backpacks or lugged them on packboards.

Bathed in light streaming in through a bomb-damaged roof, a lone American soldier, helmet in hand, stands before the altar of a village church in southern Italy. But such respites from war were rare during the Italian campaign, where soldiers like those below had to make their way warily through small mountain towns street by street.

CHAPTER

A Day in June, 1944

"You are about to embark upon the Great Crusade, toward which we have striven these many months. The eyes of the world are upon you."

EISENHOWER'S ORDER OF THE DAY TO THE ALLIED EXPEDITIONARY FORCE, JUNE 6, 1944

After more than a year of preparation, the mighty armada under Dwight Eisenhower's command was tense as a coiled spring, ready to launch the largest and most ambitious amphibious invasion in history at the beaches of Normandy in northern France. This was known as Operation *Overlord*, the long-awaited Allied assault upon German-occupied western Europe. Its goal was to open a second front to ease the pressure on the Soviets, who had been fighting Adolf Hitler's Nazi forces on the Eastern Front for nearly three years.

Eisenhower was a four-star general in the United States Army whose imposing title was Supreme Commander Allied Expeditionary Force. But to generals and GIs alike, he was simply Ike. He had gained the nickname as a boy in Kansas, despite the best efforts of his mother, who had named him David Dwight at birth and then reversed the names because she disliked nicknames. Dwight, she figured, could never be shortened. The same could not be said of the last name, however: Eisenhower was too much of a mouthful for young Dwight's friends, who quickly shortened it to Ike.

Eisenhower had scheduled the invasion's d-day—the military name for the operation's target date—for Monday, June 5, 1944. On that day and the two days following, he knew, certain conditions deemed essential for success would be just right. A late-rising full moon would facilitate the night airborne assaults intended to secure the inland areas just beyond the beaches; aircraft carrying the paratroopers could approach under cover of darkness and then identify the drop zones in bright moonlight. And a low tide at dawn would aid the seaborne forces by exposing the mines and other treacherous obstacles planted by the Germans just offshore.

Unlike the predictable moon and tide, the weather was a worrisome unknown. Throughout the month of May the conditions considered vital to the invasion had prevailed: calm seas for the small landing craft, clear skies for the aerial bombardment. On Saturday, June 3, two days before the target date, Eisenhower cabled Washington that everything appeared to be on schedule. All that remained was for the Supreme Commander to give the final go-ahead. At his command, *Overlord*'s 175,000 assault troops, 5,000 ships and smaller craft, and 50,000 vehicles, with 11,000 aircraft overhead, would embark for Normandy. Indeed, on that Saturday all the troops were aboard ship and sections of the armada already were at sea, set to sail toward the beaches that lay 60 to 100 miles distant across the English Channel.

General Dwight David Eisenhower shares a lighter moment with Prime Minister Winston Churchill during the hectic preparations for Operation *Overlord*. Churchill is modeling the uniform he designed for British air-raid wardens.

Then the weather forecast, which had been so favorable for so long, turned sour. That Saturday night Eisenhower met with his ranking subordinates for their regular twice-a-day weather briefing at Southwick House, the mansion that served as *Overlord's* forward headquarters near Portsmouth on the south coast of England. The report from his top meteorologist, Captain James Stagg of Britain's Royal Air Force (RAF), was discouraging. The 28-year-old Scotsman predicted that a series of low-pressure areas moving eastward across the North Atlantic would bring stormy weather to the Channel. The weather picture was "very disturbed and complex," he said, the worst for that time of year in a half-century.

The news proved to be no better when the group again convened early the following morning, Sunday, at 4:15. Stagg said conditions at sea would be slightly calmer than anticipated, but those overhead were a different matter. He predicted that a thick cloud cover would preclude use of the fighter planes and bombers that were considered necessary for success on the beaches. But while Stagg was speaking, the first light of the new day brightened the windows of Southwick House. And to the men gathered there that morning, things did not look all that bad. The air was still, the sky almost cloudless. Some may have recalled a recent description of the rangy, rather morose meteorologist: "There goes six feet two of Stagg and six feet one of gloom."

Eisenhower, however, trusted Stagg. They had been meeting privately for a month, and Eisenhower found Stagg "dour but canny," his predictions remarkably accurate. The forecast of heavy cloud cover was therefore particularly worrying, for Eisenhower had already decided not to send troops onto the beaches without a preliminary bombardment of the German positions from the air. The general well knew that an amphibious assault was perilous, and even *with* air support the risks were high: His own chief of staff had recently put the chance of success at only 50-50. There was nothing for it. "If the air cannot operate," Ike told the meeting, "we must postpone." No one disagreed. Eisenhower issued orders to delay D-Day for at least 24 hours. No more ships were to sail, and the prearranged signal to return to port—"Ripcord plus 24"—went out to the hundreds of craft already at sea.

As the storm Stagg had predicted gathered fury that Sunday afternoon, Allied ships struggled back through the rain- and wind-whipped sea. The strain mounted on the men who were waiting in transport ships—and on their commander. Eisenhower sought refuge in his little trailer secreted in the woods about a mile from Southwick House. Although he could have stayed in the luxury of the huge mansion, Ike preferred the privacy and modest comfort of the sparsely furnished trailer that he called his "circus wagon."

He had slept badly the night before, and now he could taste the bitter disappointment of the postponement. *Overlord* was his baby. He had first advocated this cross-channel invasion more than two years earlier when he was a Washington staff officer. But he had been so little known in those days that one U.S. newspaper had referred to him as Lt. Col. D. D. Ersenbeing. Since then he had risen like a rocket commanding the combined Anglo-American invasions of North Africa, Sicily, and Italy, and then the preparations for *Overlord*.

Eisenhower belonged to a new breed of general. As some jealous colleagues liked to point out, he had never personally led men into battle. But he was a master of logistics and planning. With great care he had overseen the buildup of a massive arsenal of weapons and supplies and the compilation of an operational plan so detailed that it required a book three inches thick to explain it. Eisenhower's greatest genius, however, lay in his ability to harness the disparate and difficult personalities of the British and American commanders who served under him. This flair was embodied in his infectious grin—a smile, it was said, worth 20 divisions. Even to the most contentious of the British leaders, Field Marshal Bernard Law Montgomery, it had "the power of drawing the hearts of men towards him as a magnet attracts the bits of metal."

Nevertheless, Eisenhower's surface amiability cloaked an explosive temper and an iron resolve that did not flinch at the tough decisions. When the RAF and the U.S. Army Air Force balked at giving him control of how their strategic bombers would be used in the preinvasion aerial campaign, Ike threatened to resign and go home. He won the battle, and the Allied bombers were assigned the role he deemed crucial—that of severing the German transportation links to the beaches in Normandy.

Far from going home, Eisenhower had embarked on the most hectic period of his life, the four months leading up to the scheduled invasion. Averaging 15 cups of coffee and four packs of cigarettes a day and only four hours of sleep a night, he visited 26 different divisions of troops, 24 airfields, and countless depots and other installations. And he had coped with myriad problems. One of the thorniest was British prime minister Winston Churchill's request to accompany the invasion fleet.

Eisenhower had refused the request, telling him that the risks were too high and that the prime minister was too important to the Allied cause. But Churchill was not one to be put off easily. He considered his options for a moment, and then he pointed out, "You have the operational command of all forces, but you are not responsible administratively for the makeup of the crews."

"Yes, that's right," replied Eisenhower patiently, acknowledging the loophole that the clever Englishman had detected.

"Well," said Churchill, "then I can sign on as a member of the crew of one of His Majesty's ships, and there's nothing you can do about it."

"That's correct," Ike conceded. "But, Prime Minister, you will make my burden a lot heavier if you do it."

Churchill remained adamant about crossing the Channel aboard the cruiser HMS *Belfast*. Just as Ike was about to concede defeat to the wily politician, however, help for the Supreme Commander arrived from an unexpected source. It came from the owner of His Majesty's ships, His Majesty himself.

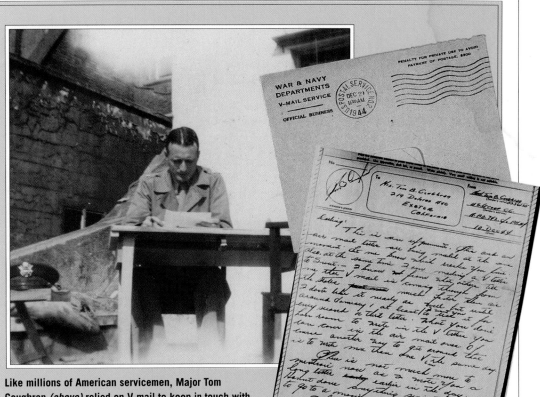

Like millions of American servicemen, Major Tom Coughran *(above)* relied on V-mail to keep in touch with loved ones. A letter sent from London to his wife in California is shown at right.

LINES OF COMMUNICATION

Letters from home were a great morale booster for American servicemen facing long separations from their families. Every ship and plane that left the United States was crammed with sacks of mail for the troops, but the volume was still so great that delivery could be delayed for months. To expedite postal shipments and to free valuable cargo space, the military developed a system called V-mail; the V stood for victory.

Beginning in June 1943, soldiers and civilians wrote to each other using a special form that served as both writing paper and envelope. Postal authorities gave the forms preferential handling en route to V-mail processing centers in the United States and overseas. There the letters were opened by machine and photographically transferred to microfilm at the rate of up to 2,500 an hour. Sixteen hundred letters could be stored on a single roll of film, a reduction of about 97 percent of their original weight and volume.

After sorting, the film was sent to the V-mail facility closest to its destination, where it was printed on photographic paper. The addressee then received a V-mail envelope containing a four-by-five-inch photograph of the original letter. The service was free for military personnel; civilians paid three cents postage. More than one billion pieces of V-mail were exchanged during the course of the war.

King George VI had been informed of his prime minister's plans to sail with the invasion force and had declared that if Churchill felt it necessary to go on the expedition, then he, the king, would have to go too. In the face of this royal intervention, the prime minister capitulated.

Dealing with Churchill was just one of what Ike himself referred to as the "Worries of a Commander." It was no wonder that he felt like "a flea on a hot griddle," as he wrote his wife, Mamie, toward the end of May. "I seem to live on a network of high tension wires." And now, with the invasion postponed for 24 hours, the tension grew almost unbearable. If D-Day had to be postponed again, beyond Tuesday, June 6, the operation might have to be put off for two weeks before a favorable tide came again, and at least a month to obtain both tide and moon. Eisenhower knew that such a delay would undercut the morale of troops all primed for action, risk loss of valuable secrecy, and clog the camps where follow-up units already were filing in to replace the first waves of assault units. The Soviet Red Army, moreover, had timed a major offensive on the Eastern Front to coincide with an early June invasion. To Eisenhower the consequences of postponement were "almost too bitter to contemplate."

That stormy Sunday afternoon Ike tried without much success to relax with one of the western pulp novels that he kept piled on a table near his bunk. Then he went outside and paced up and down a pathway near his trailer, chain-smoking and kicking at the cinders. From a distance Merrill "Red" Mueller, a reporter for NBC, watched the tall figure, shoulders slightly hunched, hands jammed deep into pockets. Looking up, Ike spotted Mueller and called out to him, "Let's take a walk, Red."

The two men strode off into the woods, the reporter quickening his pace to keep up with the general. But despite Eisenhower's request for company, he spoke barely a word. He seemed totally preoccupied with his own thoughts, and the newsman hesitated to intrude. When they returned to the trailer and Ike bade him farewell, Mueller thought

him bowed down with worry, "as though each of the four stars on either shoulder weighed a ton."

At 9:30 that night an immaculately uniformed Eisenhower strode into the oak-paneled library at Southwick House for another weather briefing. At one end of the room, a dozen senior officers lounged on couches and easy chairs, chatting quietly and drinking coffee. A fire crackled in the fireplace. The general flashed a subdued smile at his colleagues and crossed the polished floor to a table at the other end of the room. The others joined him there, and then Stagg, the chief meteorologist, came into the room. A hush fell over the group.

The meteorologist could feel Eisenhower staring at him. Stagg took a breath and began. "Gentlemen," he said quietly, "since I presented the forecast last evening, some rapid and unexpected developments have occurred over the North Atlantic." Everyone in the room perceived a glimmer of hope. The Scotsman gave the details. He predicted that a developing cold front would create a temporary break in the storm and that the rain would stop before daybreak. Then, from Monday afternoon through late Tuesday, winds would moderate and the clouds would scatter to provide clearer skies— clear enough, he forecast, for the fighters and the bombers to operate.

Stagg finished his report, and now it was time to make a decision. If the Allies were to launch the invasion on Tuesday morning, June 6, sailing orders for the fleet would have to be sent in just 30 minutes. Eisenhower started pacing the room with his chin on his chest and his hands clasped behind his back, mulling over what he had just heard. The news was not all good. Rough weather was expected to return on Wednesday, which raised questions about further air support and about the landing of reinforcements on the beachheads.

In a scene repeated at ports all over southern England in the late spring of 1944, U.S troops load the landing ships destined to ferry Eisenhower's army across the Channel. The vehicles were carefully backed into the cavernous holds so that they could be off-loaded quickly on the beaches of France.

A favorite pastime of American soldiers in England was jitterbugging at London's Rainbow Corner, a GI club near Piccadilly Circus *(right)*. An American soldier and his date *(below)* share a romantic moment in Hyde Park.

"OVERPAID, OVERSEXED, AND OVER HERE"

More than 1.5 million U.S. soldiers, sailors, and airmen had arrived in Britain by May 1944, leading American war correspondent Ernie Pyle to comment that on some streets "an Englishman stood out as incongruously as he would in North Platte, Nebraska." With their free-spending ways and gifts of nylons, perfume, and other luxuries rare in wartime Britain, the GIs turned many a woman's head; 70,000 eventually came to the United States as war brides.

Hard pressed to compete with these audacious newcomers—a British Tommy's salary was one-fifth an American GI's—the local chaps were soon repeating the unflattering description originated by a cockney comedian—"overpaid, oversexed, and over here." The GIs retorted that British discontent stemmed from the fact that they were "underpaid, undersexed, and under Eisenhower."

Americans also invaded British tourist sights in droves. Madame Tussaud's Wax Museum was a popular London destination, and the museum catered to its new clientele by adding the figures of 14 U.S. presidents plus Generals Eisenhower and Douglas MacArthur.

GIs learned to drive on the left-hand side of the road and mastered the proper use of British words like *copper,* meaning "penny," and *vest* instead of "undershirt." But most never developed a taste for the flat local beer served warm or British wartime staples such as mutton, boiled kidneys, and Brussels sprouts.

Despite their differences and the competition for women, however, the Americans and British generally got along well. The Yanks' optimism and vitality was "as good as tonic," according to one Briton, who said that "for a while the people forgot about the war."

Ike polled his subordinates one by one. His chief of staff considered it "a helluva gamble" but probably "the best possible gamble." The two British air commanders thought it "a bit chancy" and wanted to postpone. Eisenhower then turned to the only officer there dressed informally, in his trademark roll-neck sweater and corduroy pants. This was the man who would be in charge of the Allied troops on the ground in Normandy. Bernard Montgomery rarely lacked confidence in his own abilities. He showed no hesitation now. "Do you see any reason why we should not go on Tuesday?" Ike asked him.

"No," Montgomery replied emphatically. "I would say—Go!"

The polling done, the room fell silent as the officers waited for Eisenhower to reach a decision. Minutes passed before he spoke. "The question," he began slowly, "is just how long can you hang this operation on the end of a limb and let it hang there." He resumed pacing. The wind and rain rattled the windows. Then he said, "I am quite positive that the order must be given. I don't like it, but there it is. I don't see how we can do anything else."

As orders went out to the ships announcing that D-Day would be June 6, Eisenhower came over to his meteorologist, who might just have made the most important weather prediction in history. "Well, Stagg," he said, "we're putting it on again. For heaven's sake hold the weather to what you told us and don't bring any more bad news." Then he flashed a broad smile and went out. The hands of a clock on the mantel pointed to 9:45. The whole conference had taken just 15 minutes.

That night, while the invasion armada once again weighed anchor and headed for Normandy, Ike slept on his decision—fitfully. He awoke at 3:30 a.m. and made the short drive to Southwick House for one last weather briefing. It was still not too late to call back the fleet. Indeed, he thought he might have to, for the storm raged unabated. But Stagg held fast to his prediction. Wearing an uncharacteristic smile, he suggested that any change in the forecast would be "in the direction of optimism." Eisen-hower began pacing again. He thought of his eager men cooped up in transport ships and of the consequences of calling them back. After a minute or so he stopped and looked around. "OK. Let's go," he said quietly. A cheer went up from the assembled commanders. Dawn was breaking as they rushed out to their posts, and the woods were loud with the song of birds. Just as Stagg had promised, it had stopped raining.

Later that day Eisenhower sat at a small table in his trailer and scrawled a note: "My decision to attack at this time and place was based upon the best information available. The troops, the air and the Navy did all that bravery and devotion to duty could do. If any blame or fault attaches to the attempt it is mine alone." He mistakenly dated the note July 5, folded it, and put it in his wallet. Should Operation *Overlord* fail, his message to the public was ready.

A few hours before, the fate of the invasion had hung on Eisenhower's every word. But now that he had said "OK. Let's go," he was powerless to affect the outcome. That depended on the soldiers, sailors, and airmen of the Allied Expeditionary Force. In the order he addressed to them, Eisenhower stressed the overriding importance of their mission: "You are about to embark upon the Great Crusade, toward which we have striven these many months," he wrote. "The eyes of the world are upon you. The hopes and prayers of liberty-loving people everywhere march with you." To Eisenhower, the Allied effort was indeed a crusade: If it succeeded, the Third Reich's stranglehold on Europe would be broken after five long and terrible years.

Seeking to bolster morale, Eisenhower and a small group of officers and pool correspondents drove to a nearby airfield to visit paratroopers of the U.S. 101st Airborne Division. These were the men whose mission he had deemed so vital that he was willing to run the risk of predicted casualties of up to 70 percent. Together with the 82d Airborne Division, they would parachute in to provide a protective inland shield for the westernmost seaborne landing; British airborne troops, arriving by parachute and

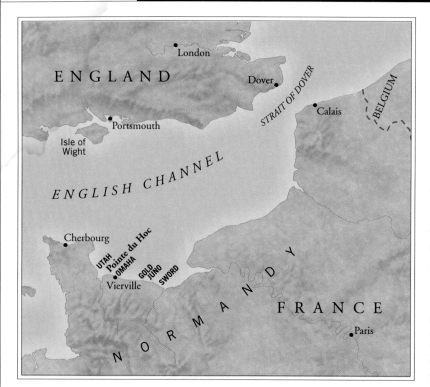

To get the 175,000 assault troops safely ashore on D-Day, the Allies mustered the largest fleet in naval history—5,000 vessels of every type, from battleships to flat-bottomed, plywood landing craft. The map above shows how the armada, setting out from various ports on England's southern coast, rendezvoused at a point called Piccadilly Circus, then headed for the five invasion beaches.

until the last plane had been swallowed up by the night. The NBC reporter Red Mueller was also on the roof, standing just a few paces away, his eyes on Eisenhower. When Ike at last turned to leave, Mueller saw that he had tears in his eyes.

Shortly after midnight, while wave after wave of transport planes carrying the airborne troops soared overhead, the great invasion armada made its way through the choppy waters of the English Channel. All the previous day vessels of all varieties had streamed from ports stretching across 150 miles of the southern British coast, from huge battleships and cruisers to the doughty little minesweepers that would clear the lanes through the lethal German minefields. There were 2,727 ships in all. In addition, the long flat-bottomed transports known as LSTs (for Landing Ships, Tank) and LSIs (Landing Ships, Infantry) carried other boats on their decks or slung over the side: the 2,606 smaller craft that would bear troops and vehicles ashore.

South of the Isle of Wight, the ships funneled into a rendezvous area buzzing with so much traffic that it was nicknamed Piccadilly Circus after the busy traffic circle in central London. There the ships formed into closely packed convoys and steamed south in five major lanes marked with lighted buoys. Each lane led to one of the five target beaches arrayed on a 50-mile stretch of the Normandy coast. The three eastern beaches, code-named Gold, Juno, and Sword, were assigned to British and Canadian forces. The two western beaches, Omaha and Utah, were assigned to the Americans.

Aboard the ships queasy stomachs abounded. The crews had served up special meals for the assault troops—fresh eggs, ice cream, and other foods that were rarities in wartime Britain—and some of the soldiers joked about transferring to the navy for the next war. Many had been at sea riding out the churning Channel for several days now. The flat-bottomed boats in particular pitched and rolled with every wave. Men gobbled seasickness pills but still found ample use for the items labeled in U.S. Army

glider, would perform a similar service behind the easternmost beach.

In the gathering dusk, Eisenhower moved among the American paratroopers as they assembled under the wings of their C-47 Dakota transport planes. He noticed with pride that "the light of battle was in their eyes." He greeted a fellow Kansan, bantered with a Texan, talked with a man from Michigan. "I've done all I can," he said to one of them. "Now it's up to you."

The paratroopers could read their commander's mood too. One man was struck by the great burden of decision that showed on Ike's face. Another tried to make him smile: "Now quit worrying, General," he called out, "we'll take care of this thing for you."

When the men began to board their planes, a somber Eisenhower made his way back to the airfield's headquarters. Around 11:00 p.m. the Dakotas began to taxi slowly down the darkened runway in single file to a position facing into the wind. From the roof of the nearby headquarters building, the Supreme Commander saluted each plane as it roared past and headed off toward France. There he waited parlance Bag-vomit. But it was not only the stormy seas that afflicted them. For the vast majority, this would be their first taste of combat.

Like thousands of others, Sergeant Robert Slaughter carried a souvenir he hoped would serve as a talisman in battle. It was Ike's order of the day, which had been handed to everyone boarding ship. Slaughter had his pals in Company D, First Battalion, 116th Infantry Regiment autograph his copy. Then he carefully wrapped the paper in plastic for protection and put it in his wallet as a souvenir and for luck on Omaha Beach.

A strapping youth six feet five inches tall, Bob Slaughter was just 19 years old. Before the war, back in his hometown of Roanoke, Virginia, he had lied about his age and enlisted in the National Guard at age 16. He was attracted by the olive drab dress uniform, the dollar a day, and the two weeks' training at Virginia Beach every summer. His new outfit,

for the invasion of Europe for nearly two years, and they were ready to go.

Now, riding the British LSI *Empire Javelin* as that flat-bottomed craft pitched and rolled, Slaughter had just finished listening to a final pep talk from his company commander, Captain Walter Schilling. A wiry Roanoke native and a strict disciplinarian, Schilling had come up through the ranks of the National Guard. Privately he was worried, having confided to an old friend the premonition that he would not make it safely through the invasion. But in his talk to the men he was so upbeat that Slaughter felt a chill run up his spine.

Throughout the invasion fleet, officers were delivering such pep talks to their troops, chaplains were saying prayers, and men were seeking out friends and relatives. Another soldier in the 29th Division, Sergeant Roy Stevens, struggled across a crowded deck to say good-bye to his twin brother.

"Now quit worrying, General, we'll take care of this thing for you."

U.S. PARATROOPER TO GENERAL EISENHOWER, JUNE 5, 1944

Company D, which specialized in heavy weapons such as machine guns and mortars, was made up of local boys—"we grew up together, went to school together and went to church together." They knew little of the larger world until the 29th Infantry Division, of which they were a small part, was called up for federal service before Pearl Harbor. Many northerners then came into the division, and Slaughter was exposed for the first time to men of different origins, like the Italian boy who introduced him to an exotic food he had never tried before—spaghetti.

Although National Guard outfits were sometimes taunted by veteran regulars as "home nannies" unfit for combat, Slaughter's regiment could trace its fighting roots as Virginia militia back to the American Revolution. During the American Civil War, it was commanded by Thomas "Stonewall" Jackson as part of his famous Stonewall Brigade. By June 1944 the Stonewallers, as Slaughter and his buddies referred to themselves, had been in England preparing

When he found him, the brother smiled at him and extended his hand. "No, we will shake hands at the crossroads in France like we planned," Roy told him. The smile and proffered hand was his last memory of his brother. He never saw him again.

A few miles to the west, on the attack transport *Bayfield*, the deputy commander of the 4th Infantry Division was talking individually to his troops. A small man with a wrinkled face and an irreverent streak that was now subdued, Brigadier General Theodore Roosevelt was remarkable in several ways. He was the eldest son of the late president whose name he bore and a cousin of the current president, Franklin Roosevelt. He was a veteran of World War I and of the Allied landings in North Africa and Sicily. At age 56 he had a bad heart and an arthritic shoulder, but he had persuaded his commander to let him go ashore at Utah Beach with the first wave of troops to "steady the boys." Having such a senior officer in the first wave would bolster morale, he said: "They'll figure that if a general is going in, it can't be that rough!"

As Roosevelt strolled quietly among the rookies crowding the deck of the *Bayfield* he spoke softly, offering words of reassurance in his deep bass voice. At length he started singing and urged others to join in. Soon all these young green troops, facing battle for the first time, were singing "The Battle Hymn of the Republic" and then "Onward, Christian Soldiers."

The Allied armada moved unmolested through the early-morning mist in a 30-mile front. To be sure, Hitler had fortified the entire German-occupied coast of western Europe. The 1,700 miles reaching from Norway in the north to the French-Spanish border was girded with sections of the Atlantic Wall, a cordon of steel-and-concrete bunkers, artillery emplacements, and beach barriers. But Hitler had long ago decided that the main Allied invasion would be aimed at Calais, 150 miles northeast of Normandy, where the Channel dividing Britain and France was at its narrowest. There, at the Strait of Dover, where the potential invasion route led directly east to Germany, he concentrated his best troops and strongest fortifications.

Hitler's belief that the invasion would come at Calais was reinforced by an ambitious campaign of deception waged by the Allies. For many months the Germans were fed a steady stream of misinformation consisting of fake radio traffic and false reports from German agents working for the British. Eisenhower even created in southeastern England near Dover a phony army group of half a million nonexistent troops equipped with inflatable tanks and sham landing craft. To lead this phantom force Eisenhower shrewdly selected Lieutenant General George Patton, whose slashing tank tactics in North Africa and Sicily had won the respect of the Germans. They considered Patton the best American general and felt certain he would spearhead any invasion. Patton was in full agreement with the German assessment of his abilities, and would have preferred a more active role. But Eisenhower, who had promised him command of a real army in France, decided to

Eisenhower spent the eve of the Normandy invasion visiting those who faced the most perilous mission—the paratroopers. Here he chats with members of the 101st Airborne Division just before they board their planes.

THE AIRBORNE ASSAULT: EISENHOWER'S BIG GAMBLE

For Operation *Overlord*, Eisenhower demanded a large airborne force to secure both flanks of the Allied beachhead against German counterattack. But landing 17,400 British and American troops by parachute and glider in enemy territory in the dark would be a tremendous risk; Eisenhower's air commander predicted casualties of 70 percent.

On the night of June 5, 1,200 planes and 850 gliders took off from England. Meticulous Allied planning quickly went awry as cloud cover over the drop zones, combined with heavy German antiaircraft fire, scattered the planes and spread the men all over Normandy. Some paratroopers, carrying up to 100 pounds of equipment, came down in marshes behind the coast and drowned, while many glider-borne infantry perished as their fragile craft broke apart on landing. Most found themselves miles from their intended targets, lost and alone in the dark. In this chaos the special training of the airborne troops paid off, as ad hoc formations went into action against any Germans they could find. British troopers blocked several key bridges and road junctions, while the Americans took the town of Ste.-Mère-Église and held the causeways behind Utah Beach. Casualties, though heavy, did not approach the dire preinvasion predictions.

Their faces blackened in order to make it more difficult for the enemy to spot them, paratroopers flash confident smiles and gestures shortly before taking off from England for their jump over Normandy.

Eight dead soldiers are laid out beside the wreckage of their glider in a Norman field. Although glider units faced risks similar to those of the paratroopers, the army classified them as regular infantry, and not until later in the war would they receive the added benefits or pay accorded to the airborne.

use Patton as a decoy to keep the Germans looking toward Dover.

The security of the Allied armada benefited as well from the unsettled weather. German commanders had been thrown off guard because they lacked observation stations west of the Continent that could have predicted the break in the storm. Two days before, on Sunday, June 4, the commander in Normandy, Field Marshal Erwin Rommel, the legendary Desert Fox in the North African campaigns, decided that the Allies could not mount an invasion in such blustery weather. He went home to Germany. For his wife he had a pair of new shoes from Paris as a fiftieth birthday gift, and for his Führer a request for tank reinforcements for his 60,000 troops in Normandy. Because of the weather the German air force—already badly crippled by the continuing air war over Europe—failed to send reconnaissance flights over the Channel. German torpedo boats likewise stayed warm and dry in port at Cherbourg, forsaking their nightly patrols.

Moreover, radar stations that almost certainly would have picked up the invasion fleet were largely put out of action the previous evening by Allied bombers. Of 92 stations along the French coast, only 18 were left operational. The Allies allowed a handful of stations to survive on purpose because they wanted them to detect the mock air and sea armada dispatched toward Calais. Bombers dropping strips of aluminum foil caused the German radar screens to register the blips of a great swarm of Calais-bound aircraft. Similarly, large barrage balloons carrying electronic reflectors and towed by motorboats created radar echoes resembling a large fleet advancing on Calais. It was 3:09 on that D-Day morning before German radar registered the truth and detected the real armada nearing the Normandy beaches. Even then German commanders suspected this was merely a diversionary operation prior to the principal effort at Calais. They ordered their shore-based guns to hold off firing until daybreak.

Nearly two and a half hours before dawn the Allied armada was preparing to unleash the assault.

THE BOAT THAT WON THE WAR

In the 1930s navy designers began producing experimental models for a fast, shallow-draft craft to transport assault troops from ship to beach, but their prototypes didn't impress New Orleans boatbuilder Andrew Jackson Higgins (inset). He labeled them tubs and said that the navy didn't know "one damn thing about small boats." Higgins himself knew a great deal about such craft. The shallow-draft boat he designed was a great success with oil companies needing to get workers and equipment to drilling sites in Louisiana's marshes and swamps. The boat could run up on muddy banks and beaches at full speed and extricate itself easily, and it was also maneuverable and stable in heavy surf. The Army Corps of Engineers and the Coast Guard used Higgins's boat, and the Marine Corps was impressed with its military potential. But the navy declined to draw on his expertise and stubbornly clung to its intention to design its own craft.

After war broke out in Europe the navy finally broke down and gave Higgins a contract to build an experimental landing craft. In a competitive trial in 1940 his prototype bested the navy's own, and he won a contract to begin production.

Assembly lines like the one below turned out more than 20,000 LCVPs, an abbreviation for Landing Craft, Vehicle and Personnel. They carried more U.S. troops and equipment ashore than all other landing craft types combined. General Eisenhower later said that without the LCVP "we never could have landed over an open beach," and he called Higgins "the man who won the war for us."

THE GUY WHO RELAXES IS HELPING THE AXIS!

The lead transports put down anchor seven to 12 miles off their target beaches, and the troops prepared to transfer to the smaller landing craft that were lowered over the side. Nearly half of these craft were known as Higgins boats (technically LCVPs, for Landing Craft, Vehicle and Personnel), named after Andrew Higgins, the New Orleans entrepreneur who created them. Propelled by a diesel engine and made largely of plywood, these boxy 36-foot-long boats, which could carry up to 36 men, proved so valuable to Allied invasions that Eisenhower later dubbed Higgins "the man who won the war for us."

On some transports the Higgins boats were slung over the side on booms and lowered into the water with only one man aboard, the coxswain, who operated the craft. Then, in the inky darkness, assault troops had to scramble down cargo nets strung down the transport's side and leap down into the craft. The typical soldier was laden with more than 50 pounds of equipment: steel helmet, M-1 rifle, ammunition belt, canteen, backpack with a shovel for digging trenches, rations and first-aid kit, grenades and gas mask hanging from his assault jacket, and an inflatable life belt around his waist. Thus encumbered he had to try to time his jump for the shortest distance, catching the crazily bobbing boat on the crest of a wave. Even if his timing was good, he risked broken limbs and worse.

Other transports, such as the *Empire Javelin* carrying Bob Slaughter and his fellow Virginians, allowed a smoother disembarkation. The landing craft could be boarded from the ship's deck over the rail and then lowered gently into the water by long curved steel arms called davits. The descent of Slaughter's boat and some 30 other landing craft assigned to the Stonewallers went smoothly, with one bizarre exception. One craft became stuck halfway between deck and water. This position placed the boat directly below the outlet emptying sewage from the transport's latrines. For nearly a half-hour while the unwelcome stuff streamed down upon their heads, the men aboard yelled, cursed, cried, and laughed. Then, mercifully, the boat resumed its descent to the water and moved safely away from the *Empire Javelin.*

Awaiting the signal to move, the swarms of landing craft circled their mother ships. Misery rode these boats pitching to and fro in the unfriendly sea. Waves quickly swamped some of them, and the occupants had to keep bailing with their steel helmets. One young soldier, less impressed with his means of transportation than was Eisenhower, was heard to grumble, "That guy Higgins ain't got nothin' to be proud of about inventin' this goddamned boat!"

The landing craft were so crowded that everyone had to stand jostled together in their bulky outfits. Even their uniforms were uncomfortable. The cloth had been impregnated with a chemical that would ward off any poison gas used by the enemy, and it felt stiff and clammy and gave off a vile smell when wet. The wait was even worse. The actual assault was scheduled to begin at 6:30 a.m. on the American beaches in the west, one hour after low tide; H-hour was an hour later for the British landings in the east, where the tide turned later. Many troops had to wait for two hours or more, endlessly circling in the rough seas, before making the run in to the shore.

About 5:20 a.m., as the first light pierced the eastern sky, the men in the boats heard the throb of engines overhead and then the thunder on the land ahead. To their cheers, thousands of fighters and bombers struck at the beaches and inland targets. Then, about 5:35 a.m., German shore batteries opened up, and the Allied warships—not due to fire until dawn, 15 minutes later—loosed a barrage. Salvo after salvo poured out from 68 Allied destroyers anchored three miles offshore and from six battleships and 20 cruisers a few miles out. The huddled foot soldiers watched as the orange fire from the gun muzzles of the warships flashed in the gray dawn.

Roosevelt and his men at 6:20 a.m. were rushing through the early-morning mist toward Utah, a beach running roughly north-south at the base of the Cherbourg Peninsula. Behind their craft the battleship *Nevada,* reborn after being severely

Two members of a U.S. landing party help an exhausted survivor of a sunken landing craft to shore. German shell-fire, mines, and beach obstacles caused many casualties before the troops even had a chance to disembark from their small boats.

damaged at Pearl Harbor, blasted away with its 14-inch guns. The men crammed in the Higgins boats—sodden, seasick, and scared—swore that the shells passed so near overhead they created a vacuum that lifted their craft out of the water.

The naval bombardment lifted on schedule, and at 6:31 a.m., almost exactly on H-hour, 20 landing craft carrying the first wave of Roosevelt's 4th Division lowered their steel ramps, and 600 GIs, the first amphibious assault troops to land in France on D-Day, jumped off into the waist-deep water. Holding their rifles in the air they waded through 100 yards of surf to the dry sand beyond. The tide was a long way out, and in front of the soldiers

lay a stretch of firm, gently sloping yellow sand 500 yards wide that was strewn with beach obstacles and surmounted by a 100-yard belt of low dunes. It was all going as smoothly as a practice landing, and there was surprisingly little response from the Germans.

Stomping back and forth with the walking stick that he carried because of his bad heart and arthritis, the oldest man on the beach urged on the troops. Armed only with a pistol and wearing a wool knit hat because he hated steel helmets, General Roosevelt ignored enemy fire and vigorously took command. As he had predicted, his presence inspired the scared and seasick young soldiers, driving them on by example and galvanizing them with his sharp tongue. One man, struggling with the equipment from his heavy-weapons company, confessed later that he kept going only because he was more afraid of old Teddy than of the enemy.

With his cane Roosevelt pointed out targets for the tanks, which followed the first wave of infantry. The armor included conventional Sherman tanks, which plowed ashore through five feet of water, as well as the special amphibious models, which swam up to the beach from a mile or so out, thanks to a propeller and canvas flotation collar.

Roosevelt directed the armor and some infantry toward a German stronghold that was the center of opposition for this part of the beach. Situated behind a low concrete sea wall about 300 yards from the water's edge, it consisted of a heavily armed blockhouse, bunkers, and a series of trenches. Its fortifications had been shattered and its arsenal of guns mostly disabled by the prelanding bombardment. But a machine gun emplacement had sur-

vived in a half-buried old French tank turret, and it was harassing the beach, pinning down incoming assault troops. A blast from the 75mm gun on one of the American Shermans scored a direct hit on the tank turret. The Germans then tried to man their 88mm cannon; it fired once and jammed. Finally, as a last resort, they launched the miniature, radio-controlled tanks known as Goliaths. These child-sized vehicles were stuffed with up to 200 pounds of explosives and then directed at the enemy. But their delicate guidance electronics had been disrupted by the bombardment, and the Goliaths crawled about aimlessly, earning the nickname doodlebugs from the Americans.

The tank-led assault finished off the German stronghold. A dazed young officer who emerged from the ruins was being taken prisoner when shrapnel from a German shell fired from artillery 10 miles inland ripped open his side. A GI gave him a gauze dressing for the wound and a cigarette. When General Roosevelt came up, the German saluted

Despite painful arthritis, 56-year-old Brigadier General Theodore Roosevelt (at far left) insisted on landing with the first wave of his 4th Infantry Division on Utah Beach. He died of a heart attack a few weeks later and was posthumously awarded the Medal of Honor for his initiative and courage during the invasion.

smartly. Roosevelt automatically started to return the salute. Then, thinking better of this sign of respect, he dropped his half-raised arm and gruffly ordered the prisoner escorted to the beach to await transport to England.

Roosevelt climbed to the top of the dunes beyond the sea wall to look for the landmarks shown on the map of his landing position. He scanned the landscape, but the landmarks he was looking for were nowhere to be seen. He said to an officer with him, "We're not where we're supposed to be." He was right: They had indeed landed in the wrong place. Smoke and dust from the bombardment had obscured landmarks onshore, and the resulting navigational errors, combined with a strong tidal current, had taken the assault craft to a landing more than a mile south of their target.

to be a good one, and Roosevelt decided to go with it. "Gentlemen," he announced to his two senior field commanders. "We'll start the war from here!"

To clear safe paths for the follow-up landings, teams of demolition experts and combat engineers came in soon after the first wave. Wading through waist-deep water, each man carried up to 75 pounds of explosives on his back, so much that Sergeant Richard Cassiday had to jettison the six cartons of cigarettes he intended to carry inland for the purpose of barter with the French citizenry. Dodging fire from distant German artillery, the teams affixed charges to the beach obstacles, wired them together, and blew them up. Some of the obstacles were simply heavy logs driven into the sand with mines attached to the tips. Others, called hedgehogs, consisted of three or four short steel rails that were

"We pushed two thousand yards inland, then hit the marshlands. The Germans had flooded them. They were from three to ten feet deep, and we had to wade through them.... Our mission was to reach the paratroopers."

SERGEANT RICHARD SOVER, UTAH BEACH

From one point of view the off-course landing had been a blessing, since German defenses were much weaker here than at the intended point farther north, which bristled with shore batteries. But the old general now found himself facing a critical choice. Wave upon wave of troops—nearly 30,000 of them, and 3,500 vehicles—were due to follow him ashore. He could redirect his present forces and the follow-up troops northward up the beach to the prescribed landing place. Or his division could continue to land on this relatively calm stretch of sand and proceed straight inland.

The problem was that only one road led off the beach at this point, risking a bottleneck of the men and matériel that would soon be coming ashore. Farther north, there were several exit roads off the beach, but Roosevelt knew that they would be fiercely defended. Either choice was a gamble. The hand fortune had dealt him that morning appeared

welded together at their centers; the rails had jagged ends designed to rip open the bottoms of landing craft. The largest obstacles, however, were the Belgian gates, steel frames 10 feet wide and seven feet high with explosives strapped to them that would be triggered upon impact.

As the teams worked their way up the beach, members sometimes had to risk their lives to shove away troops who wandered too near the explosions. Near the sea wall, Sergeant Cassiday saw a short man, an officer, pacing back and forth perilously near a set of wired obstacles. "Go knock that bastard down!" Cassiday shouted. "He's going to get killed."

"Do you know who that is?" a teammate asked.

"Yes, it's Roosevelt," Cassiday replied, "and he's going to get killed."

The general moved on, uninjured, and his demolition teams continued to clear the obstacles. By mid-morning they had opened up a series of safe lanes

50 yards wide through which a constant stream of vehicles poured onto the beach and up the dunes. Roosevelt was still in the thick of it. Leaning on his cane and smoking a pipe—"as unperturbed as though he were in the middle of Times Square," thought one observer—he stood directing the oncoming traffic. The old soldier seemed to be thoroughly enjoying himself. "Keep right on this road," he yelled out to one vehicle. "You're doing fine! It's a great day for hunting, isn't it?"

Exuberant though he might be, Roosevelt knew that his gamble might still be unsuccessful unless traffic could be kept constantly moving along the single road inland. If the vehicles piled up, a German counterattack could wreak complete havoc. Tanks equipped with bulldozers ruthlessly shoved any vehicle that stalled or had been hit by shellfire off the road into the marsh.

Then, around 11:00 a.m., Roosevelt received good news: Two other exits off other stretches of Utah were now in American hands, and the GIs moving inland through them had met up with elements of the 101st Airborne Division, which had landed on top of the bluffs behind the beaches the previous night and had been fighting to capture a number of key coastal villages. The essential linkup between the troops who came from the air and those who came from the sea had been achieved, putting the squeeze on the Germans.

By late afternoon Roosevelt had also made it all the way through his exit. Eager to keep his men advancing forward, he hitched a ride on the hood of a jeep to see what was going on up ahead. Spotting a colonel along the way, Teddy suggested, "Let's go up to the front."

"We *are* at the front!" replied the colonel. "See those two men?" he said, pointing just 50 yards ahead. "They are the leading scouts."

"Let's go talk to them!" said Roosevelt.

The gamble had paid off. The beachhead at Utah had cost fewer than 200 casualties. Roosevelt's leadership would be rewarded five weeks later by Eisenhower, who promoted him to the command of his own division. But Roosevelt would die that same day of a heart attack, without ever learning of his promotion. He was buried at the American cemetery just six miles from Utah Beach.

The successful landing on Utah depended in part on the achievement of a different kind of assault mounted a half-dozen miles to the east. There a force of 225 Rangers, new elite troops modeled after the British commandos and trained in special assault tactics, were assigned a monumental task. They were to land on a rough shingle beach, scale the sheer face of a 100-foot-high prominence named Pointe du Hoc that jutted out into the Channel, and disable the battery of five big coastal guns reported to be positioned on top. Eisenhower wanted this task completed by 7:00 a.m., 30 minutes after H-hour, for the guns were said to be effective up to 10 miles, and thus able to zero in on both American beaches—Utah to the west and Omaha to the east—and even threaten the Allied armada offshore.

Lieutenant Colonel James Rudder, the Rangers' commander, was in courage and verve a younger version of General Roosevelt. The 34-year-old Rudder was a former rancher, college football coach, and star lineman at Texas A&M. Although he had "a steely-eyed look when he was not pleased," as one of his Rangers put it, he was also beloved as "the big brother for everyone." His highly motivated men were all volunteers and a cocky bunch. A few days before the invasion, one of them had written a letter to a girl in Paris asking for a date; the soldier told her that he expected to be there sometime in early June. But the man's boss was far from complacent. In fact, so concerned was he about the dangers of the assault that Rudder insisted on leading it himself. "If I don't take it," he told his superior, "it may not go."

Even with Rudder riding in the lead landing craft, there was still a good chance that it would not go. Rudder lost two of his boats to the swamping waves on the way in. The rest of his flotilla drifted so far off course because of navigational errors and the strong current that his Rangers did not land at the

Members of an army Ranger battalion crowd together in their landing craft prior to going ashore at Normandy. Like other Allied soldiers, Rangers were issued invasion scrip to use in France. The example shown here (inset) bears the signatures of 5th Ranger Battalion officers.

base of the cliff until 7:10 a.m. This was 40 minutes late, which gave the defenders time to reman the guns that they had abandoned after the earlier bombardment from sea and air.

Seeing the Rangers land, a German machine gunner posted atop the cliff immediately began to sweep the beach, killing or wounding 15 Rangers. The rest of the men hit the ground, all except for a six-foot-four English commando officer, "a great big, black-haired son of a gun—one of those staunch Britishers," thought Rudder. The officer had helped train the Rangers, and now he walked the beach, encouraging those around him. "How in the world can you do that when you are being fired at?" one Ranger called out to him.

"I take two short steps and three long ones," the commando replied simply, "and they always miss me." But just then a bullet from the German machine gunner hit him in the helmet and knocked him to the ground. The Englishman shouted a profanity in the direction of the enemy, then crawled forward like everyone else.

Rudder had known it wasn't going to be easy. Looking up at the cliff he remembered the first time he had seen aerial photographs of Pointe du Hoc, and the navy officer who had told him that "three women with brooms could keep the Rangers from climbing that cliff." To help prove the navy man wrong, Rudder's men had brought along a versatile arsenal of climbing aids. They had tubular steel ladders in four-foot sections for quick assembly, rocket-propelled ropes, and 100-foot-long extension ladders furnished by the London Fire Department that were fitted at the top with machine guns and mounted on amphibious trucks. But the beach sloped away sharply from the foot of the cliff, and none of the ladders could be positioned close enough to it to reach all the way to the top.

With the ladders unusable the Rangers were left with their ropes. Rocket guns mounted on the landing craft launched steel grappling hooks, or grapnels, attached to the ropes and sent them flying up toward the cliff. Some of the grapnels fell short of the mark because of the weight of the water-soaked ropes they were pulling, but others shot up in a high

arc, came down on the top of the cliff, and sank their hooks securely into the ground.

As the Rangers began climbing the ropes hand over hand, German troops at the top of the cliff cut some of the ropes and leaned out over the edge to fire rifles and machine pistols and lob down hand grenades. "Boys, keep your heads down," Rudder shouted. "Headquarters has fouled up again and issued the enemy live ammunition!"

Most of the Rangers made it through the fire and grenades and were on the summit in 15 minutes. Rudder quickly established a command post at the edge of the cliff and ordered a message radioed out to sea: "Praise the Lord." This was the prearranged signal for bringing in a backup force of 500 additional Rangers once Rudder and his men had reached the top. But the time was now 7:30 a.m.— 30 minutes too late. The reinforcements were gone.

After two days of bitter fighting at Pointe du Hoc, the army Rangers were finally relieved by other American units. Here the Rangers herd German prisoners down the face of the cliff. The American flag is displayed to protect against shelling by U.S. ships and planes.

If the signal was not received by 7:00 a.m., the back-up troops were to land at Omaha Beach, three miles east, and then try to reach the summit of Pointe du Hoc by the landward route. Until they made it through, Rudder's men would have to go it alone.

Atop the summit, Rudder found a moonscape, a plateau cratered by 10,000 tons of Allied bombs and shells. Despite sporadic firing from a scattering of defenders, the Americans closed in on the German fortifications. They found a massive concrete observation post, a network of trenches eight feet deep, and railroad tracks for handcarts hauling ammuni-

tion. But the emplacements held none of the big guns they had expected—only protruding telephone poles meant to fool aerial reconnaissance.

Although the big German guns were gone, the Rangers found the machine gun responsible for the 15 casualties suffered earlier on the beach. Rudder wanted to get rid of it by directing fire from the nearby destroyer *Satterlee,* but all his radios were out of commission. A communications officer had brought along an old World War I signal lamp for just such an occasion and began to blink out a message to the destroyer by Morse code. After a couple

of adjustments directed by the communications man, the ship's five-inch guns blew the German machine gun off the cliff.

The Rangers now turned to their second mission, which was to prevent German reinforcements from moving eastward to Omaha Beach on a highway that ran parallel with the water's edge. They fought their way inland to the highway, and after setting up a roadblock they sent out small patrols to scout the area. A two-man team was moving cautiously through the middle of an apple orchard about 200 yards from the highway when the lead man hissed to his partner, "Here they are! Here are the goddamned guns!" Covered with camouflage netting were the big guns, five 155mm cannon with shells stacked nearby, that the Rangers had expected to find at the top of the cliff. The weapons were pointed toward Utah Beach and ready to fire. The two Rangers spotted a group of German soldiers about 100 yards away; they were about to come forward to man the guns.

The Americans acted quickly. They bashed in the gun sights and dumped in grenades to destroy the firing mechanisms. Then they hightailed it back to their buddies at the roadblock.

It was now 9:00 a.m., and the Rangers had accomplished both of their missions on Pointe du Hoc. They had blocked the inland highway and silenced the big guns that threatened the entire American invasion. Casualties were so heavy—70 percent killed, wounded, or captured—that after fighting off repeated German counterattacks that day scarcely 50 men were still available for combat. They kept looking to the east, toward Omaha and the 500 Rangers who were supposed to reinforce them. None came. For on that embattled beachhead, American forces were embroiled in D-Day's fiercest struggle.

Allied planners had targeted the beach code-named Omaha only because they felt they had to. It would be dangerous to leave a 20-mile gap between Utah Beach in the west and the British Gold Beach in the east, and Omaha was the only feasible place for a landing; sheer cliffs and rocky offshore reefs ruled out every other site. No one liked the beach: Four miles long and crescent shaped, it was closed in at both ends by sheer cliffs, and steep bluffs as high as 150 feet blocked the way inland elsewhere along the crescent. Tanks and other vehicles could climb off it only at five ravines—the Americans called them draws—that sloped up gradually to small villages on the plateau behind the beach. Omaha was a natural killing ground.

Though the planners knew that the Germans had taken advantage of this favorable terrain, reconnaissance photos had failed to reveal the full extent of the defenses. In fact, Omaha was by far the most heavily fortified of the five beaches assaulted by the Allies. Belts of Belgian gates, hedgehogs, and other obstacles guarded the outer beach. Hundreds of mines planted on the beach and bluffs awaited the trespasser. Scores of concrete-lined pillboxes, gun casemates, and firing pits studded the plateau and the steep sides of the draws leading up to it. From these strongpoints, 60 artillery pieces, 85 machine guns, and 40 mortars covered every inch of the beach.

To neutralize the defenders' advantages of terrain, the Allies carefully designed a one-two-three punch of naval shelling, aerial bombing, and tank support. None worked. Shells from the sea bombardment merely pocked the thick concrete casemates atop the bluffs. Salvos of rockets that were supposed to terrify the defenders and create instant foxholes on the beach for the assault troops fell short, plopping harmlessly into the water. Some 13,000 bombs dropped by hundreds of American planes fell too far inland, in part because the area was obscured by clouds and also because the airmen were fearful of hitting the beach-bound assault troops. A flotilla of 29 amphibious tanks intended to blast open the way for the first wave of infantrymen was launched more than three miles from the beach. But the wind-whipped sea ripped their canvas flotation collars and flooded their engines. Twenty-seven of them sank in quick succession, taking most of their crews with them.

Braving a hail of machine gun and mortar fire from concealed German positions, American infantrymen struggle through the surf off Omaha Beach. Casualties among the first wave were horrendous; the survivors were pinned down, and the success of the landing was in doubt for several hours. "Many of my friends died thinking we had lost," recalled Dan Whisten of the 29th Infantry Division.

Other mishaps and miscalculations disrupted the precise landing plan. The transports were anchored 12 miles offshore in order to be out of range of the big guns at Pointe du Hoc, and during the long run to the beach 10 landing craft carrying more than 300 men swamped in the six-foot-high waves. Many of the rest of the craft were unavoidably pushed off course by as much as a mile and a half by wind and tidal current.

The nature of the reception that awaited them was also a matter of miscalculation. "Polish and Russian volunteers and overage German Home Guard would be the underdog opponent" was the briefing given the young sergeant Bob Slaughter and his Virginia buddies. In fact, undetected until too late by Allied intelligence, an enemy division that fit this description recently had been reinforced by one that did not, a crack German unit with service on the Russian front.

To the troops coming ashore in the landing craft, however, it seemed impossible that any of the defenders could have survived the massive Allied bombardment. Not a shot was heard from the enemy. Riding in one of the boats was novelist and war correspondent Ernest Hemingway. He recalled the looks of surprise and happiness on the faces of the GIs as they watched the battleship *Texas* go to work. "There would be a flash like a blast furnace from the 14 inch guns of the *Texas*, that would lick out far from the ship," Hemingway reported. "Then the yellow brown smoke would cloud out and, with the smoke still rolling, the concussion and the report would hit us, jarring the men's helmets. It struck your ear like a punch with a heavy, dry glove."

Their faces lighted by the flashes of the guns, the infantrymen marveled at the sight. Peering out from beneath their helmets, they reminded Hemingway

In this famous image of D-Day by photographer Robert Capa, Private First Class Edward Regan of the 116th Regiment, 29th Infantry Division takes cover in the surf at Omaha Beach. Capa landed with the first wave of troops and took about 70 pictures in all. Unfortunately, a darkroom technician's error ruined all but 11 frames.

of "pikemen of the Middle Ages to whose aid in battle had suddenly come some strange and unbelievable monster." Over the roar of the landing craft's diesel engines, he heard the reaction of one soldier: "Look what they're doing to those Germans! I guess there won't be a man alive there."

The GIs closed to within 600 yards of the beach, and still there was no answer from the enemy guns. On came the little steel boats, 100 yards more. And then the Germans opened up.

On the left of the assault force, coming in to the eastern half of the beach, was a regiment of the 1st Infantry Division, the famed Big Red One. These were veterans of the amphibious landings in North Africa and Sicily and virtually the only Americans in the amphibious assault who were combat tested. But nothing had prepared them for Omaha. At 6:30 a.m., right on the scheduled H-hour, their landing craft grounded on sand bars 50 yards from shore, and the ramps crashed down for unloading. The occupants charged into chest-deep water—and into fire so intense that most of the officers, first off the boats, went down before they could even reach the beach. The streams of machine gun bullets converged from the bluff in front of them and from both flanks. Artillery shells exploded in showers of sand and water. Many men, already exhausted by seasickness and dragged down by their 50 pounds or more of equipment, struggled futilely in the waves and drowned. Others crouched behind the beach obstacles. Some ran or crawled across 300 yards of sand to temporary shelter behind a low sea wall that was about halfway between the place where the GIs were landing and the Germans waiting on the bluffs. Cold, wet, and scared, their units scattered and leaderless, the Americans huddled together behind the wall.

Things were even worse at the other end of Omaha. In front of the draw leading to the village of Vierville, units of the Stonewallers were making their run in to the shore. Guiding on the village's church steeple, the first half-dozen landing craft were right on target. They were also heading into a corridor of death, straight toward enemy fortifications on the bluffs protecting the vital Vierville exit. Before the landing craft reached the beach one boat swamped and went down, and another either struck a mine or took a direct hit from a German artillery shell and simply disintegrated, killing its entire 30-man assault team.

By the time the other four craft hit the sands of Omaha, German bullets were beating a steady tattoo on the ramps and sides of the boats. Nevertheless, they pushed onward—the ramps were lowered, and the men leaped into the icy water. One sergeant had his left hand up above the water, struggling to get his balance. A bullet hit him in the knuckle, then another passed through the palm of his hand. "They're leaving us here to die like rats!" cried a man beside him in the water. Another bullet bored through the sergeant's left thigh and smashed into his hipbone before he was able to reach the beach, and his heavy pack was hit a couple of times. One bullet severed the chin strap of his helmet.

Another soldier—loaded down with a pistol, a shovel, a life jacket, a canteen, a block of dynamite, and an 80-pound flamethrower—stepped off his landing craft and immediately disappeared under the water. "I was unable to come up," he recalled. "I knew I was drowning and made a futile attempt to unbuckle the flamethrower harness." Just then he felt a buddy grab the flamethrower and drag him forward to shallower water. Half drowned and coughing violently, he slowly made his way to the beach. There he heard a sound he did not recognize, a *sip sip,* like someone sucking on his teeth. He realized with terror that it was the sound of German machine gun bullets cutting into the wet sand.

Not far away a sergeant had taken momentary shelter behind one of the German beach obstacles, well aware that he had to push on to the sea wall if he was to escape the heavy enemy fire. As he was catching his breath, a private fell down beside him, his face white with fear. "He seemed to be begging for help with his eyes," recalled the sergeant. "His look was that of a child asking what to do." He told the soldier, "Gillingham, let's stay separated as much

Sergeant Robert Slaughter lied about his age to join the National Guard at 16 and was part of the early landing at Omaha Beach. "Landing craft exploded. Men went up in flames. Some outfits didn't have enough men left to whip a cat with," he recounted later. Slaughter narrowly escaped being a casualty himself: "I felt something hit my jacket. Later, I noticed a couple of bullet holes in the cloth—but none in me."

as we can, because the Germans will fire at two quicker than one."

Gillingham did not reply. Then the sergeant heard the whistle of an incoming shell and dived facefirst into the sand. He could feel the shrapnel fly all around him. When he looked up, he saw that it had blown off Gillingham's chin. It was time to move. With a hand to his chin, the private ran with the sergeant to the sea wall. There he gave the wounded man a shot of morphine and stayed with him until he died. "The entire time," the sergeant remembered, "he remained conscious and aware that he was dying."

Such casualties were common to all the first-wave units that morning. One company was particularly hard hit: Within 10 minutes of H-hour all but seven or eight of its 197 men were killed or wounded. Many had not fired off a single shot. Twenty-three of the dead were from the little Virginia town of Bedford, the company's original National Guard home. With horror the unit's only surviving officer looked around at the bodies of dead GIs gently nudging against one another in the cold water. By the time he crossed the beach to the cover of the sea wall, he himself had been hit three times.

Another wave of GIs—Sergeant Bob Slaughter and his comrades from Company D—entered this lethal corridor in front of the Vierville draw at 7:10 a.m. When they were still 1,000 yards offshore, artillery fire bracketed their boats, sending high plumes of water into the air around them. In the lead craft Captain Walter Schilling, the company commander whose pep talk had so inspired Slaughter, was still trying to reassure his men. "See," he remarked to one of them, "I told you it was going to be easy." Just then an 88mm shell scored a direct hit on the ramp of the landing craft, and Schilling's earlier premonition that he would not survive Omaha proved tragically true. He was killed instantly before ever setting foot on the beach.

In Slaughter's boat the British coxswain was worried about the perils of beach obstacles as well as the enemy artillery. Suddenly he announced his intention to lower the ramp even though the craft was still several hundred yards offshore. From his place in the front of the craft Slaughter heard another sergeant speak up. "These men have heavy equipment," he said. "Please take them all the way in."

"But we'll all be killed!" the coxswain pleaded.

The sergeant took out his .45 Colt pistol, put it to the sailor's head, and repeated, *"All the way in!"*

When the craft grounded on a sand bar 25 yards from the beach, the water was so rough that when the ramp was lowered it bucked up and down violently. One man jumped off and was killed when the ramp slammed down upon him. When Slaughter's turn came he hesitated. He wanted to time his own leap into the water so that he could jump into the trough of the wave. But the teenager was taking too

Nearby another 19-year-old was recovering from his morning's ordeal. Private Harold Baumgarten had wanted to let the Nazis know just who they were up against: On his field jacket he had drawn a Star of David and below it had written, "The Bronx, New York." But so far this day the Germans were getting the better of things. Baumgarten had taken a bullet through the top of his helmet, and another bullet had hit his rifle as he waded ashore. His buddies were dying all around him. One man lay sprawled on the wet sand, his head toward the enemy, his face to the sky. He was screaming, "Mother, Mom!" Another, known to everyone as "Pilgrim," had a gaping wound on his forehead and was down on his knees as if praying. The deadly interlocking fire of the Germans cut him in half.

Baumgarten pressed on, taking refuge behind

> *"There were dead men floating in the water and there were live men acting dead, letting the tide take them in....It became apparent that it was time to get the hell away from that killing zone and get across the beach."*
>
> SERGEANT ROBERT SLAUGHTER, VETERAN OF OMAHA BEACH

long, blocking the exit and endangering the men behind him. He finally jumped, inflated his life jacket, and let the tide carry him in through a surf that had turned red with blood.

Slaughter knew that he had to get onto the beach and safely across it to the shelter of the sea wall but was "scared to death" of trying. Keeping as low to the ground as his six-foot-five-inch frame would allow, he headed over the sand. On the way he stumbled in a tidal pool and his rifle accidentally fired, barely missing his foot.

Once behind the sea wall, Slaughter spread out his raincoat so he could clean his sand-clogged rifle. Only then did he notice the bullet holes in the coat and his assault jacket. He lighted a cigarette from a package he had carefully wrapped in plastic, then he rested before attempting to move beyond the wall. For the first time he looked behind him and saw the 5,000-ship armada looming offshore.

one of the obstacles on the beach. He fired one shot at an enemy helmet glinting in the sunlight up on the bluff, and his damaged rifle broke in two. He could hear the whine of enemy shells all around him, and he raised his head to curse the Germans. But just as he did, a shell exploded 20 yards in front of him. The force of the blast caught him full in the face, shattering his upper jaw and blowing away his left cheek. Teetering on the verge of passing out, Baumgarten washed his face with cold Channel water and struggled to reach the sea wall, where a medic dressed his wounds.

All along the four miles of Omaha Beach, from the National Guard rookies from Virginia in the west to the veterans of the Big Red One in the east, men were composing themselves—or just trying to stay alive. By the disorganized and frightened hundreds they crowded against the low sea wall and a high embankment of stones near it. Among the

At the close of D-Day with Omaha Beach secured, French civilians gather to examine the bodies laid out in rows awaiting transport back to England. In the distance, barrage balloons protect the invasion fleet from attack by low-flying German planes.

Stonewallers only a quarter of the radios were working, and the officers who had survived scrambled from group to group trying to regain contact. Beyond the wall lay thick coils of barbed wire, a flat and wide-open stretch of marshy ground, and then the treacherous bluffs from which the entrenched German gunners threatened their every move.

Back toward the water the beach was a chaos of men, alive and dead, and the twisted wreckage of equipment littering the water's edge. Ernest Hemingway, watching from his landing craft off the eastern end of Omaha, saw American tanks go ashore, only to be stopped by the enemy gunners. "They were crouched like big yellow toads along the high water line," he wrote of the Shermans. "I saw three tanks coming along the beach, barely moving, they were advancing so slowly. The Germans let them cross the open space where the valley opened onto the beach, and it was absolutely flat, with a perfect field of fire. Then I saw a little fountain of water jut up, just over and beyond the lead tank. Then smoke broke out of the leading tank on the side away from us, and I saw two men dive out of the turret and land on their hands and knees on the stones of the beach. They were close enough so that I could see their faces, but no more men came out as the tank started to blaze up and burn fiercely."

Jeeps, trucks, and other vehicles were also coming ashore now, trying to find a place to land on a strip of sand that was steadily shrinking as the tide

rose. Demolition teams labored frantically to clear the beach obstacles for the new arrivals. But the teams were taking terrible casualties, as high as 40 percent, and had managed to open up only a half-dozen lanes across the beach, well shy of the 16 the assault plan called for. And until the troops massed in the shelter of the sea wall could wrest the five heavily defended draws from the Germans, there was no way inland from the beach, no place to go.

At 8:30 a.m. Omaha was so hopelessly clogged by the tens of thousands of men that had come ashore that the navy beachmaster closed the beach to all new landings and ordered incoming boats to turn around. Hundreds of craft circled offshore "like a stampeding herd of cattle," thought one observer. Up on the plateau the Germans watched it all with mounting hope. One enemy commander was so confident, in fact, that he even turned down an offer of reinforcements. Jubilant German gunners, seeing the boats turn around and head back out, thought for a moment that the Americans were actually abandoning the beach.

Just such a possibility passed through the mind of the general who commanded the American troops that morning. Lieutenant General Omar Bradley, Eisenhower's West Point classmate and close friend, was a desperately worried man. From the bridge of the flagship USS *Augusta,* a dozen miles offshore, he peered anxiously through binoculars at the smoke-shrouded beach, his ears plugged with cotton against the roar of the ship's guns bombarding

Jubilant headlines announce the long-awaited invasion of Europe. The special "invasion issue" of the underground newspaper *The Free Dane (above, right)* reveled in the Allied triumph: "Joy and expectation all over Denmark. It had happened—the big one. . . . So there was joy in our hearts from the early hours of June 6th—and we just could not hide our joy, despite informers and other vermin."

the bluff. He could see frustratingly little, but the fragmentary reports coming in alarmed him. According to the plan, his troops should have been a mile inland by this time, and Bradley could not confirm that they controlled even 100 yards of sand. As the morning wore on he began to fear that his forces had suffered an "irreversible catastrophe." He considered the possibility of relieving the congestion by transferring the men and matériel that had not yet landed to Utah or to the three British beaches. And he even thought about the unthinkable—evacuating Omaha.

Even as Bradley agonized, "praying that our men could hang on," his soldiers were doing more than that. In groups large and small, acting independently and with little cohesion, men were attacking the bluffs. One of the first groups was led by Captain Joseph Dawson, a 30-year-old Texas geologist. As a company commander Dawson had been first off his landing craft when he came ashore about 7:00 a.m. in the eastern part of Omaha. The policy that officers were the first to leave the boat often proved fatal for them, but it saved Dawson's life. Moments after he jumped into the water a shell struck his craft and killed 30 men.

Determined to keep on going, Dawson reached the stone embankment, where survivors from other boats in his company joined him. They were situated between the draws leading to the villages of Colleville and St. Laurent, and though this area was not as heavily defended as the exits themselves, it was still a dangerous place. Deciding that "there was nothing I could do on the beach except die," Dawson began looking for a way inland.

Barring the way off the sand was a double apron of barbed wire fences. Dawson's men assembled Bangalore torpedoes—metal pipes filled with high explosives—and pushed them through the wire. At a pull on the ignition cap the pipes exploded, cutting an opening through the barbed wire.

Ahead of them lay a raised path leading across a low, marshy area and on up the bluff. The Germans had mined the path thickly, so Dawson led his group across the marsh. Still in the lead he started up the bluff. Crawling from one patch of brush to another he got to within 30 feet of an enemy machine gun before the Germans saw him and swung their weapon around. Dawson managed to scramble to cover behind a fold in the bluff's face. He tossed one grenade up, then another, and the gun fell silent. Dawson waved up the rest of his men and climbed onto the crest, where he found Germans sprawled dead in their trenches. It was now about 8:30 a.m., and Dawson figured he was the first American to get from the beach to the top of the bluff.

Near the other end of Omaha, still pressed up against the sea wall, Sergeant Bob Slaughter was

the face of the bluff, though steep, had folds and other irregularities where the assault troops could take shelter as they climbed. By 8:00 a.m. Canham's troops had moved over the sea wall, through the barbed wire, and across 150 yards of marshy flat, and were climbing the bluff single file.

At the same time, Canham's superior, Brigadier General Norman Cota, was working the beach a little to the west. He was the assistant commander of the 29th Division, and like his counterpart over on Utah Beach, Teddy Roosevelt, more than 50 years old. Known as Dutch for his roots in the Pennsylvania Dutch country, he was ordinarily a relaxed and affable man. But now he was all business.

Cota had realized that there was no hope of opening the exits by frontal assault as had been the plan. He concluded that he would have to organize men to scale the bluff between exits and attack the strongpoints guarding them from the rear. Along

"Don't die on the beaches, die up on the bluff if you have to die, but get off the beaches or you're sure to die. You men are Rangers and I know you won't let me down."

BRIGADIER GENERAL NORMAN COTA, OMAHA BEACH

watching another officer in action. To Slaughter, the scrawny and bespectacled Colonel Charles Canham, commander of the Stonewallers, didn't look like a soldier. But in a preinvasion memo Canham had at least sounded like one: "There is one certain way to get the enemy out of action and that is to kill him." And when the colonel came ashore, he did so blazing away with a Browning automatic rifle. After that weapon was shot out of his hand, he put a makeshift sling on his wounded right hand and clutched a .45 Colt pistol in his left. With a soldier following behind to reload the pistol after he emptied it, Canham stalked back and forth screaming for his officers to "get the hell off this damn beach and go kill some Germans."

In fact, this stretch of the western beach to the left of the Vierville exit afforded possibilities for doing just that. Smoke from grass blazing on the crest of the bluff obscured the enemy's view. Moreover,

the wall he saw a group of soldiers and demanded to know who they were. They were Rangers, part of the group who, if all had gone according to plan, would have reinforced their comrades at Pointe du Hoc. "If you're Rangers," snapped Cota, "get up and lead the way!" Though it was debatable whether these elite soldiers needed Cota's prodding, scores of Rangers headed up the bluff, pulling along in their wake leaderless infantrymen from the first wave. Cota's remark that day inspired a new Ranger motto: "Rangers lead the way."

Well over 600 men had climbed the bluff overlooking Omaha Beach by midmorning and were heading inland. Leading a mixed group of Rangers and a number of Stonewallers, Cota battled his way into the village of Vierville. Around 11:00 a.m. Charles Canham entered the town, only to find Cota striding down its narrow

The Liberation of Paris

Paris endured more than four years of occupation by the Nazis. The Germans confiscated most of France's coal supply for their own use, and by 1944 electricity flowed for only one hour a day. Food shortages were widespread, and Parisians learned to eat dishes like heifer's udder, sheep lungs, and alley cat.

In late August, German resistance in front of Paris crumbled and the Allies prepared to move in. Fortunately the German commander ignored Hitler's order to raze the city, and there was only sporadic fighting as most of the garrison withdrew or surrendered.

On August 25, as French and American units rolled toward the city center, thousands of Parisians swarmed over the tanks and jeeps, kissing and hugging their liberators. An American captain said, "A physical wave of human emotion picked us up and carried us into the heart of Paris. It was like groping through a dream."

The 28th Infantry Division marches down the Champs Élysées with the Arc de Triomphe in the distance *(top)*, while other American soldiers lucky enough to take part in the liberation *(above)* enjoy a smoke and a drink in a Paris bistro. The vast majority of front-line GIs continued pursuing the German army across France.

main street, twirling a pistol on his index finger like some old-time gunfighter.

Cota's next move was to test the German defenses in the draw running between Vierville and the beach. Picking his way through the mines that carpeted the draw, Cota descended toward the beach, where he found an enormous concrete wall 12 feet high and 14 feet thick at the base blocking the entrance to the draw. It had to be demolished so vehicles could be driven to the top of the bluff. Down on the beach Cota spotted a bulldozer laden with TNT but no driver. He accosted some soldiers sitting at the sea wall: "Who drives this thing?"

No one answered.

Shells were still falling nearby, and none of the troops wanted to get anywhere near a bulldozer that was full of TNT.

"Well, can anyone drive the damn thing?"

Silence.

Cota then spelled out the necessity of getting the explosives down to the Vierville draw and finally asked in exasperation, "Hasn't anyone got guts enough to drive it down?" A soldier with red hair stood up and said, "I do."

"That's the stuff!" yelled Cota, slapping the man on the back. "Now let's get off the beach."

The deadlock on Omaha was breaking at last. Cota with his Rangers and Stonewallers began clearing the Vierville draw at the far western end of the beach. To the east, Dawson had gotten rid of the German machine gunners near the St. Laurent draw, paving the way for it to be blasted open shortly after noon. The American troops were starting to look like an army again.

But the good news was late in reaching the anxious Omar Bradley out on the *Augusta*. At 1:30 p.m. he received his first favorable report: "Troops formerly pinned down on beaches advancing up heights." Bradley could breathe easier. His troops were at last making headway. Now there was no question of abandoning Omaha.

That night the GIs were digging in at Omaha Beach. By 11:00 p.m. Bob Slaughter was crouched in a shallow foxhole on the bluff. He could hear the reassuring sounds of men and vehicles moving inland and the pounding of the surf on the shore. Intermittent enemy sniper and artillery fire was punctuated by hundreds of small explosions as the weary Americans detonated the half-pound blocks of TNT they carried to blast out foxholes.

Looking out to sea Slaughter spotted his first hostile aircraft of the day, a single-seat fighter plane. It flew over the entire Allied fleet, and thousands of tracer bullets illuminated the night, as if every ship in the English Channel had fired on the defiant pilot. The German plane flew off unscathed—how, Slaughter couldn't imagine. He thought he had never been so tired in his life. He had been awake since 2:00 that morning; it had been a long day.

Back in England the Supreme Commander had not given a command all day. At 7:00 that morning an aide went to Ike's trailer with the news that the troops had begun landing on the beaches of Normandy. He found the general propped up in bed smoking a cigarette and reading a western novel. All day Eisenhower paced the floor of the trailer, alternating between anxiety and elation, while the reports filtered in: the successes by the Americans on Utah and Pointe du Hoc, by the British on Gold and Sword, and by the Canadians on Juno. And then, finally, came word from bloody Omaha—of victory snatched from near disaster, though at a terrible cost. Of the more than 9,000 Allied casualties on D-Day, Omaha made up a third.

Eisenhower would have no need now for the note in his wallet taking full responsibility for the failure of the invasion. Nearly 160,000 of his men were safely ashore in France that night, and he was able to sleep soundly for the first time in days. Tomorrow he would cross the Channel to see the beachheads for himself. Then he would start giving commands once more, mapping the campaign that, after eight weeks of hard fighting to break free of the hedgerows of Normandy, would lead in late August to the liberation of Paris. ◆

Bombing the Nazis around the Clock

"We were riding Ray Clough's left wing when he got hit. He dropped out, and twenty seconds later he burst into flames. Brown got hit and disintegrated: a great sheet of flame and then a hole in the formation."

LIEUTENANT RAY WILD, OCTOBER 14, 1943

American airmen began swarming into England in the spring of 1942 to join their Royal Air Force counterparts fighting the Luftwaffe. For three years Hitler's air force had controlled the skies over Europe, although the RAF had some success with its strategic bombing campaign against aircraft factories, oil plants, rail yards, and other facilities critical to Germany's ability to make war.

British and American commanders were united in principle, but they disagreed over bombing strategies. The Americans strongly favored daytime precision bombing, which their B-17 Flying Fortresses had been built for. The British responded that they had already tried daytime bombing and found it far too costly in men and planes;

the Allies should limit their attacks to nighttime area bombing. President Roosevelt and Prime Minister Churchill settled the issue when they met at Casablanca in January 1943. They committed the Allies to an around-the-clock bombing campaign that would wrest air superiority from the Germans and gut their essential war industries. The British would bomb by night and the Americans by day.

Young American airmen like the crew of the *Yankee Queen* shown above faced grave danger every time they took off for Germany, especially in the early months following the U.S. entry into the European air war. It took remarkable courage, for the fliers had a 1 in 3 chance of making it through their 25-mission tour of duty.

READY FOR TAKEOFF

Whether crews flew out of England with the Eighth Army Air Force or, beginning in late 1943, out of Italy with the Fifteenth, they followed the same routine. Up before dawn, the crews assembled after breakfast to hear an operations officer describe the day's target, the weather, and the antiaircraft fire and enemy fighters they could expect to encounter.

After the briefing, airmen picked up the 60 pounds of clothing and equipment needed for the mission: a life jacket; a parachute; and, for the -40°F temperatures and thin air found at high altitudes, an electrically heated flight suit, a fleece-lined leather suit to wear over it, gloves, and an oxygen mask.

By the time a flight crew reached its plane at the hardstand, ground crews had repaired any previous damage, serviced the four engines, fueled the plane, and loaded it with bombs and ammunition. Aboard, the flight crew ran through a preflight checklist, then taxied out to the runway to wait its turn as the mission's bombers took off at intervals of 30 to 60 seconds. On a large mission, the formation in which the bombers flew could stretch across 200 miles of sky.

Pilots *(right)* **in the all-black 332d Fighter Group based in Italy listen during a briefing before a mission in 1944. The highly decorated squadron escorted Allied bombers on hazardous missions over Germany. Above, an Eighth Army Air Force navigator plots a mission course to avoid known concentrations of antiaircraft guns.**

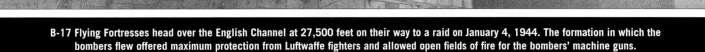

"Up early for an 03.30 briefing. Take-off at 07.10. Again I'm navigator and not minding it too much. With this being our 13th mission I anticipated a hot one but didn't say much to the rest of the crew, I guess they were sweating it out enough themselves."

SECOND LIEUTENANT WILLIAM DUANE'S DIARY ENTRY AFTER A RAID ON SEPTEMBER 28, 1944

B-17 Flying Fortresses head over the English Channel at 27,500 feet on their way to a raid on January 4, 1944. The formation in which the bombers flew offered maximum protection from Luftwaffe fighters and allowed open fields of fire for the bombers' machine guns.

LITTLE FRIENDS

Fighter planes, called little friends in air force parlance, flew with the big, heavy bombers to protect them from enemy aircraft. But the capacity of the fighters' fuel tanks was limited, and Eighth Army Air Force bombers taking off from England had to depend on their own defenses for much of a mission, since the range of the fighters stopped near the German border. The Luftwaffe fighters often waited to attack un-til the bombers' escorts had turned back.

By the summer of 1943, Hitler had strengthened German air defenses in reaction to the Allied around-the-clock bombing, and Allied bombers flying beyond the range of their little friends were suffering badly. Between October 8 and 14, 1943, called Black Week because it was the worst week on record, Americans lost a total of 148 bombers on four raids. It was so bad that flights deep into Germany were suspended for the time being.

The Americans found two solutions to cut their bomber losses. One was the P-51 Mustang, a new long-range fighter that could fly the eight-and-a-half-hour trip from England to Berlin and back. Drop tanks, auxiliary gas tanks, were added to other fighters to extend their range another 100 miles.

A new chapter in the air war in Europe began on February 20, 1944, when 1,000 bombers and almost as many fighters headed to Germany on the first raid of what came to be called Big Week. Now fighters could escort the bombers to their targets and then home, and only 21 American bombers were lost that day—a rate well below the 5 percent deemed acceptable. By April 1944 the long-range fighters had won air superiority for the Allies over Germany and Western Europe. On the eve of D-Day, General Eisenhower was able to reassure his troops, "If you see fighting aircraft over you, they will be ours."

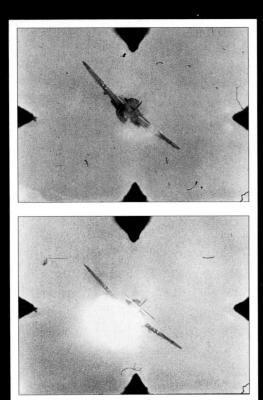

A camera mounted in the wing of an American fighter photographs the Messerschmitt-109 following close on its tail *(top left)*. Hit by American fire, fuel tanks on the Messerschmitt's belly burst into flames *(middle)* that grow into a great ball engulfing the plane *(bottom)*. As Allied air power accelerated, Germany was increasingly hard pressed to replace planes and pilots lost in combat.

"After dropping our bomb load we ran into some fairly accurate flak, ...and at 1230 a twin-engine Me-110 started to make a frontal attack on us. Out of nowhere a P-51 came blazing down and the 110 blew up in a burst of smoke about 600 yards in front of our aircraft."

LIEUTENANT DARRELL GUST, NAVIGATOR, JANUARY 11, 1944

Flying in close formation, Mustangs from the Eighth Army Air Force head off to escort heavy bombers. Pilot Donald Blakeslee *(right),* who flew with the RAF before the United States entered the war, scored most of his 15½ air victories in P-51 Mustangs. He shared credit for one of his hits with another pilot.

Controlled by the bombardier from his windowed compartment in the nose of the airplane *(below)*, bombs are released through the open bomb bay of a B-17 Flying Fortress. To ensure against accidental explosions, bombs carried three safety devices.

Delivering the Payload

Flying bombers in formation 250 feet apart took tremendous strength and concentration, so a pilot and copilot shared the work. The gunners kept them informed about the location of the German fighters, which usually broke off and let the flak guns take over when the bombers neared their target. Once the bombers had started a bombing run they stayed on course and could not take evasive action against flak, an abbreviation of the German for antiaircraft shells and guns.

When the formation began its run, the pilot in the lead plane of the lead squadron turned on the automatic pilot, controlled by the Norden bombsight, a top-secret device operated by the bombardier. Americans liked to brag that it could drop a bomb into a pickle barrel from 20,000 feet. The bombsight automatically released the bombs at a preset reading, and bombardiers in the rest of the formation released theirs when they saw the lead plane drop its payload. Once the bombs were away, the pilot resumed control. Precision bombing was not always precise; weather and navigation mistakes and other errors caused many bombs to miss their target.

"*Never in my life did I have to work as hard as flying a B-17 in formation. Vernon Sahm and I took 15-minute turns, and each used to look at the clock and when the turn was over, each dropped the wheel with relief. Twenty-year-old fellows in top physical shape could not keep up over 15 minutes!*"

WILLIAM G. RUSSELL, 447TH BOMB GROUP PILOT, EIGHTH ARMY AIR FORCE

Coming in unusually low to make its attack, a B-24 Liberator skims over the smokestacks of an oil refinery at Ploieşti, Romania, during a raid on August 1, 1943. Of the 177 Liberators assigned to the mission, 54 were lost.

A Mission's Multiple Hazards

While the Luftwaffe fighter pilots posed a serious threat, a big plane had a measure of defense in its machine guns. But it was defenseless against flak. Traveling as far as six miles, the 22-pound shells burst into 1,500 deadly fragments that could pierce the skin of airplanes, shatter windows, and set fire to fuel, causing planes to explode.

Weather, accidents, fatigue, stress, and the mistakes of green pilots added to the toll taken by flak and by the Luftwaffe. From August 1942 to the end of the war, 20,000 American airmen died over Europe. During some missions, especially before the advent of long-range fighters, losses were horrendous. In a strike against Nazi ball-bearing factories in Schweinfurt, Germany, on October 14, 1943, the rate reached 40 percent.

A B-24 Liberator bursts into flames and spills out its bombs over central Germany after being hit by flak. In 1944 German flak destroyed 3,501 American planes, almost 600 more than the toll taken by German fighters. B-24s were more vulnerable to flak than B-17s because they could not fly as high.

A waist gunner, one of two gunners in the midsection of a B-24 Liberator, watches for enemy aircraft through a portal in the plane's midsection. One gunner was stationed in the tail and one in the ball turret under the plane. When attacked, the navigator and the bombardier manned the nose guns, and the flight engineer took over the gun in the upper turret.

"*The sight of those ugly black bursts leaves you with a numb helpless feeling. All you can do is try and concentrate on your job and pray that in all that steel flying around there isn't a piece with your number on it.*"

LIEUTENANT GORDON COURTENAY, 398TH BOMB GROUP BOMBARDIER, U.S. EIGHTH ARMY AIR FORCE

Smoke pours from one engine of a B-24 as it flies through black puffs of flak over Vienna on October 13, 1944. Luftwaffe fighter pilots preyed on exposed and crippled planes, but this one made it back to its base in Italy.

Crew members of *The Worry Bird* cluster near their plane after a mission *(left)*. Following a hard flight, airmen watched anxiously to see who would—or would not—return. Below, an exhausted gunner still wearing his flight gear eats a sandwich.

COMING IN ON A WING AND A PRAYER

As planes returned to England or Italy at the completion of a mission, fighters and bombers separated and flew on to their various bases. Once over home base, bombers with wounded men aboard fired a flare gun to signal that they needed to land first. On the ground, the airmen shed layers of clothing, looked over their planes, and rehashed the flight before heading to debriefing sessions. Engineers and sheet-metal workers quickly assessed planes for damage, and mechanics were soon at work on the necessary repairs and maintenance.

Intelligence officers debriefed the crews as a group. Each member, beginning with the pilot, reported his experience. The intelligence officer ran through a checklist of questions designed to gather information that might reveal new enemy tactics or technological development; the Allies and the Germans were warring with each other to improve radar and other critical military capabilities. Intelligence officers sent their "flash reports" to headquarters, where staff specialists analyzed the information and used it to plan the next mission in the air war over Europe.

*"Our ground crews were waiting and waiting at their hardstands. And **nothing** was coming back.... These people had worked their butts off preparing these aircraft.... They really thought of themselves as part of a team with the flight crews. And when the other half of the team didn't come back, it was a hard thing to take."*

Lieutenant John F. Bell after a raid on Schweinfurt, Germany, October 14, 1943

Firefighters spray thousands of gallons of foam on *Golden Gaboon*, a B-24 Liberator that crash-landed at an Eighth Army Air Force base in England following a mission to Germany. The crew escaped unharmed. A shortfall of fuel or damage from enemy fire made crash-landings a frequent occurrence.

CHAPTER 3

TAKING THE WAR TO GERMANY

"I'm going to be an awful irritation to the military historians, because I do things by a sixth sense. They won't understand."

GEORGE S. PATTON JR.

One day between the wars, Colonel George Patton took his family to visit a Civil War battlefield near Fredericksburg, Virginia. They were accompanied by a German military attaché, General Friedrich von Boetticher, a longtime friend of Patton's who was also a learned student of American history. As was the custom on these outings, Patton assigned each member of his family a position—his wife, Beatrice, being from Massachusetts, was appointed as representative of the Union forces; his children, as his 25-year-old daughter Ruth Ellen recalled, "were somebody's troops."

A group of tourists with a guide was nearby, and as Patton began explaining the battle, Ruth Ellen noticed one elderly man with muttonchop whiskers begin to lose interest in what his own guide was saying and start to listen to Patton. Her father finished his speech by saying that he was Confederate general Jubal Early and would retire with his aides to a rise of ground a short distance away.

Von Boetticher, reading from a book on the battle, countered that Early, according to the book, had been in another part of the field at the time, and he and "Georgie," as Patton was known to his intimates, began to discuss the question. The old gentleman with the tour party had drifted away

from his group and had drawn close to the Pattons. Finally, the man could stand it no longer. "The young gentleman is quite right," he said. "General Early was on that nearby rise. I was in that battle." Patton turned his attention to the stranger. "Of course General Early was on that rise," Patton explained calmly. "I saw him there myself!" The odd statement elicited no surprise among those present, Ruth Ellen noted—and von Boetticher dutifully took out a pen and methodically made the correction to the text of his book.

Reincarnation. Patton rarely spoke about the subject, but from an early age it permeated his being and colored his approach to life—and to war. Throughout his childhood his father and other friends and family, some of whom had themselves seen action during the Civil War, had filled him with vivid tales of the heroic Pattons of Virginia who had bravely fought and died for the Confederacy. Young Georgie listened in rapt attention to these stories, as well as to stirring accounts of the campaigns of Hannibal, Julius Caesar, Napoleon Bonaparte, and other great captains of the past, read to him by his parents and by a doting spinster aunt whom he called Nannie. By the age of eight, young Georgie was convinced not only that he was born to carry on

Wreathed in stars and wearing what he called his war face, General George S. Patton Jr. looks every inch the soldier. "By his own opinion," wrote a journalist who knew him well, "he was an obstreperous, fighting, cantankerous bastard—and proud of it!"

97

his family's illustrious military tradition, but that he had lived many times before, always as a soldier, always dying gloriously in battle.

So compelling was his drive to fulfill his destiny to be a great battlefield leader that when his wealthy prospective father-in-law objected to his daughter's becoming a soldier's wife, Patton was prepared never to marry rather than give up his chosen profession. The anguished suitor poured out his heart in a letter to his parents. "All my life I have done every thing I could to be a soldier for I feel inside that it is my job and that war will come," he wrote. "There is inside me a burning something. . . . I wake up at night in a cold sweat imagining that I have lived and done nothing." By the time World

him to fight here once more, this time at the head of a great conquering army.

An hour after leaving England Patton's plane touched down on a landing strip near Omaha Beach—"a hell of a way to make an amphibious landing," he muttered to one of his aides. For by July 6, a month after D-Day, the successful Allied amphibious invasion of Adolf Hitler's Europe had been followed by the establishment of beachheads on the Norman coast. And only now was George Patton getting into the game. Indeed, he was lucky to be seeing any of the action at all.

A year earlier Patton had been in line to become the senior American field commander for the Normandy operation. His successes against the Germans

> *"All my life I have done every thing I could to be a soldier for I feel inside that it is my job and that war will come. There is inside me a burning something....*
> *I wake up at night in a cold sweat imagining that I have lived and done nothing."*
>
> CADET PATTON IN A LETTER TO HIS PARENTS, JANUARY 17, 1909

War II came along, after two long decades in the peacetime army, George Smith Patton Jr. was well into his fifties, and he felt as if he had been training—and waiting—a lifetime for the challenge.

The morning of July 6, 1944, Patton, now a general and the commanding officer of the U.S. Third Army, boarded a C-47 Dakota transport plane in southern England and took off for France. Packed away in his luggage were the books that he always kept close at hand: a volume of Kipling's poems, a biography of Civil War leader Jeb Stuart, and the Holy Bible, which his Aunt Nannie had spent so many hours reading to him. With him too came an overwhelming sense of personal destiny. Here he was in France, the country of Charlemagne, William the Conqueror, and Napoleon, a land fought over by great warriors, like Julius Caesar and Attila the Hun. And Patton believed that he, too, had fought here, in a previous life. He sensed that *his* time had come again—that God had chosen

in North Africa and Sicily had convinced his superior, Supreme Commander Dwight Eisenhower, that Patton should play a key role in the invasion of Europe. But his notoriously quick temper had been his undoing. While visiting field hospitals in Sicily in August 1943 Patton had slapped two GIs who he thought were malingerers. It was scandalous conduct for an officer, and the incident caused a furor when it was reported in the American press. Patton's career would have been over without the intercession of Eisenhower, who declared, "I can't afford to lose my best general."

Eisenhower and Patton had been friends since they were stationed together at Camp Meade, Maryland, shortly after the end of World War I. Patton was five years older and, having served with the American Expeditionary Force to France in 1917, had the combat experience that Ike lacked. But he had always felt that Eisenhower would someday be his superior. Anticipating how a future war might be conducted, Patton used to tell his friend kiddingly, "Ike, you will be the Lee of the next war, and I will be your Jackson."

But as a consequence of the slapping incidents, Ike had passed over Patton when looking for a commander of U.S. ground forces for D-Day. The post had gone instead to General Omar Bradley, who had served under Patton in North Africa and Sicily—and who had serious doubts about his new subordinate's style of leadership.

The two men were a study in contrasts. Where Bradley was homespun and businesslike, Patton was flamboyant and rash. He liked to ride in an open jeep marked by oversized white stars and equipped with a klaxon. His perfectly tailored battle jacket and jodhpurs, his gleaming helmet with its firmament of stars, the ivory-handled six-shooters at his hip were all part of the image. So was his menacing expression—what he called his war face—which he had perfected by practicing in front of a mirror. As he told Bradley on one occasion, "I'd rather be looked at than overlooked."

Bradley was scornful of Patton's theatrics and condemned his generalship as reckless and irresponsible, but he also recognized his subordinate's complexity and described him as a "Jekyll and Hyde" figure "living a role he had set for himself 20 or 30 years before." Although Patton was deeply religious, widely read, and a writer of poetry, his speeches were nonetheless laced with profanity and vulgarity, and usually accompanied by great fanfare, including an honor guard and band. His message was always aggressive. "Every waking minute, he was playing the indomitable, inimitable, and incomparable professional warrior," wrote a reporter who knew him well. "He played the part so boldly that much of it became a reality."

The differences in style between the cautious, predictable Bradley and his showman subordinate were apparent the moment that the Third Army commander stepped off his transport plane near Omaha Beach. Patton was immediately surrounded by soldiers, sailors, and news correspondents, all of

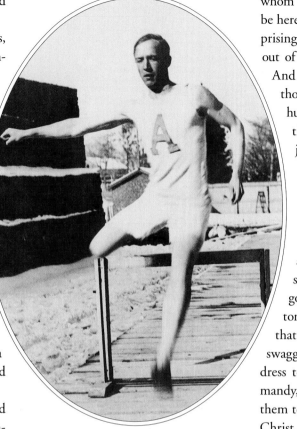

THE SOLDIER-ATHLETE

At West Point, George Patton was a mediocre student but excelled at individual sports such as swimming, riding, shooting, cross-country running, and track events. His athletic prowess won him a berth on the U.S. team at the 1912 Olympic Games in Stockholm. The 27-year-old Patton competed in the modern pentathlon, which consisted of a steeplechase, pistol shooting, a grueling swimming race, fencing, and, finally, a 4,000-meter cross-country run. Patton was still in the competition when the run began, and he was the first to reenter the stadium for the last stretch. But heat, humidity, and dehydration were too much for him, and he slowed to a walk and fainted after crossing the finish line. Although he didn't win a medal, Patton finished a very respectable fifth out of 43 athletes.

whom wanted to get a glimpse of him. "I'm proud to be here to fight beside you," he told them in his surprisingly high-pitched voice. "Now let's cut the guts out of those Krauts and get the hell on to Berlin. And when we get to Berlin," he continued, his thoughts turning to the German leader and his humble origins, "I am going to personally shoot that paper-hanging goddamned son of a bitch just like I would a snake."

Larger than life, George S. Patton had arrived, and his Third Army was not far behind him. Observing him supervising the unloading of tanks on the beach, one sailor said, "When you see General Patton you get the same feeling as when you saw Babe Ruth striding up to the plate. Here's a big guy who's going to kick hell out of something." But Patton wanted to imbue his whole command with that same fighting zeal, to mold it in his own swaggering image. In the general's welcoming address to the Third Army upon its arrival in Normandy, he said of the Germans: "Some day I want them to raise up on their hind legs and howl: 'Jesus Christ, it's the goddam Third Army and that sonofabitch Patton again!'"

Three weeks after Patton's landing in France, Eisenhower persuaded a reluctant Bradley to turn the Third Army loose—and during the summer of 1944, Patton's results spoke for themselves. His army attacked without letup, dashing more than 400 miles across France in 26 days, killing, wounding, or capturing more than 100,000 Germans and destroying some 500 tanks and 700 guns with a loss of only 16,000 men.

George Patton had never been happier—or busier. His columns were racing along roads that had at one time been tramped by the legions of Rome. "If Caesar chose those routes," he declared, "they must be good." It seemed like Patton was everywhere. He made frequent visits to the front, all the time praising, inspiring, and, when necessary, reprimanding his men. According to one officer, "His spirit permeated the whole organization. You

had a feeling that Third Army was going in only one direction—forward."

The visits to the front line also had another, more symbolic purpose. In Patton's view, they were to "show the soldiers that generals can get shot at." He always tried to return after dark, sometimes in a small Piper Cub aircraft, because he thought that a commander should be seen only going to the front, never coming away from it. "If you want an army to fight and risk death," he said, "you've got to get up there and lead it. An army is like spaghetti. You can't push a piece of spaghetti, you've got to pull it."

The highly irregular technique Patton used to "pull" his army caught the imagination of the press, which found an unlikely new hero in the officer who had slapped a pair of GIs in Sicily. "A fiction writer couldn't create him," a United Press reporter mused. "History itself hasn't matched him. He's colorful, fabulous. He's dynamite. On a battlefield, he's a warring, roaring comet."

As the Third Army's victories continued, Bill Mauldin, the famed GI cartoonist for *Stars and Stripes,* arranged to go see Patton, though with some trepidation. The general detested Mauldin's "goddamned cartoons" because he thought they demeaned the American soldier, and he had threatened that "if that little son of a bitch sets foot in Third Army I'll throw his ass in jail."

Patton made a memorable first impression on the 22-year-old Mauldin: "His hair was silver, his face was pink, his collar and shoulders glittered with more stars than I could count, his fingers sparkled with rings, and an incredible mass of ribbons started around desktop level and spread upward in a flood over his chest to the very top of his shoulder, as if preparing to march down his back too." With Patton

Sandwiched between two colossal egos, the temperate General Omar Bradley looks as Field Marshal Bernard Montgomery casts a critical eye at Patton's ivory-handled revolver. Patton considered "Monty" too cautious in pushing the Germans. He repeatedly complained to Bradley, his superior, that the British share of the Allies' overtaxed resources was too large and argued that channeling more to his army would produce better results.

was his dog, a white bull terrier named Willie, short for William the Conqueror. Patton had picked him up at a pound in England, and he had traveled over to France with the general. "If ever dog was suited to master this one was," Mauldin observed. "Willie had his beloved boss's expression and lacked only the ribbons and stars. I stood in that door staring into the four meanest eyes I'd ever seen."

Patton reveled in the attention being showered on him by the media. And while critics called him a prima donna and dubbed him Old Blood and Guts, Patton's soldiers came to love him, even as they chafed at his insistence that everyone not actively engaged with the enemy be clean-shaven and wear polished boots, necktie, and helmet. Instead of identifying themselves by their unit as most GIs did, his troops simply proclaimed, "I'm with Patton."

The end of 1944 saw "the goddam Third" and six other Allied armies—more than two million men in all—crowding up against the 400-mile-long, steel-and-concrete West Wall that Hitler had built along the Rhine River on Germany's western frontier to the Swiss border. Many Allied intelligence analysts figured the Germans were on their last legs. In five years of warfare they had lost almost

From Normandy the Allies swept across France, Belgium, and Luxembourg to the German frontier, where they were halted by supply shortages, worsening weather, and the defenses of the West Wall *(red line)*. On December 16 the Germans launched a tremendous counteroffensive in the Ardennes region.

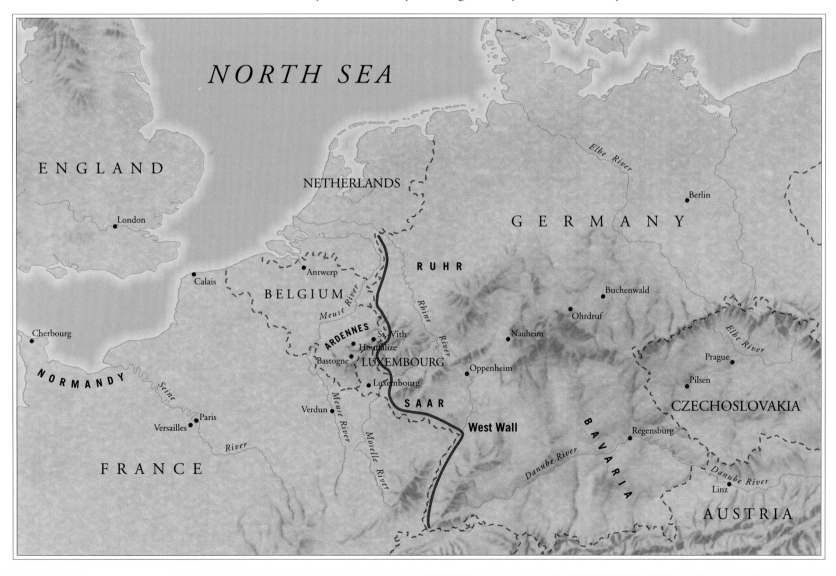

three and a half million men, the vast majority of them on the Eastern Front fighting the Soviets. Their air force had been so severely reduced by attrition that it had ceased to be a meaningful threat. And Hitler's appointment of 69-year-old Field Marshal Gerd von Rundstedt as commander in chief of the Western Front further lulled Eisenhower and his generals into complacency. Given Rundstedt's reputation for conservative strategy, the Allies expected only careful defensive operations west of the Rhine, assuming he would hold back his strongest forces to defend the West Wall and the Rhine.

Eisenhower had determined that the main Allied drive against those defenses would be made by Britain's Field Marshal Bernard Law Montgomery in the north, with secondary attacks farther south by Bradley. "Monty" would thrust through Belgium toward the Ruhr, Germany's industrial heartland. While protecting the British right, Bradley was to push east toward the Saar, Germany's vital mining region. The only place the Allies were on the defensive was in the Ardennes, the heavily forested mountain range southeast of the Meuse River between Luxembourg and Belgium.

The Ardennes was a hostile place of steep ravines, thick tree cover, rivers running through deep, narrow valleys, and few roads or trails. Despite the German success in coming through the region in the blitzkrieg that overwhelmed France in 1940, the American commanders still considered it impassable to large armored forces. Bradley, with Eisenhower's blessing, had confidently thinned the lines there so that the First Army could be concentrated north of the region while Patton's Third Army was poised opposite the Saar to the south. As a result, the 90-mile Ardennes front was held by only 83,000 men, largely elements of Major General Troy Middleton's VIII Corps. Many were green troops and the others were veterans who had been sent there for rest, which led one officer to joke that the sector had been turned into a "nursery and old folks' home."

Although there were only enough men in the Ardennes to hold a few strongpoints linked by occasional patrols, Eisenhower and Bradley were focused on the upcoming offensive and did not want to borrow troops from other sectors to beef up the area. When Middleton complained that his sector was undermanned, Bradley responded: "Don't worry, Troy, they won't come through here."

Bradley was only echoing what he had been told by his intelligence officers. Even the usually skeptical Montgomery sent a rosy assessment to his troops: "The enemy is at present fighting a defensive campaign on all fronts; his situation is such that he cannot stage major offensive operations."

Patton felt otherwise, however. His own offensive into the Saar region was scheduled to kick off on December 19, when he planned to burst through the West Wall and unleash his tanks on the flat terrain that lay west of the Rhine. But all the time he had cautiously kept a watch over his left shoulder, fearing that the Germans might launch a spoiling attack to derail his offensive.

His instincts proved correct. On December 9 Patton's intelligence chief called a special briefing to report a huge buildup of tank and infantry divisions on the eastern side of the Ardennes. Staring at the detailed battle maps that his intelligence officer kept meticulously up to date, Patton contemplated the news for a minute or two. Then he declared that until the German intentions became clear, the Third Army's offensive would proceed as planned with one proviso: Planning would begin at once to counter any threat in the Ardennes sector. "We'll be in a position to meet whatever happens," he told his staff.

Patton's foresight would pay immense dividends. But even he underestimated the size and scope of the German plans. This would be no spoiling attack but a full-fledged offensive, a fight that would come to be known as the Battle of the Bulge.

The offensive in the Ardennes sprang from the evil genius of Adolf Hitler. During the late summer, when Germany's military situation looked the darkest, the Führer had begun laying the groundwork for a bold counterstroke to regain the

THE FÜHRER'S DECLINING HEALTH

By the fall of 1944, the once vigorous Adolf Hitler looked gaunt and irresolute, and with good reason. The western Allies were racing across France while the Soviets hammered at the eastern borders of the Reich. In July a bomb planted in his headquarters had nearly killed him, and the attempted assassination deepened his already acute paranoia. His official diarist noted that Hitler "had suddenly grown old, his complexion looked unhealthy, he often stared vacantly, his back was bent, and his shoulders sunken, as if an invisible weight was crushing him."

But perhaps the real reason for Hitler's changed appearance had more to do with an eccentric regimen he was following than with the changing fortunes of war or his paranoia. Plagued by stomach cramps, headaches, insomnia, jaundice, dental problems, and possibly Parkinson's disease, Hitler turned to his personal physician of nine years, Dr. Theodor Morell, who had made a fortune manufacturing chocolate vitamins and claimed to have discovered penicillin, only to have British agents steal the secret from him. He nurtured Hitler's well-known hypochondria by prescribing as many as 28 different medications including amphetamines, extracts from bull testicles, and probably morphine, along with some of his own patent medicines. Morell's quackery undoubtedly hastened the physical and mental decline of his patient, who, in the words of an SS bodyguard, looked "closer to 70 than to 56."

initiative in the west. It would take place when the winter weather would interfere most with the Allied air forces. "Fog, night, and snow," he said, would offer a "great opportunity." Hitler had decided that the attack should come out of the Ardennes, with the Belgian city of Antwerp, which had become the Allies' chief port of supply, as the designated target. The grand design called for German tanks—panzers—to split the American and British armies with a lightning attack and push the British to the edge of the North Sea.

Such a catastrophe, Hitler reckoned, would rip the fragile Allied coalition apart, set them to squabbling over who was to blame, and allow Germany time to turn back to face the Russians, who were already closing in on Germany's eastern borders. "Never in history," Hitler told his senior commanders, "was there a coalition like that of our enemies, composed of such heterogeneous elements with such divergent aims. Ultracapitalist states on the one hand; ultra-Marxist states on the other. On one hand, a dying empire, Britain; on the other, a colony bent upon inheritance, the United States." Hitler believed these conflicts of interest were potentially fatal: "If now we can deliver a few more heavy blows, then at any moment this artificially bolstered common front may suddenly collapse with a gigantic clap of thunder."

Hitler gave the plan the code name Watch on the Rhine to lead Allied intelligence into thinking that the Germans were merely preparing their defenses to prevent a breakthrough across the great river barrier, a ruse he reinforced with his appointment of the venerable Field Marshal Rundstedt. The attack would be aimed squarely at the American soldier, whom Hitler considered the weak link in the Anglo-American alliance. From his twisted Nazi viewpoint, the United States was too mongrelized to produce top-quality fighting men.

But Hitler's own soldiers were in short supply. To scrape together a new army, he began calling up surplus workers from business and industry, conscripting youths and old men, and pressing into the ranks rear-echelon troops as well as airmen and sailors who had been idled by lack of fuel for their planes and ships. He created new armored formations by pulling veteran SS panzer divisions out of the line on the Eastern Front. These units—which were made up of the most fanatical and ideological of the Nazi troops—were given top priority in the distribution of the tanks that were currently coming off the production lines in record numbers despite the Allied air raids.

To sow confusion and terror among the American troops, Hitler organized a force of infiltrators who were dressed in captured American uniforms and equipped with captured American tanks, jeeps, arms, and identification. They were to race to the Meuse, seize several bridges, commit sabotage, and generally create havoc. In addition, a 1,000-man parachute force was to land behind U.S. lines to open the roads for German armor and to block American units from interfering with the panzers' progress. An early goal of the panzer corps was to seize two major road junctions in the Ardennes, the towns of St.-Vith and Bastogne.

The impact of the German whirlwind would push as much as 50 miles deep into U.S.-held territory, forming the bulge that would give the battle its name. Fought in the worst winter northern Europe had had in nearly four decades, the struggle would call forth superhuman efforts from American GIs and put the lie to Hitler's racist notions about the capacity of Americans to fight. It would also be the finest hour for the Allied general the Germans feared the most: George S. Patton Jr.

Mere seconds before 5:30 a.m., in the foggy darkness of December 16, an American soldier in an observation post in the Ardennes saw strange, flickering points of light in the distance. But even as he telephoned his company commander to report the phenomenon, the din of bursting shells explained what the flashes were: Nearly 2,000 German guns had begun what would be a 90-minute bombardment of the American positions.

Powered by 250,000 men, fully half of the German forces available on the Western Front, Hitler's desperate offensive roared into motion against the unsuspecting Americans. Up and down the Ardennes front shells screamed in over the U.S. positions, the ground trembled, trees splintered, and ugly black patches appeared in the six-inch blanket of snow. GIs leaped out of sleeping bags, quickly grabbed their weapons, and dived for foxholes. Forward observers reached for field telephones, only to discover that their lines were dead, the wires cut by the shelling. Switching over to radios, they

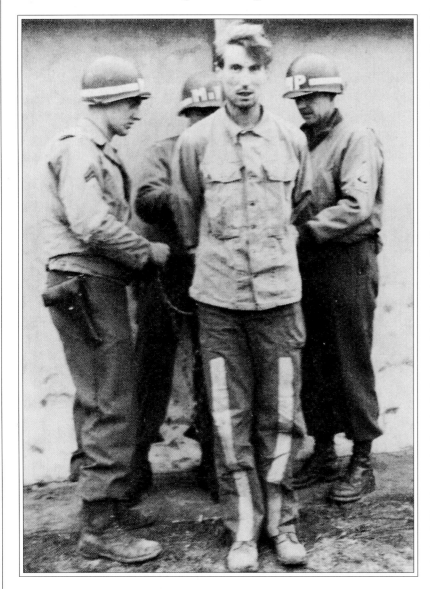

MPs tie German commando Manfred Pernass to a stake shortly before his execution by firing squad. In an attempt to alarm and mislead their captors, Pernass and his comrades fabricated the story that other commandos were seeking to kill General Eisenhower.

found their wavelengths were jammed by the martial music of German bands.

At first no one knew what to make of the shelling. Inexperienced troops thought it was "outgoing mail"—friendly fire. Even veterans were baffled; it didn't seem possible that the meager German force said to be holding the front could manage such a heavy bombardment. Then the shelling let up and the morning mists of the Ardennes were bathed in an eerie glow. The Germans had switched on searchlights, bouncing their powerful beams off of low-hanging clouds in order to illuminate the American positions. German infantrymen advanced through this false dawn—spectral figures in snow-white camouflage suits—and behind them rumbled their terrible Tiger tanks.

Hitler had achieved his surprise. GIs everywhere were engaged in desperate combat, but the general disruption of communications led most units to assume the attacks were purely local. Until the radio network began to function again, companies were cut off from their battalions, battalions from their regiments, and regiments from their divisions. It was

difficult for any of the field commanders, much less the U.S. high command at Versailles, outside Paris, to form a clear picture of what was going on. But General Bradley knew that he desperately needed to get tank reinforcements to the Ardennes. On the evening of December 16 he telephoned Patton. "The Germans are attacking toward St.-Vith," he said. "I've got to take 10th Armored away from you."

Patton was furious. Bradley had taken units away from him in the past, and Patton did not want to lose another just when the Third Army was about to go on the offensive. Moving the 10th Armored Division to the north, he told Bradley, "would be playing into the hands of the Germans."

"Ike said you'd yell your head off," Bradley told him. "But I've got to do it. This is serious." Despite his frustration, Patton followed orders and promptly dispatched the tanks.

Eisenhower and his staff knew that Bastogne, a drab market town of 3,500 inhabitants, would be critical to the defense of the Ardennes. Seven paved roads radiated from the town's central square, including the main east-west highways running from

Puffs of dust from the concrete wall behind them mark the moment of death for Pernass and two other commandos. Just before the fatal volleys rang out, one of the Germans shouted in a clear, steady voice, "Long live our Führer, Adolf Hitler!"

The formidable German King Tiger was the largest and heaviest tank of World War II. Shells from its 88mm cannon had a devastating effect on Sherman tanks *(inset)*, while its own six-inch-thick steel armor made it almost impervious to American guns. One Sherman sergeant reported scoring 14 direct hits on a King Tiger without causing any damage.

the German border to the Meuse River. On December 17 the Supreme Commander ordered his reserve forces, the 82d and 101st Airborne Divisions, to rush toward Bastogne. Meanwhile, the man in the thick of things, General Middleton, was making plans to throw up roadblocks in the path of the Germans moving toward Bastogne, St.-Vith, and other critical crossroads.

Up and down the Ardennes front the fighting was a confusing series of small-unit actions with pockets of outnumbered and outgunned Americans fighting for their lives and for control of the road junctions that would let the Germans move north and west to Antwerp. In some areas the GIs were outnumbered by 7 to 1. When they had to withdraw from one position, the Germans were often so close that the shootout looked like a Wild West affair, with soldiers leaping aboard any vehicle they could grab—armored cars, tanks, half-tracks—or taking off on foot. In the numbing cold, the sluggish vehicles could move at only about 10 miles an hour, so the Americans—hanging on with one arm while firing with the other—had to run a gantlet of enemy troops on both sides of the road in slow motion.

In other places the withdrawal was a more orderly affair, taking full advantage of a tactic known as skinning the cat. This procedure involved units' being pulled back through their rear battalions, which would cover their withdrawal. The movement would then be repeated, with the rear battalions falling back through the former front-line units, until the entire force had safely withdrawn to a more secure position.

At the northern end of the Ardennes front, however, a German task force consisting of more than 100 tanks and about 5,000 veteran SS troopers broke through the weakly defended U.S. lines and rolled west toward the Meuse. The SS troopers left a gruesome trail: more than 300 American prisoners of war and 100 Belgian civilians murdered in cold blood in a dozen different locations.

News of the massacres spread rapidly, with electrifying effect. American resolve stiffened. Some units vowed that they would take no prisoners in SS uniform. Two German airdrops—a small paratroop landing and a phony drop consisting of 300 dummies—created confusion briefly in the American rear areas. But the German panzers had overextended themselves, and U.S. reinforcements rushed down from the north to cut them off. Despite efforts to capture them, however, 800 of the SS men escaped back through the lines.

The Americans suffered their worst disaster in the central Ardennes when a panzer army made a major breakthrough against a division of General Middleton's green troops; stranded and cut off, more than 7,000 men surrendered to the Germans on December 19. Elsewhere in this part of the front, veteran U.S. units fought fierce delaying actions, holding up the attackers for two days before eventually pulling out. The resistance by outnumbered and outmaneuvered GIs had managed to slow the enemy tanks and granted the American command time to defend St.-Vith and Bastogne, which the attackers had expected to capture early in their offensive, December 18.

Meanwhile, at the southern end of the front, American infantry and armor put up stiff resistance, yielding ground slowly as their isolated outposts were either overrun or pushed back and blunting the German attack as long as five days in some places. Together with elements of the 10th Armored Division sent by Patton they established a new line of defense blocking the way south to Luxembourg City, a key road and rail junction. This southern shoulder, together with the matching shoulder in the north, restricted the enemy onslaught to the central portion of the Ardennes, where the panzers had achieved sizable gains. But the Germans would have to funnel all their strength into the middle, on a much smaller network of roads than they had planned on, and thus they would be much more vulnerable to blocking actions by American units.

The evening of December 18 Omar Bradley put through another call to the commanding officer of the Third Army. General Patton was to meet with the rest of the top Allied commanders at Verdun the next day. The purpose of the meeting was to formulate a strategy to counter the German thrust in the Ardennes. But by the time that Patton arrived in the French city, he had already decided what the U.S. response should be.

A potbelly stove did little to dispel the chill of the dank room in an old French army barracks where the commanders gathered the next morning, and most of them kept their coats on, like travelers in a dingy railway station.

Dwight Eisenhower, who had recently been promoted to the rank of five-star general, looked pale and grim and snapped irritably at two late arrivals. He had come from Allied headquarters at Versailles, where rumors were circulating that German commandos disguised as GIs were roaming the countryside with orders to assassinate him. The general's staff took the reports seriously, and Ike had traveled to Verdun in a bulletproof car.

The Supreme Commander tried to lighten the mood, his own as well as that of those around him. "The present situation," he told his generals, "is to be regarded as one of opportunity for us and not disaster. There will be only cheerful faces at this conference table." General Patton, who had arrived wearing his war face, grinned wolfishly. "Hell, let's have the guts to let the sons of bitches go all the way to Paris," he said. "Then we'll really cut 'em off and chew 'em up!" The remark drew only forced smiles. "No," Eisenhower responded quietly. "The enemy will never be allowed to cross the Meuse."

The generals decided on a simple strategy of containment and counterattack. Advantageous conditions were already developing for such a strategy, for the northern and southern ends of the American front were firmly anchored. From these positions, U.S. forces would mass along both flanks of the bulging German breakthrough, to keep it from widening any further. The Allies would then cut through the bulge and block the enemy troops heading toward the Meuse. The counterattack, Eisenhower decided, would be launched initially by the Third Army, which was to slice northward through the German flank to relieve Bastogne, where 13,000 men, under the command of the 101st Airborne, were trapped in a circle five miles in diameter.

Eisenhower turned to Patton. "George, I want you to command this move—under Brad's supervision, of course—making a strong counterattack with at least six divisions. When can you start?"

"As soon as you're through with me," Patton shot back. The Third Army commander had done his homework. Whereas the other generals had come to the conference for the purpose of working out a solution, Patton had met with his staff that morning—and already possessed one. In fact, as he explained to Eisenhower, he knew of three; he had only to telephone his chief of staff, Brigadier General Hobart Gay, to set in motion the plan he had made for a thrust of 60 to 70 miles toward Bastogne. Ike then asked him when he could attack. "On December 21," Patton replied confidently, "with three divisions."

The other generals stirred in disbelief. Some laughed at the typical Patton bravado, others shuffled their feet nervously. But one of Patton's aides detected a current of excitement leap through the room. This was vintage Patton. He was proposing a movement of enormous size and complexity, requiring him to pull three divisions totaling more than 100,000 combat and support troops out of line, wheel them 90 degrees northward, and launch an attack, all in two days and in bitter weather and bad road conditions.

"Don't be fatuous, George," Eisenhower said. "If you try to go that early, you won't have all three divisions ready and you'll go piecemeal. You will start on the twenty-second and I want your initial blow to be a strong one! I'd even settle for the twenty-third if it takes that long to get three full divisions."

Enjoying the attention, Patton lighted up a cigar and pointed to the German penetration on a map. "Brad," he said, addressing Bradley directly, "the Kraut's stuck his head in a meat grinder and this time"—he turned his fist in a grinding motion— "I've got hold of the handle."

In two hours the talking was over. As Patton left the meeting to make his call to Hap Gay, Eisenhower walked him to the door. "Funny thing, George," the Supreme Commander said, "every time I get another star, I get attacked." The new five-star general had received his fourth star in early 1943, just before U.S. forces were hit hard by Erwin Rommel's Afrika Korps at the Kasserine Pass in Tunisia. Patton, who had been called in to revitalize the troops on that occasion, slyly reminded his superior, "And every time you get attacked, Ike, I have to bail you out!"

Patton spent the next three days racing from one Third Army unit to another, fine-tuning the plans and exhorting his men to "drive like hell" toward Bastogne. If other commanders might have felt overwhelmed at the task that lay before them, Patton positively exulted at the opportunity that the German offensive had bestowed on him. Unlike Bradley's request that he give up the 10th Armored Division, this was a chance for Patton to run the show with his entire army. "Destiny sent for me in a hurry when things got tight," he wrote in his diary. "Perhaps God saved me for this effort."

The biggest and longest fight in the Battle of the Bulge was shaping up at Bastogne by December 20. Under the command of a quiet Mississippian named Brigadier General Anthony McAuliffe, the paratroopers of the 101st Airborne had

Bad weather and narrow mountain roads slowed traffic to a crawl behind the front lines during the Battle of the Bulge. An ambulance *(right)* carrying wounded to the rear eases past a convoy of jeeps and trucks rushing reinforcements forward. Such delays infuriated Patton, who on more than one occasion leaped from his jeep to direct traffic himself.

helped blunt the advance of a crack panzer division. In the process, however, the Americans had become surrounded in the town. That evening the corps headquarters, 15 miles to the southwest, called the 101st for a status report. But an officer in Bastogne, aware that the Germans were monitoring American radio transmissions, was reluctant to give a straight answer. Still headquarters insisted on a report. "Visualize the hole in a doughnut," replied the quick-thinking officer. "That's us!"

Although such a predicament might have seemed hopeless to some troops, the men of the 101st were not unduly alarmed: Airborne divisions were accustomed to dropping behind enemy lines and holding out until relief forces could break through. The 101st had performed such a role on D-Day, parachuting in behind enemy lines and causing disruption until the in-

Medical supplies were almost nonexistent. The 101st's medical company had been overrun by the Germans on December 19, and only eight doctors and 44 medics had escaped capture. The wounded were being cared for in a makeshift clinic, and virtually the only painkiller on hand was brandy. Fortunately it was in generous supply.

On December 21 the weather turned colder, freezing the muddy roads and fields and making it easier for tanks and vehicles to move. The Germans took the opportunity to consolidate their forces and did not attack that day. On December 22 McAuliffe received word that one of Patton's armored divisions was beginning its final drive from the south. American troops throughout the Ardennes took heart. "That's good news," said one sergeant manning a forward infantry outpost northeast of Bastogne. "If

"If you don't understand what 'Nuts' means, in plain English it is the same as 'Go to hell.' And I will tell you something else—if you continue to attack, we will kill every goddamn German that tries to break into this city!"

COLONEL JOSEPH HARPER TO A GERMAN MAJOR SENT TO DEMAND THE SURRENDER OF BASTOGNE

fantry troops that had landed at Utah Beach could link up with them. In fact, the same officer who described their position as a doughnut hole confidently told his comrades that Bastogne was a "textbook situation" for the 101st. The paratroopers deployed in a defensive circle on the outskirts of the town, placing their artillery in the center, and braced themselves for the German attack.

What did worry the men, however, was the lack of supplies. Artillery shells were so short that McAuliffe ordered them severely rationed. To a protesting officer he said, tongue in cheek, "If you see 400 Germans in a 100-yard area, and they have their heads up, you can fire artillery at them. But not more than two rounds." Rifle ammunition was low as well. And the food supply was dwindling fast, except for tons of flour that had been found in a Bastogne granary. The flour made good flapjacks, and the men ate flapjacks until they were sick of them.

Georgie's coming, we've got it made!" Reflecting on the moment years later, an officer said, "I know of no other senior commander in Europe who could have brought forth such a response."

McAuliffe got a second message that day, this time from the enemy. At about 11:30 a.m. a sergeant near the American perimeter spotted several Germans walking toward him and immediately got on the field telephone to his command post. "There're four Krauts coming up the road," he reported. "They're carrying a white flag. It looks like they want to surrender."

Far from surrendering, however, the Germans had brought an ultimatum for the American commander. The message, written in clumsy English, had been typed out on two sheets of paper. The Germans—a major, a captain, and two enlisted men—were detained and the message was passed through to General McAuliffe at division headquarters. "To the U.S.A. Commander of the encircled town of Bastogne," the message began. "The fortune of war is changing. This time the U.S.A. forces in and near Bastogne have been encircled by strong German armored units. There is only one possibility to save the encircled troops from total annihilation: that is the honorable surrender of the encircled town."

"Aw, nuts!" grunted McAuliffe. He dropped the papers on the floor and strode out of the room. But his staff brought him back, reminding him that the German emissaries were still waiting for a reply. "Well, I don't know what to tell them," the general said in his soft Mississippi drawl.

"That first remark of yours would be hard to beat," suggested one of his staff officers.

"What was that?" McAuliffe asked.

"You said 'Nuts!' "

"That's it!" said the general, snapping his fingers.

Everyone in the room burst into laughter. Gleefully, a sergeant typed up the answer on a sheet of 8½-by-11-inch bond and passed it to the general.

"Will you see that it's delivered?" McAuliffe asked one of his officers, Colonel Joseph Harper.

The colonel glanced at the message and beamed. "I'll deliver it myself!" he said, and headed off to the command post where the German major and captain waited. The major took the paper and read its eight typed words: "To the German Commander: Nuts! The American Commander."

The Germans were thoroughly puzzled. "The reply," Harper told them helpfully, "is decidedly not affirmative." Seeing they were still mystified he explained further. "If you don't understand what 'Nuts' means, in plain English it is the same as 'Go to hell.' And I will tell you something else—if you continue to attack, we will kill every goddamn German that tries to break into this city!"

The officers saluted formally. "We will kill many Americans," the German captain declared frankly. "This is war."

"On your way, bud!" growled Harper. Then he added impulsively, "And good luck to you." As the Germans marched away, Harper wondered why on earth he had wished good luck to people who were determined to kill him.

Patton was immensely pleased when he heard about McAuliffe's cheeky response to the German ultimatum, perhaps because it sounded like something Patton would have said himself. "Any man who is that eloquent deserves to be relieved," he said. "We shall go right away."

The damp, foggy weather broke on December 23 and the day dawned bright, clear, and very cold. At midday the first signs of relief for Bastogne came into view, as more than 200 C-47 transports began an airdrop of about 240,000 pounds of food, ammunition, and medical supplies. When the transport planes had finished the drop, 82 Thunderbolt fighter-bombers that had escorted them wheeled and hammered the Germans ringing the town, streaking in low with napalm, fragmentation bombs, and machine gun fire. Over the course of the next two days, the Battered Bastards of Bastogne, as McAuliffe's men had taken to calling themselves, endured a pounding by German artillery, two attacks by enemy bombers, and another ground assault.

Meanwhile, Patton's armored spearhead was fighting its way to the city's outskirts. From a hill located outside of the town, one of the force commanders could see the C-47 transports dropping their cargo into Bastogne. The officer could not bear to turn away from an object that was so tantalizingly close. In the day's last light, he made the decision to press on.

Sitting in the open turret of the lead American tank, a sharp-eyed lieutenant spotted some men jumping into foxholes in front of him. Although they didn't look like Germans, he couldn't be sure. He stood up and yelled at the men, and after a few moments a figure approached cautiously, with his rifle at the ready. When he reached the tank, the man grinned: "Second Lieutenant Duane J. Webster," he announced, "326th Engineers, 101st Airborne Division."

A short time later other tanks made their way through to a 101st observation post. General McAuliffe was there waiting to greet them. "How are you, General?" a tank officer asked.

"I am mighty glad to see you," McAuliffe said.

Patton had done it. He had reached Bastogne. In what would be the highest praise he ever gave of Patton, Omar Bradley later wrote, "His generalship during this difficult maneuver was magnificent. One of the most brilliant performances by any commander on either side in World War II. It was absolutely his cup of tea—rapid, open warfare combined with noble purpose and difficult goals." Then came the irresistible dig: "He relished every minute of it, knowing full well that this mission, if nothing else, would guarantee him a place of high honor in the annals of the U.S. Army."

Bastogne was still surrounded except for the 300-yard-wide corridor that Patton's spearhead tanks had punched into the town. Within 24 hours 40 truckloads of supplies were brought in and 22 ambulances carrying 652 wounded men were taken out. Meanwhile, less than 40 miles to the northwest of Bastogne, German panzers had fought their way to within a few thousand yards of the Meuse. There they were beaten back with huge losses. With that the bulge stopped growing. Now Eisenhower wanted to cut the Germans off at the knees. While the First Army drove southward, Patton continued his lunge to the north. The two American armies were to link up at Houffalize, a village in the center of the German breakthrough, cutting the bulge in two across its midsection.

Hitler was forced to admit that his great counterstroke had failed, and on January 8 he reluctantly authorized the withdrawal of his troops before they were all cut off and captured. The Americans, in Patton's words, were now "chasing a sinking fox and

Draped in improvised winter camouflage, three American half-tracks hug the edge of a snowy field. Belgian civilians donated bedsheets and lace-trimmed tablecloths, many of them precious heirlooms, to provide concealment for American soldiers and vehicles.

babbling for the kill." But it took another week of hard fighting in terrible weather before the First and the Third U.S. Armies finally met at Houffalize.

On the same day that Hitler ordered the retreat, Patton was riding back from the front in his open jeep. It was a dark, horribly cold afternoon, and the weather had prevented him from flying back to the rear, as he preferred to do. Careful not to be more warmly dressed than his men, Patton wore only a parka, and he sat straight as a ramrod in the biting air, with his arms folded.

On the way to the rear, Patton's jeep came upon a truck that had gone into a ditch and gotten stuck in the snow. A GI who had been riding in the truck later described the scene to Patton's wife: "His face was awful red and he must have been about froze riding in that open jeep. He yelled to us to get out and push, and first I knew, there was General Patton pushing right alongside of me. . . . he never asked a man to do what he wouldn't do himself."

During that cold ride Patton also passed a truck carrying a Third Army combat team toward Bastogne. When the men recognized the stern and solitary figure sitting in the back of the jeep, they leaned out of their truck and began cheering wildly. For a moment the war face dropped, and despite himself the general smiled and waved back to them. But tears filled his eyes; he knew that many of these men would be dead tomorrow. The fleeting encounter was, Patton wrote later in his diary, "the most moving experience of my life."

The Battle of the Bulge was over, and Patton paid tribute to his troops: "During this operation the Third Army moved farther and faster and engaged more divisions in less time than any other army in the history of the United States—possibly

Their fatigue clearly showing, two soldiers from the 80th Division consume a lunch of cold rations and lukewarm coffee while sitting on the frozen ground. Unlike most GIs who fought in the Battle of the Bulge, they are wearing warm waterproof galoshes. Trench foot and frostbite were rampant, accounting for almost a third of the casualties in one division.

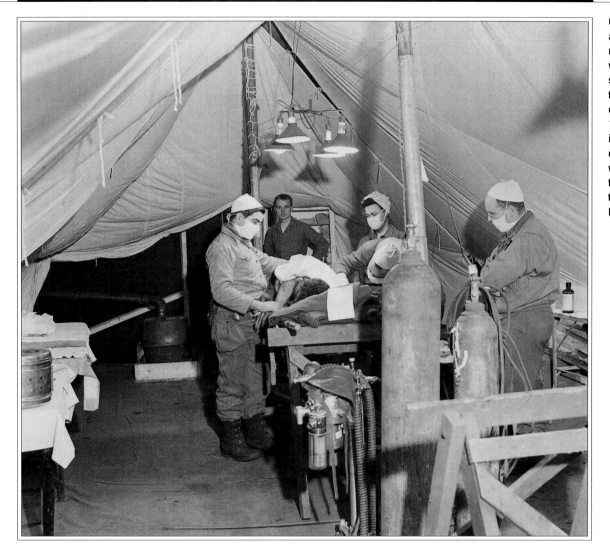

Operating in a tent, army surgeons and a nurse work to save a wounded soldier. After surgery at Ardennes field hospitals like this one, which handled 1,000 casualties during one 63-hour period, the critically wounded were transferred to larger facilities farther behind the lines for further care.

in the history of the world. No country can stand against such an army." Among the 650,000 Americans who took part in the fighting, 81,000 were killed, wounded, or captured. On the German side, there were as many as 100,000 casualties out of the 500,000 troops that took part in the action. Not only had Hitler failed to reach Antwerp, he had failed even to seize the interim prize of the Meuse. Moreover, the western offensive that was his brainchild hastened his nation's collapse. When the Red Army launched its attack against Germany's Eastern Front on January 12, Hitler's army was nearly finished as an organized fighting force, and the Soviet offensive enjoyed swift success.

Patton knew that the end of the war was near, and he was ready to head for Berlin. During February the Allied armies, reinforced to 3.7 million men, fought their way back to the lines they had held in early December. They now faced a German defense reduced to about one million men by losses in the Battle of the Bulge and by transfers of some of the best troops to the Eastern Front.

The next target for the Allies was the great natural barrier of the Rhine, Germany's traditional frontier in the west. The question of how to get there was a divisive one, however. The British favored a single "full-blooded" thrust under Montgomery's command, using most of the available fighting men,

Hunching down in their assault boats in order to avoid the fire of German troops on the east side of the Rhine, Third Army soldiers race across the river at Oppenheim.

American as well as British, to slash into northwestern Germany and cross a 20-mile section of the Rhine north of the industrial Ruhr district. Beyond the river at this point lay the level terrain of the north German plain, which would offer, Montgomery pointed out, relatively easy access to the interior of the Reich. The Americans, on the other hand, continued to favor a "broad-front strategy," which called for the Allied armies to move into Germany simultaneously all along the western border and to cross the Rhine at several widely separated places, thereby providing a choice of directions for the follow-through.

To the British, the broad-front plan smacked of a slapdash, attack-everywhere-at-once approach, summed up by one anonymous wag as "have a go, Joe," the usual salutation by London prostitutes to passing Yanks. The Americans, for their part, viewed the single-thrust plan as an attempt by Montgomery

to hog the main show while the American role was downgraded. One of the British plan's provisions specified that those U.S. troops not allotted to Montgomery's purposes were to remain in positions of static defense—in short, sidelined.

The quarreling of his generals irritated Eisenhower, who complained privately that he had to "arrange the blankets smoothly over several prima donnas in the same bed." His solution to the dispute was characteristic: He gave each contending party some, but not all, of what each sought. Montgomery won top priority for his offensive in the north but lost the attempt to take overall command and to impose a static defense on U.S. forces not involved in his operation. Instead, these forces were to go on what was called the "aggressive defensive."

Patton was livid when he heard the orders. "What's the defensive?" he demanded. "Nobody ever successfully defended anything. Look at Hadri-

The Germans destroyed bridges along the Rhine to slow the Allied advance, but engineers quickly built pontoon bridges like the one shown here, and tanks, jeeps, and other vehicles began rolling into the German heartland.

an's Wall. Look at the Great Wall of China and the Maginot Line." For Bradley, the bad news was that he would have to furnish several divisions to support Montgomery's southern flank. However, the "aggressive defense" approved for Bradley's other forces could be interpreted as authorizing a "limited offensive." Whatever it meant exactly, the term would give George Patton plenty of room to maneuver.

Montgomery launched his drive to the Rhine from Holland on February 8, with the understanding that only after the British had reached the river would Patton's Third Army strike eastward. Patton despaired. "The Third Army wants to fight," he told Bradley. "It can do so victoriously if it is allowed. That's all we're asking. The chance to fight for our country and lick the goddamned Hun whom we've got on the run."

Bradley knew that he could not permit Patton to launch such an offensive. But he wanted as badly as Patton to see the Americans across the Rhine and into the heart of Germany before—or at least along with—the British. And so Bradley winked at the Third Army's preparations for an "aggressive defense," which amounted to plans for a full-blown assault. Patton had a scare when he was suddenly ordered to report to Eisenhower at Bastogne; he was sure that Ike had discovered his intentions and was about to stop him. However, to his immense relief, Patton found that he was wanted only for some official photographs with other generals in the ruins of Bastogne. On February 7, the day before Montgomery's scheduled jump-off toward the Rhine, Patton launched his own attack.

For the next three weeks Patton moved ever deeper into Germany, his men taking 1,000 German prisoners a day. Occasionally he would check in with Bradley, as he did on February 27, asking if he could keep going. Bradley told him that he had his blessing to continue, until "higher authority"—that is, Eisenhower—ordered him to call Patton to a halt. In the meantime, Bradley added, he intended to keep away from the telephone. By March 7 Patton's men were looking across the Rhine.

A week later the Third Army turned south, overrunning German towns along the west bank of the river. Patton was headed toward the little town of Oppenheim, in the heart of the Rhine wine country. Napoleon had crossed the Rhine near Oppenheim. But of more immediate interest to Patton was the town's barge harbor, which was hidden from the view of the Germans on the other side of the river. On the night of March 22, his infantrymen stole through the town's cobbled streets to the little harbor. There the shadowy figures piled into rafts and assault boats and slipped across, quickly overwhelming the small force of Germans defending the opposite bank.

The next morning, while Third Army engineers set to work building bridges across the river to speed the passage of added infantry and tanks, Patton got Bradley on the phone. "Brad," he said, lowering his voice, "don't tell anyone, but I'm across!"

"Well, I'll be damned," responded a stunned Bradley. "You mean across the Rhine?"

"Sure am," Patton replied. "I sneaked a division across last night, but there are so few Krauts around they don't know it yet, so don't make any announcement. We'll keep it a secret until we see how it goes."

Later in the day, Patton had second thoughts. He called Bradley again: "Brad, for God's sake, tell the world we're across. I want the world to know that the Third Army made it before Monty starts across!" Happy to comply, Bradley announced the news to press and radio correspondents at his headquarters.

That night, under the cover of an immense aerial and artillery barrage that lighted 40 miles of horizon, the British launched their assault at a river crossing north of the Ruhr. Patton had trumped Montgomery's ace.

On March 24 Patton started across the Rhine himself by way of a pontoon bridge his engineers had built. Halfway to the other side, he paused, unzipped his fly, and urinated in the river. "I have been looking forward to this for a long time," he said, looking around him with great satisfaction. He followed up with a second, more seemly symbolic act. On reaching the east side of the river he fell to the ground on one knee and grabbed two handfuls of dirt. Raising his fists high Patton declared, "Thus, William the Conqueror!" in imitation of that Norman king's gesture when he landed in England in 1066. "See," William had said, falling on his face and clutching the ground, "I have taken England with both hands!"

Four days later Allied troops were pouring across the Rhine at six major bridgeheads along a 200-mile front. Since the Battle of the Bulge the Third Army had seized nearly 6,500 square miles of territory from the enemy, captured more than 140,000 soldiers, and killed or wounded 99,000 more, eliminating almost all of two German armies. Patton told the troops, "The highest honor I have ever attained is that of having my name coupled with yours in these great events."

In their triumphant advance into Germany, the Allies encountered unspeakable horror. In April the Third Army liberated the first of the huge Nazi concentration camps, at Ohrdruf, and Patton, Bradley, and Eisenhower came to witness firsthand the evil that flourished in Hitler's regime. When he saw the starving slave laborers and the unburied corpses, Bradley was speechless. Patton vomited against the side of a building. Eisenhower ordered that as many GIs as possible should visit the camp. "We are told the American soldier does not know what he is fighting for," he said. "Now, at least, he will know what he is fighting against." Patton wanted to go further. He insisted that the local German townspeople see for themselves what their government had done. He forced them to dig graves and bury the dead. When the mayor of Ohrdruf and his wife saw the inside of the camp, they were so overcome that they went home and hanged themselves.

Patton was poised to race Montgomery to Berlin, but it was not to be. The Allies had divided postwar Germany into zones of occupation, and the Soviets were to get Berlin; the American armies were to halt at the Elbe River. Eisenhower had kept the news from his generals, probably be-

"In the period from January 29 to March 22, 1945, you have wrested 6484 square miles of territory from the enemy. You have taken 3072 cities, towns, and villages....You have captured 140,112 enemy soldiers, and have killed or wounded an additional 99,000, thereby eliminating practically all of the German 7th and 1st Armies. History records no greater achievement in so limited a time....The highest honor I have ever attained is that of having my name coupled with yours in these great events."

GENERAL GEORGE PATTON
TO THE MEN OF THE THIRD ARMY,
MARCH 23, 1945

cause he did not want to deal with their reactions. Patton's, as it turned out, was surprisingly mild. When Eisenhower remarked that he could not understand why anyone would want to capture the German capital, with all its problems, Patton did not answer immediately. Then he gripped Eisenhower by the shoulders and looked at him searchingly. "Ike," he said, "I think history will answer that question for you."

Thus, by the middle of April the Third Army had reached its eastern stop line in Germany. Its advance across Hitler's Reich had been fast, though not fast enough to suit Patton. His armor had broken past organized opposition and was steadily making 15 to 20 miles a day with minimal losses when Eisenhower and Bradley told him he was going too fast. To Patton the admonition seemed overcautious, and he had reason to reflect on an entry he had made earlier in his diary: "When those two get together, they get timid."

The belligerent Patton was badly in need of a new fight, and Bradley gave him the most appropriate assignment he could. The Third Army was to veer southeastward along Czechoslovakia's western border, aiming toward Linz, Austria. On the way, Patton was to look for the rumored national redoubt, a stronghold in the Bavarian Alps where there was supposedly a large force of fanatical Nazis who were determined to resist the Allies to the bitter end. He was to destroy the redoubt—assuming that it actually existed—then link up with the Russians at or near Linz.

Patton was less than delighted by the mission. The general was convinced—rightly, as it turned out—that there was nothing to the rumors of a national redoubt. And as for the Russians, Patton wanted to fight them rather than greet them. Bradley did mention informally a possibility that excited Patton—that the Third Army might get the job of invading and liberating at least a portion of Czechoslovakia. In a way this inducement only increased Patton's frustration, however. As his patrols into Czechoslovakia discovered on April 17, he could reach Prague, the capital, in just three days, and take it in one or two more.

But the fate of Czechoslovakia was being worked out between Eisenhower and the Soviets. By late April agreement had been reached on an American advance to a line that ran through the town of Pilsen. On May 4 Eisenhower passed the word to Bradley, who granted Patton permission to make the move into Czechoslovakia.

To lead Patton's advance, the U.S. V Corps, on the Czech border facing Pilsen, was transferred on May 4 from the First Army to Patton's Third. The unit's commander, who had served with Patton in Sicily, sat down to dinner shortly after learning of his transfer and remarked to his staff, "Well, I'll give us about 12 hours before General Patton calls up and tells us to attack." Minutes later, the phone rang. It was Patton. He had orders. The V Corps was to attack Pilsen in the morning. The commander returned to his dinner. "Well, I missed that one," he said. "Instead of 12 hours it was 12 minutes!"

The war in Europe was drawing to a close. The Americans had halted at the agreed line in Czechoslovakia, and Patton was thinking about a transfer to the Pacific. "I should like to be considered for any type of combat command from a division up against the Japanese," he wrote to the Joint Chiefs of Staff. "I am sure that my method of fighting would be successful. I also am of such an age that this is my last war, and I would therefore like to see it through to the end." Patton knew, however, that his chances of getting a crack at the Japanese were slim—not because of his abilities but because of General Douglas MacArthur. "There is already a star in that theater," he grumbled to one of his senior officers, "and you can only have one star in a show."

The idea of having to cooperate with the Communists depressed Patton further. He was convinced that the western Allies had made an error of historic proportions in ceding so much of Europe to Stalin. On May 8—the day the European War officially ended—he addressed a group of reporters at the Third Army headquarters in Regensburg, Bavaria.

UNCOVERING THE HORROR

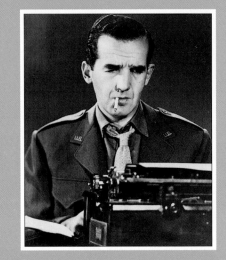

CBS newsman Edward R. Murrow (above) was in Germany traveling with the Third Army in April 1945 and went in with the troops who liberated the Nazi concentration camp at Buchenwald on April 12. His eyewitness report, broadcast in the United States on April 15, is excerpted here:

Permit me to tell you what you would have seen, and heard, had you been with me on Thursday. If you are at lunch, or if you have no appetite to hear what Germans have done, now is a good time to switch off the radio, for I propose to tell you of Buchenwald. . . .

We entered. . . . Men and boys reached out to touch me, and they were in rags and the remnants of uniform. Death had already marked many of them, but they were smiling with their eyes. I looked out over that mass of men to the green fields beyond where well-fed Germans were ploughing. I . . . asked to see one of the barracks. . . . When I entered, men crowded around, tried to lift me to their shoulders.

They were too weak. Many of them could not get out of bed. I was told that this building had once stabled eighty horses. There were twelve hundred men in it, five to a bunk. The stink was beyond all description. . . .

As we walked out in the courtyard, a man fell dead. Two others—they must have been over sixty—were crawling toward the latrine. I saw it but will not describe it.

In another part of the camp they showed me the children, hundreds of them. Some were only six. . . . An elderly man standing beside me said, "The children, enemies of the state." I could see their ribs through their thin shirts. . . .

We went to the hospital; it was full. The doctor told me that two hundred had died the day before. I asked the cause of death; he shrugged and said, "Tuberculosis, starvation, fatigue, and there are many who have no desire to live. . . ."

There were two rows of bodies stacked up like cordwood. They were thin and very white. Some of the bodies were terribly bruised, though there seemed to be little flesh to bruise. Some had been shot through the head, but they bled but little. All except two were naked. I tried to count them as best I could and arrived at the conclusion that all that was mortal of more than five hundred men and boys lay there in two neat piles. . . .

I have reported what I saw and heard, but only part of it. For most of it I have no words. . . .

If I've offended you by this rather mild account of Buchenwald, I'm not in the least sorry.

Enraged by what he saw at Buchenwald, Patton ordered that the mayor and other prominent residents of the nearby city of Weimar be brought to see firsthand what the Nazi regime had perpetrated there. Some averted their eyes, others broke down and cried; most maintained they had no idea what was going on in the camps.

Atop a massive 274mm German railroad gun still draped in the tattered remnants of camouflage netting, Seventh Army troops survey the scene of victory. As they crossed Germany, the conquerors collected souvenirs from piles of surrendered German weapons, fished in streams with hand grenades, and "liberated" bottles of good Rhine wine.

"They have allowed us to kick hell out of one bastard," he complained in his squeaky falsetto, "and at the same time forced us to help establish a second one as evil or more evil than the first." The sacrifice of so many thousands of American boys made it all the more tragic. "I wonder how the dead will speak today when they know that for the first time in centuries we have opened Central and Western Europe to the forces of Genghis Khan," he continued, with tears welling in his eyes. "I wonder how they feel now that they know there will be no peace in our times and that Americans, some not yet born, will have to fight the Russians tomorrow, or 10, 15, or 20 years from tomorrow."

Patton made no effort to hide his disdain for America's erstwhile ally. At a military parade in Berlin hosted by the Soviets, Patton was seated next to Marshal Georgy Zhukov, the Red Army's most prominent general. As a long line of huge T-34 tanks rumbled past the reviewing stand, Zhukov turned to Patton and remarked, "My dear General Patton, you see that tank, it carries a cannon which can throw a shell seven miles."

"Indeed?" responded Patton, not the slightest bit impressed. "Well, my dear Marshal Zhukov, let me tell you this, if any of my gunners started firing at your people before they had closed to less than 700 yards I'd have them court-martialed for cowardice!"

Instead of a command in the Pacific, Patton was assigned the administrative and political task of rebuilding the German state of Bavaria, where before long his genius for explosive statements got him into deep trouble. When asked at a press conference why he had retained so many former Nazis in high governmental positions, Patton defended his actions with an unfortunate political analogy. "The way I see it, this Nazi question is very much

Pallbearers, including Master Sergeant William Meeks *(front left)*, General Patton's orderly and confidant for 10 years, carry his casket from the railroad station in Luxembourg City. From there it was driven to the American military cemetery, located in nearby Hamm. Beatrice Patton is seen walking behind her husband's casket.

like a Democratic and a Republican election fight," he explained. "To get things done in Bavaria, after the complete disorganization and disruption of four years of war, we had to compromise with the devil a little. We had no alternative but to turn to the people who knew what to do and how to do it. I don't like the Nazis any more than you do. I despise them. In the past three years I did my utmost to kill as many of them as possible. Now we are using them for lack of anyone better until we get better people."

Patton's statement made front-page headlines back home, and this time even Eisenhower could not save him from the ensuing outrage. Given Pat-

ton's apparent indifference to the Allied program of denazification, the Supreme Commander had no choice but to sack him both from his beloved Third Army command and from his military governorship, a move that brought an end to their 25-year friendship. With no more battles to fight, Patton reluctantly accepted command of the U.S. Fifteenth Army, a skeleton headquarters operation in Nauheim, Germany, that was charged with compiling the history of the fighting since D-Day. Deeply hurt, he determined to resign from the army as soon as the assignment was completed so that he could speak freely against the dangers of a Soviet presence in Europe.

The war for which he had spent most of his life preparing was over. But Patton seemed unable to accept the fact. On the day that Germany's surrender was formalized, he had remarked to an aide, "The best end for an old campaigner is a bullet at the last minute of the last battle." That bullet had not come, and the old campaigner was wondering what his future would be in a world that was now at peace. When the Japanese surrendered on August 14, Patton wrote to his wife: "Another war has ended and with it my usefulness to the world."

Sunday, December 9, 1945, dawned raw and clear. It was four years after the bombing at Pearl Harbor and the beginning of U.S. involvement in World War II, and one day before George Patton was to return to the United States to celebrate the Christmas holidays. To get Patton's mind off his frustrations, his loyal chief of staff, Hap Gay, had suggested a day of pheasant shooting. And so, early that morning, the two friends set out from Nauheim in the general's black Model 75 Cadillac on the 80-mile drive to the hunting area. They were in no hurry. Along the way, Patton stopped to visit the site of some Roman ruins, and to spend a brief time alone with his own thoughts.

A little before noon, they had another dozen or so miles to go before reaching their destination. The big Cadillac was proceeding at a leisurely pace and Patton, who was sitting in the backseat, was leaning forward so he could get a better view of the wrecked military vehicles that littered both sides of the road. "Look at all the derelict vehicles!" he said. "How awful war is. Think of the waste." Just then, the general's 19-year-old driver took his eyes off the road for an instant. When he looked up again, he saw a two-and-a-half-ton U.S. Army truck that had approached from the opposite direction making a left-

Patton's English bull terrier, Willie, lies mournfully beside his master's personal effects awaiting shipment to the United States. Patton acquired the dog in 1944, and thereafter Willie was his constant companion, following the general to conferences, eating his food, and sharing his bed.

hand turn directly in front of the Cadillac, no more than 20 feet away. The young man jammed on the brakes and turned the car sharply to the left. Although the Cadillac hadn't been moving at more than 30 miles an hour and the truck was doing no more than 10, there wasn't enough time to avoid a collision, and the car's front right fender struck the right bumper of the truck.

Patton, perched on the edge of his seat, was thrown forward and then backward, striking his head against either the front seat or the roof of the car. The blow didn't knock him out, but he was bleeding heavily from his forehead. General Gay and the driver were uninjured.

"My neck hurts," Patton said to Gay. Then, "I'm having trouble breathing, Hap. Work my fingers for me." Gay massaged Patton's fingers, moving them back and forth several times. "Go ahead, Hap," he repeated. "Work my fingers." Patton had felt nothing, and both men realized the seriousness of the injury. Gay sat holding his old friend until a young medic arrived. As he bent down to examine the general, Patton whispered, "I think I'm paralyzed."

Patton was rushed to the best hospital available, the 130th Station Hospital of the Seventh Army, which was located some 20 miles away, in Heidelberg. Though he hadn't spoken a word during the ride, he seemed to recover some of his zest at the hospital. As a doctor began working on him, he heard Patton whisper to himself, "This is a damned ironical thing to happen to me." Another doctor, seeing his lips move, asked what he wanted. "I don't want a damned thing, Captain," Patton said, smiling. "I was just saying, 'Jesus Christ, what a nice way to start a vacation.'"

The doctors determined that the blow to Patton's head had crushed his upper vertebrae, paralyzing him from the neck down. Over the next several days specialists looked for any ray of hope—and found none. Still, when Beatrice Patton arrived, she found her husband looking remarkably good under the circumstances and despite the formidable apparatus holding his body in traction. His temperature was

down to 100, he was breathing easily, and his pulse was a steady 70.

When this small, wiry woman walked into the room, he said in a clear, firm voice: "Good to see you, Bea. I'm afraid this may be the last time we see each other." They were behind closed doors for only half an hour, but it was all they needed, after 33 years of marriage, to put everything necessary in order. "You always know what's best for me," he had told her many times in the daily letters he wrote when they were apart.

Several weeks before the accident Patton had written to a friend that "it had always been my plan to be killed in this war, and I damned near accomplished it, but one cannot resort to suicide." Now the end had come, and Patton knew it. Those around him in the hospital were awed by his good humor and by his sense that the struggle was over. He told one of the nurses that all the fuss over him was a waste of taxpayers' money because he was "fated to die" within a fortnight. The great warrior seemed at last to be at peace. On the afternoon of December 21, 1945, George S. Patton Jr. died peacefully in his sleep.

Beatrice had initially planned to bring her husband's body home for burial. But when she learned that no American serviceman who died in Europe during the war had been returned to the United States, she immediately changed her mind. "Of course he must be buried here," she said. "I know George would want to lie beside the men of his army who have fallen."

So it was that on the day before Christmas, Patton's flag-draped coffin was placed in a half-track and carried to the unfinished American military cemetery on the outskirts of Luxembourg City. Thousands of his beloved Third Army troops were already buried there. In a driving rain and raw gusty wind, General Patton's body was lowered into a grave dug by German prisoners of war in the thick, red clay of the Ardennes beside that of a Third Army soldier from Detroit who had been killed in action during the Battle of the Bulge. ◆

FRANKLIN AND ELEANOR: THE WAR YEARS

Meeting Franklin Roosevelt, said Winston Churchill, was like opening your first bottle of champagne. Countless others also found FDR's effervescence, wit, and charm a heady experience. His rare vitality had survived a tragedy that would have caused many to abandon their dreams and retreat to a life of invalidism. In Franklin's case, it helped him and his wife, Eleanor, reach the pinnacle of American politics.

In 1921, at the age of 39, Franklin was stricken with polio and paralyzed from the waist down. He never again walked unaided and stood up only with great difficulty, using his upper body to bear all of his weight. His legs were kept straight by metal braces that locked at the knees and helped disguise how profoundly polio had affected him.

Undaunted, Franklin emerged from the experience, wrote a reporter, "a man softened, cleansed, and illumined with pain," and with far greater sympathy for the underprivileged. Eleanor shared Franklin's idea of enlarging the scope of government to serve as guardian of the public welfare. Encouraged by her husband and his associates to become Franklin's eyes and ears, Eleanor embraced the job wholeheartedly, and soon became a national leader for social reform in her own right.

The Roosevelts were loved and despised in equal measure by Americans. Eleanor was deemed by a poll to be "the target of more adverse criticism and the object of more praise than any other woman in American history." Similarly, Franklin was considered a savior in some quarters, in others an opportunist. But the voters had faith enough to elect him to their highest office four times, a span so long that, it was said, an entire generation grew up knowing no other president.

As the war in Europe raged and pressure on the United States mounted, Franklin and Eleanor carried on with characteristic aplomb, attending Easter services on April 13, 1941. Just one month later Roosevelt declared an unlimited national emergency and called for "the strengthening of our defense to the extreme limit of our national power and authority."

The Weather—
Partly cloudy continued
warm, showers possible
Temperatures possible to-
day. Highest, 88 lowest 70
Complete record and forecast on page 2

VOL. 97   NO. 81.

St. Joseph Gazette

ST. JOSEPH, MISSOURI, WEDNESDAY MORNING, MAY 28, 1941

FINAL EDITION

PRICE TWO CENTS

NATIONAL EMERGENCY DECREED

...ate Hangs in Balance

BOMBERS

F. D. R. Warns Hitler, Says U. S. Will Guard Supplies for Britain

AMERICA'S WAR BEGINS

As soon as Winston Churchill heard the first sketchy report of an attack in the Pacific on December 7, 1941, he telephoned the White House. "Mr. President, what's this about Japan?" the prime minister asked tersely. Roosevelt replied, "They have attacked us at Pearl Harbor. We are all in the same boat now."

Roosevelt had hoped for an event that would spur the nation into action and had complained about his isolationist countrymen, "It's a terrible thing when you're trying to lead, to look over your shoulder and find no one there." Although he was stunned by the magnitude of the losses at Pearl Harbor, he and the nation rallied quickly, and seemingly overnight, America's isolationism was replaced by a fervid desire to go to war.

Roosevelt asked Churchill to come to Washington to discuss their new alliance, and they spent three weeks together. A map room was built on the ground floor of the White House, and top-secret information was delivered there around the clock. After working most of the day they would stay up into the night, talking, drinking, and smoking.

Eleanor, with four sons who would be going to war, did not share the enthusiasm of the president and the prime minister. When they huddled over the pins and markers showing the location of Allied and enemy forces, she observed, "They looked like two little boys playing soldier. They seemed to be having a wonderful time, too wonderful in fact."

Wearing a black armband to mourn his mother's recent death, Roosevelt holds a joint press conference with Churchill, seated at the president's right, to announce the alliance of Britain and the United States. When Churchill began talking, reporters toward the rear of the crowd asked him to stand up so they could see him. To their delight, the prime minister accommodated them by standing on his chair.

F.D.R., Churchill Give World Victory Message

(Text of addresses by President Roosevelt and Prime Minister Churchill on page 6.)

By Robert G. Nixon
Staff Correspondent International News Service

WASHINGTON, Dec. 24.—President Roosevelt and Prime Minister Churchill, in joint Christmas messages broadcast throughout the world, tonight dedicated the English-speaking" which must democracies to the stern task of labor and suffering" which must winning victory over the forces lie ahead before the "ultimate of Hitlerism, and the perpetu... victory" can be won,

The Examiner Wishes You a Merry Christmas

IN THE NEWS

Los Angeles Examiner

VOL. XXXIX—NO. 14

LOS ANGELES, THURSDAY, DECEMBER 25, 1941

Examiner Building, 1111 S. Broadway

Remember PEARL HARBOR

Two Sections—Part I—FIVE CENTS

James Roosevelt, who rose to the rank of lieutenant colonel in the marines by the war's end, stands arm in arm with his father. FDR's casual air here belies the tremendous effort he was exerting. An iron grip on his son's arm and a cane, plus braces that kept his legs from buckling, allowed the president to stand.

In 1942 Roosevelt traveled nearly 9,000 miles on an inspection and morale-boosting tour, visiting military bases, shipyards, and tank and aircraft factories. On one stop *(below)* FDR addressed workers at Henry Kaiser's Portland shipyard, accompanied by Kaiser, second from the left in the backseat, and Kaiser's son, standing beside the driver's door.

ELEANOR, ON HER OWN

The war increased Eleanor's public-service activities. Saddened at sending boys off "to die for a 'way of life,'" she added the welfare of the American GI to her list of fervent causes. She crisscrossed the country and traveled around the world to use her considerable influence on their behalf. No request or detail seemed too small for Mrs. Roosevelt to address. She persuaded the State Department to turn its diplomatic reception area into a sleeping room for traveling servicemen and helped draft a more sympathetic version of the president's "next of kin" letter.

Continuing her longtime commitment to civil rights, Eleanor fought for broader opportunities for Negro soldiers. She relentlessly petitioned her husband and the War Department to end segregation in the armed services, noting the irony of the fact that America was at war with Germany to combat its concept of Aryan racial superiority while subjecting many of its own citizens to racism.

And, mindful of the needs of mothers who had gone to work with the coming of war, she launched an effective campaign for day-care centers and after-school programs.

Many efforts produced far-reaching and lasting results; others did not. Mrs. Roosevelt found that she could not alter the hostility directed at Japanese Americans after Pearl Harbor, nor did she persuade America to open its doors wide to the thousands of refugees fleeing before the Nazi advance through Europe.

On her first wartime trip abroad Eleanor reviews a unit of England's Air Transport Auxiliary. The First Lady admired the British women's involvement in the war effort, and she endeared herself to this unit by dismissing her car and walking the length of the parade ground in the pouring rain.

DAILY EXPRESS MONDAY OCTOBER 26 1942

The American troops give Mrs. F.D.R. a big hand

1,000 doughboys greet the First Lady . . .

HIYA, ELEANOR!

By VIVIEN BATCHELOR

In the South Pacific, Australia, and New Zealand, Mrs. Roosevelt visited hospitals that were filled with wounded American soldiers. Thinking her a do-gooder, Admiral William Halsey dreaded her arrival but was won over by Eleanor's warmth and dedication. "When I say she inspected those hospitals," he wrote, "I mean that she went into every ward, stopped at every bed, and spoke to every patient."

On the home front, Eleanor pushed for assistance for the many women who needed to work to support both the war effort and their families. Here the First Lady stands amid a group of children served by a government-sponsored day-care center in Greensboro, North Carolina.

NEW YORK

Herald Tribune LATE CITY EDITION

THE WEATHER

Vol. CII No. 35,136

WEDNESDAY, JANUARY 27, 1943

Roosevelt, Churchill in Casablanca 10 Days, Goal Is 'Unconditional Surrender' of Axis; Giraud, DeGaulle There, in Accord on Aims

Casablanca Roosevelt Flies

Winston Churchill studies Roosevelt's face as the president watches the sun set over Morocco's Atlas Mountains. At the airport the next morning to see FDR off, Churchill confided to an associate, "He is the greatest man I have ever known." On the plane home *(below)* Roosevelt celebrated his sixty-first birthday with close friend and adviser Harry Hopkins, seated opposite, and two of his military advisers.

THE ALLIES CONFER

Franklin traveled abroad several times to confer with Allied leaders, and in January 1943 he and Churchill met in Casablanca, Morocco. To Roosevelt's disappointment, Joseph Stalin declined to join them, claiming it was impossible for him to leave home while the brutal Battle of Stalingrad was being fought.

Casablanca was a security man's nightmare, filled with agents of the Axis powers. It was also close to the front in North Africa, where the Americans and British had gained a foothold against the Germans and were pushing them hard. When he touched down

in Morocco, FDR became the first president to visit a war zone since Abraham Lincoln.

Roosevelt grew relaxed and effusive in the sun-drenched city on the Atlantic. It may have been his expansive mood that prompted him to make a startling announcement at the end of the conference calling for nothing less than "unconditional surrender by Germany, Italy, and Japan." Churchill was shocked and angry that Roosevelt had said such a thing without consulting him, and he feared it might make the Germans fight even harder.

Churchill overcame his anger at FDR's indiscretion and persuaded him to visit Marrakech. "I must be with you," he told FDR, "when you see the sunset on the snows of the Atlas Mountains." The belvedere Churchill had in mind was a six-story tower overlooking the mountains. The stairs were too narrow for Roosevelt's wheelchair, so two aides carried him to the top. Churchill, an accomplished artist, later painted the scene from the tower and presented it to FDR. It was, Churchill's daughter recalled, the only painting Churchill made during the war.

Looking old and drawn, Roosevelt talks with Soviet foreign minister Vyacheslav Molotov in 1945 at the Yalta Conference as Churchill, with his trademark cigar, looks on *(right)*. The Russian, British, and American leaders attending the conference, which was held in the Crimean resort town of Yalta on the Black Sea, laid the groundwork for the postwar division of Europe.

Franklin loved to drive his own car, a Ford equipped with hand controls, and once took Churchill on a wild ride around Hyde Park, driving madly as he tried to lose his Secret Service agents. Here, the passenger is FDR's beloved Scottish terrier, Fala.

With seven of his grandchildren, FDR, just back from a difficult Big Three conference at Teheran, celebrated Christmas in 1943 at Hyde Park for the first time since becoming president. Though he read Dickens to the children and broadcast a fireside chat to the nation on Christmas Eve, Eleanor expressed concern about his lack of vigor: "I don't think he longs to get back and fight," she wrote.

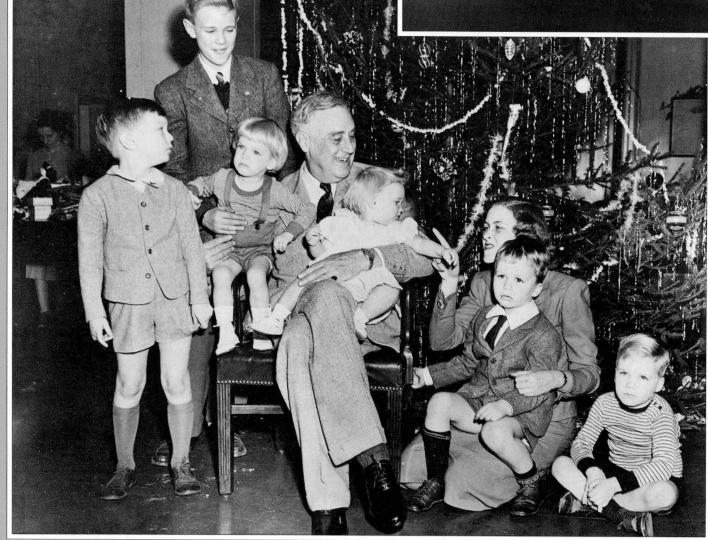

AN OCCASIONAL RESPITE

"All that is within me cries out to go back to my home on the Hudson," FDR was fond of saying. Springwood, the 2,000-acre estate along the river in Hyde Park, New York, where he was born and raised, seemed to be a wellspring of security and happiness for Franklin. He used the 35-room house and its grounds as a refuge, especially during his Washington years. Here Roosevelt could unwind, sleeping late, eating and drinking with gusto, and socializing with his many visitors.

FDR's mother, Sara, who lived at Springwood until her death in 1941, managed the household firmly and served as its ever decorous hostess. On occasion Franklin and Eleanor managed to circumvent Mrs. Roosevelt's strict conventions. A journalist wrote of enjoying cocktails with the president and other guests in a cloakroom in the usually dry residence, laughing and giggling "as if we were all bad children having a feast in the dorm at night." Eleanor scandalized Sara by entertaining England's King George VI and Queen Elizabeth at a Hyde Park picnic featuring hot dogs and beer.

On the whole, Franklin welcomed the order and serenity of his mother's home. But Eleanor couldn't help feeling stifled in her mother-in-law's "Big House" and longed for a place of her own where she would be mistress. When Franklin had a cottage built for her on the estate, a grateful Eleanor wrote to him, "The peace of it is divine."

Observing a ritual that began when he first ran for the presidency, Franklin Roosevelt, with daughter Anna and Eleanor at his side, took his place on the porch of his Hyde Park home on election night in 1944 and in front of his friends and neighbors acknowledged victory in his fourth campaign for the presidency.

EXTRA
ROOSEVELT IS DEAD

Battle Flares on East Front

Only Los Angeles Newspaper With All Leading News Services—Associated Press, International News, United Press, Dow-Jones

LOS ANGELES EVENING
HERALD Express

NIGHT FINAL

HERALD-EXPRESS BUILDING 1243 TRENTON ST. Zone 15   The Evening Herald and Express Grows Just Like Los Angeles   HERALD-EXPRESS PHONE Richmond 4141   HERALD-EXPRESS PHONE Richmond 4141

VOL. LXXV   THURSDAY, APRIL 12, 1945   NO. 15

Tears streaming down his grief-stricken face, navy accordionist Graham Jackson played "Going Home" as the president's coffin left the compound in Warm Springs on its way to Washington. Jackson had been engaged to play at a barbecue for Roosevelt on the day the president died.

THE END OF AN ERA

On April 12, 1945, the president sat reading in his favorite armchair in the living room of his house at the polio rehabilitation center he had helped establish in Warm Springs, Georgia. Nearby, an artist painted his portrait. It was almost lunchtime, and the posing session was drawing to a close when Franklin brushed his hand across his brow, then held the back of his neck. "I have a terrific headache," he said, then slumped over in his chair.

Only three months into his fourth term and one month before Germany surrendered

unconditionally, Franklin Delano Roosevelt suffered a cerebral hemorrhage and died. Eleanor, in the middle of a day of appointments and speaking engagements in Washington, was called to the White House and told of her husband's death. Mindful of her responsibilities, she first cabled her sons, saying, "He did his job to the end as he would want you to do," then sent for Vice President Truman.

Eleanor traveled to Warm Springs and accompanied her husband's body north to Washington. The funeral service took place

in the East Room of the White House, where the body of Abraham Lincoln had lain at the end of another bitter war. From there the funeral cortege traveled to New York. At every point along the way, thousands of mourners, many weeping, stood by the tracks to catch a last glimpse of their president. "I felt as if I knew him," recalled one soldier. "I felt as if he knew me—and I felt as if he liked me." The cortege stopped at last in the garden at Roosevelt's beloved Springwood. Franklin was home.

Pulled by six white horses and flanked by a military escort, the black-draped caisson bearing President Roosevelt's coffin passes the White House portico. At Eleanor's request, the Episcopal bishop officiating at the simple White House service quoted from FDR's first inaugural address: "Let me assert my firm belief that the only thing we have to fear is fear itself."

CHAPTER 4

SUNSET IN THE EAST

*"Among the Americans who served on Iwo Island,
uncommon valor was a common virtue."*

ADMIRAL CHESTER NIMITZ, MARCH 17, 1945

L ethal Japanese fire raked the landing site as Joe Rosenthal struggled toward cover. With each step, the Associated Press photographer sank ankle deep into the black volcanic ash and cinders that terraced up steeply from the water line. A portly five feet five inches and 150 pounds, and so nearsighted his draft board had deemed him 4-F, unfit for service, Rosenthal cut an unlikely figure in combat. But for the past year, the 33-year-old Californian had been following American fighters onto the beaches of Guam, Peleliu, and Angaur, earning a reputation for taking good pictures during the heat of battle.

Suddenly Rosenthal heard a clang and saw the helmet of the marine in front of him spin off into the air as the man faltered forward another two steps, then fell. The photographer reached a shell hole and dived into it, heart hammering. Catching his breath, he adjusted his thick spectacles and peered around. To his left a dead marine lay facing up the slope, stopped in midcharge, weapon still at the ready. Rosenthal wanted the shot, but it was no good from where he was. Scuttling cautiously from one shell crater to the next, he maneuvered himself into a better position and saw another man lying near the first. The photographer stood, framed the scene in his camera, and waited. When another

marine ran past, his shutter clicked—a picture, Rosenthal thought, "of the living taking over for the fallen dead." It was a fitting portrait for February 19, 1945: D-day on Iwo Jima.

Before it ended, the battle for this tiny speck of volcanic rock, lying just 660 miles southeast of Tokyo, would cost the marines more dearly than any other in their history. And the tenacity of Iwo's Japanese defenders would give military commanders and politicians in the United States yet another indication, if one was needed, that an invasion of Japan's home islands would exact a price the American people might not want to pay.

Iwo Jima was the latest in a succession of Pacific islands the marines had begun wresting from Japanese control two and a half years earlier. Before that the United States had been scrambling against the enemy's assaults and losing badly, forced to retreat from Guam, Wake, and the Philippines. But in June 1942, when the Japanese sent more than 100 warships to attack Midway Island, only 1,000 miles northwest of Honolulu, the United States mounted a furious airborne defense that finally began to turn the tide in the Pacific war *(pages 32-37)*.

Two months later the first American offensive came at Guadalcanal, an island in the Solomons.

In a moment that came to symbolize hard-won American triumph in the bloody, island-by-island war in the Pacific, five marines and a navy corpsman raise the American flag atop Iwo Jima's Mount Suribachi on February 23, 1945. Shot by Associated Press photographer Joe Rosenthal, the picture offered badly needed hope in a time of mounting American casualties.

In May 1943 America launched a two-pronged attack in the Pacific, with Douglas MacArthur sweeping through the Bismarck Archipelago, New Guinea, and the Philippines, and Chester Nimitz taking the Gilbert, Marshall, and Mariana Islands. Iwo Jima and Okinawa would be the last two battlegrounds before the planned invasion of Japan itself.

Here, 1,000 miles northeast of Australia, the Japanese had begun constructing an air base. Enemy fliers who were taking off from Guadalcanal would be able to strike at islands still in Allied hands and in addition could harass Allied ships that were carrying men and matériel to Australia for the Pacific offensive. They could also attack Australia itself. Faced with this dire threat, the U.S. Joint Chiefs of Staff sent in the marines. But the Japanese held their ground ferociously. For six months the island's fate hung in the balance before Allied forces eventually prevailed.

With the Japanese drive south now halted, positions reversed. Japan soon found itself fighting a two-pronged Allied attack in the Pacific, launched in 1943. As American submarines torpedoed enemy ships and virtually destroyed Japanese supply lines, General Douglas MacArthur commenced his drive through the Southwest Pacific, taking the Bismarck Archipelago and New Guinea and, in October 1944, reclaiming the Philippines. At the same time, Admi-ral Chester Nimitz attacked in the Central Pacific, moving through the Japanese-held Gilbert and Marshall Islands to the Mariana Islands, 1,300 miles southeast of Tokyo. The Marianas—Guam, Saipan, and Tinian—captured in August 1944, would serve as air bases for America's newest long-range bomber, the B-29 Superfortress.

The island-by-island campaign followed a pattern that the Japanese came to know well. American naval and air bombardment softened up Japanese troops holed up in elaborate bunkers; ground forces landed to clear them out; and swarms of Seabees (naval Construction Battalions, or CBs) came ashore to build strategic airfields. As Japanese losses mounted—losses that Tokyo could ill afford—Japan grew ever more determined and desperate. Nowhere was this desperation more apparent than on Iwo Jima. As one Japanese officer put it, "Iwo Jima is the doorkeeper to the Imperial capital." And Japanese forces pledged to block this doorway to Tokyo with their lives.

American bombing raids that had started the previous August by February 1945 had turned the already ugly island into a moonscape. A mere eight square miles, Iwo had no natural source of fresh water, and its scarce vegetation consisted largely of brambles. The smell of rotten egg was everywhere, a by-product of bubbling sulfur springs and sulfur refining operations. Mount Suribachi, a dormant volcano at the island's south end, had left a dual legacy that would try marine souls: ash and cinders that turned the landing beach into a slippery quagmire, and a honeycomb of caves that the enemy would use to deadly advantage.

In December, as the United States stepped up its bombing, General Tadamichi Kuribayashi, the Japanese commander on Iwo, had ordered everyone and everything underground. The previous summer the general had set his engineers to work expanding the island's natural caves and building others. The engineers designed ventilation systems for an intricate complex of interconnecting caves, man-made tunnels, and masked gun positions. One installation inside Mount Suribachi itself stood seven stories deep. Kuribayashi's intention was simple, and in keeping with his samurai heritage: The best he could do for his emperor was to defend the island to the death. As a result, each Japanese soldier's position would become his grave, and his military shrine.

Kuribayashi also instructed his soldiers to hold their fire until a significant number of American troops were onshore. Thus, when the first wave of marines hit the beach at 9:05 the morning of the 19th, they encountered surprisingly light resistance. Billowing yellow gray clouds of smoke and dust from the prelanding bombardment still hung over the island, and many wondered whether any Japanese had survived the unprecedented shelling. But marines clawing their way up from the beach to the airstrip that was their first objective felt their skin crawl with the sense of being watched by invisible eyes. Then the enemy opened fire—not only from caves and tunnels but from camouflaged blockhouses, pillboxes, and bunkers that infested every hillside and ravine. One

marine major watching the landing wondered "how anybody could live through such heavy fire barrages."

Marines scrambling to make their own cover on the exposed beach found another enemy: the volcanic ash. It was like "trying to dig a hole in a barrel of wheat," one frustrated survivor recalled. Thousands fell. Those who made it through the night awoke at dawn to a nightmarish landscape. Bodies lay everywhere, torsos cut nearly in half and limbs flung several yards away.

The sheer volume of dead produced gruesome problems. A burly machinist's mate from Michigan,

Mount Suribachi can be seen at the bottom of this intelligence map, formed from a dozen photos taken by camera-equipped B-24s during several bombing runs on August 17, 1944. Notations indicate the positions of crucial enemy airfields, ammunition storages, automatic weapons (AW), and antiaircraft guns (AA).

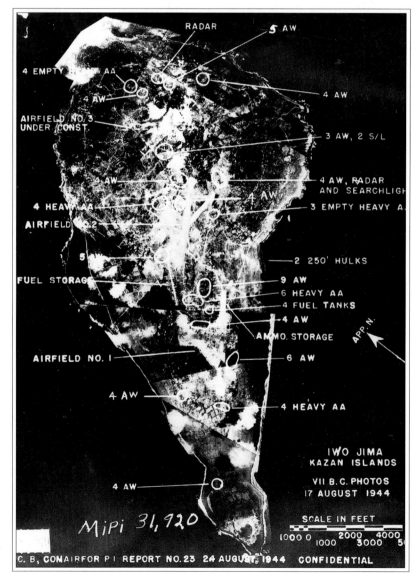

Alphenix J. Benard, trying to drive a tractor onto the beach from a landing craft, found his way blocked by the bodies of several Americans. Knowing he had no choice, Benard drove over them. The crews of two other boats circled Iwo for a couple of days, trying desperately to get an officer to issue orders for the disposal of their cargo: flag-covered stacks of bloating corpses. After he had finally helped bury these comrades far out to sea, one sickened crewman swore he could drink a gallon of whiskey and never feel a drop of it. Gagging on the stench of sulfur and decaying bodies, more than one marine swore he was in the depths of hell. And that odor was soon mixed with the horrifying smell of roasting flesh as Americans used flamethrowers to burn the hidden enemy from his lair.

But on the morning of February 23, exhausted American fighters looked up from the grim landscape and suddenly burst into cheers. "They've just raised the flag on Suribachi!" someone yelled. Tears wore tracks down some dirty faces, and men jumped recklessly out of foxholes to spread the news. The island's south was secured.

Joe Rosenthal was in a landing craft on his way to shore on February 23 when he heard that a marine patrol was heading for the top of Suribachi to plant the flag. Ever since D-day the photographer had been returning to the island to record the marines' struggle, sending his film on the daily mail plane to Guam, where the AP would develop and evaluate his photos for publication. On this morning he reached shore after 10:00 a.m. to find he had just missed the patrol taking the flag to the summit. Realizing he could not follow without protective firepower, he persuaded marine combat reporters Bill Genaust and Bob Campbell to accompany him on the climb.

Sliding and sinking into Iwo Jima's soft volcanic ash, marines inch their way up a 15-foot slope leading from the landing beach on D-day. After an initial period of light enemy fire, hidden Japanese guns poured down a deadly rain from the flanks of 550-foot-high Mount Suribachi *(far left)*, causing one regiment to report: "Machine gun and artillery fire heaviest ever seen."

Halfway to the top they ran into Lou Lowery, a photographer for the marine magazine *Leatherneck.* "You guys are late!" teased Lowery. From Lowery, Rosenthal learned that the marines had raised a small flag around 10:20 a.m. It had been a historic moment for the Americans—the first time during the war that U.S. forces had seized land under Tokyo's direct control. And Lou Lowery, not Joe Rosenthal, had shot it.

Knowing he had been scooped, Rosenthal continued halfheartedly up the mountain. He'd come this far; the least he could do was get a picture of the flag. It was rough climbing: The sandy ground, which was covered with rocks and brambles, constantly shifted underfoot. Several times they had to dive for cover when the marines up ahead shouted, "Fire in the hole!" before tossing grenades into a cave where enemy snipers might be lurking. Finally, just before noon, the journalists crested the lip of the crater. They could see the small Stars and Stripes blowing in the wind.

Rosenthal spied an officer at the base of the flagpole with a triangle of bright cloth folded under one arm. "What's doing, fellas?" he inquired of the marines who were gathered there. "We're going to take down that flag and put this one up," one answered. Their battalion commander had ordered the raising of a second, larger flag for morale purposes. Or as the sergeant who delivered the second banner had put it, "Colonel Johnson wants this big flag run up high so every son of a bitch on this whole cruddy island can see it."

To get a full view of the flag going up, Rosenthal dropped back about 35 feet. But the ground sloped down into the crater, and finding he could not get the bottom half of the action in his frame, the short photographer piled up rocks and Japanese sandbags to build himself a perch. The men were dragging a second flagpole—a heavy length of pipe—into place as Rosenthal climbed up on his rock pile and began adjusting lens and speed settings. Just then Bill Genaust, wielding a movie camera, wandered across his field. "I'm not in your way, am I, Joe?"

Genaust called. As Rosenthal glanced over, he caught the flagpole's movement from the corner of his eye, swung his camera clear, and clicked.

"That is how the picture was taken," Rosenthal would say later about the photo that made him famous. "And when you take a picture like that you don't come away saying you got a great shot. You don't know." Indeed, after sending his film off as usual, Rosenthal didn't even see the result of his accidental genius for more than a week.

On February 25 readers across America unfolded their Sunday newspapers to a stunning photograph: On a distant Pacific island, a group of U.S. marines struggled together to plant a large, wind-blown American flag over Japanese territory. The image generated a tidal wave of emotion among the American public—a surge of pride, concern, and hope for final victory.

Americans following the war news back home desperately needed that hope as Iwo Jima's casualty figures also hit the front pages: On D-day alone, 2,500 marines had fallen. And the dying was far from over. The U.S. flag might be flying over Mount Suribachi, but the battle for control of the rest of the island had just begun.

As days passed, and the Americans pushed northward to take the island's two airfields, Iwo took its toll of experienced officers and men. Officers of lower rank took charge of companies and platoons as their superiors fell, one right after another, to enemy fire. But filling the decimated ranks meant sending in green troops. On March 8 Major Robert Kriendler, a personnel officer, shook his head over the casualty reports. "They get killed the day they go into battle as brand-new replacements. Seventeen years old—four months, six months, after they've enlisted—and they are dead."

At Motoyama 1 and 2, Hill Peter, Turkey Knob, the Amphitheater, Hill 383, the Meat Grinder, Cushman's Pocket, Kuribayashi's Cave the Americans fought an enemy that did not know the word *surrender.* The marines would clear a sector by day—only to have the Japanese sneak through their

Smoke and rubble fill the air as a charge of TNT, set by marine demolitions experts huddled behind a boulder, seals the entrance to an enemy cave on Iwo Jima. The Japanese "stayed in their tunnels and their molehills to the deathly end, and we had to go in and dig them out or burn out or seal them in," noted combat correspondent Robert Sherrod. "There was nothing else for us to do."

tunnels and retake it in the night. There was no respite, even for those units that had been relieved of forward duty. So cunningly hidden were enemy positions that no one could ever be sure where an attack would come from. "Front lines? There aren't any goddam front lines. This whole island is a front line," said one U.S. fighter. "Seldom on Iwo, from D-Day until the battle was over, did you see the enemy," another recalled, "just the sights and sounds of deadly fire from his weapons."

After a while, the constant vigilance and fear of death or mutilation marked even the toughest marines. "They were bearded and hunched over," wrote one combat correspondent of the men on Iwo Jima. "Their clothes were dirty and torn, their eyes watery and distant, their hair matted, . . . and their mouths were open as if they were having trouble breathing." But the American fighters kept going, yard by yard, sustaining their momentum through sheer will power. "Few of us would have admitted we were bound by the old-fashioned principle of death before dishonor," a marine later confessed, "but it was probably this, above all else, that kept us pressing forward."

Gritty determination could not shield the marines, however, and thousands fell as they moved across the island. Beneath the roar of enemy guns and mortars came the frequent cries for medical aid: "Corpsman! Corpsman!" Risking their own lives time and again, navy corpsmen answered those desperate pleas, finding a way to reach the fallen marine, bind his injuries, and transport him to a surgical unit not far from the fighting. Rarely had American fighters received more immediate medical care in the midst of battle—and rarely had the casualty rate among surgeons and corpsmen been so high.

Badly wounded men were evacuated to Guam, but not all of them wanted to go. They begged the medical attendants to patch them up enough to continue fighting. Leaving Iwo meant abandoning comrades still under fire. "I think you might need me," one injured lieutenant told his superior, "and that's what I'm here for."

Navy flight nurse Jane Kendeigh checks an injured American fighter as she readies him for evacuation from Iwo Jima to Guam on March 6, 1945. Three shell-shocked victims wait at her right.

FLYING TO SAVE LIVES

When Ensign Jane Kendeigh stepped from a C-54 transport plane onto a U.S.-held airfield on Iwo Jima she ignored the exploding enemy shells. The 23-year-old navy flight nurse was focused not on danger to her but on her mission: Get the wounded back to the hospital on Guam. Only after the men were safely aboard and the plane was headed south did Kendeigh, who had never landed on a battlefield before, feel her knees shake.

Navy and army flight nurses could not indulge in fear as they repeatedly braved the war's battlefields to evacuate the wounded. Patients often counted as much on a nurse's demeanor as on her skills. During a flight from Saipan to the Marshall Islands, army lieutenant Victoria Pavlowski, who had been administering painkillers and checking temperatures, suddenly felt the plane reel, its port engines dying. She grabbed a litter to steady herself as her patients' eyes turned anxiously toward her. Keeping her face calm, she bent down and spoke to one of the wounded, smiling. Reassured, the men around her relaxed, and moments later the engines sputtered back to life.

Survival also depended on a nurse's ability to react quickly and improvise. When Lieutenant Stella Hawkins's plane crash-landed on an island near Guadalcanal, wreckage sliced open a patient's neck. Hawkins slid a tube down his throat and siphoned out blood and mucus with an ear syringe. She kept him and other patients alive until help arrived. After assisting her charges into the rescue dinghy, she realized there was no room for her. Unfazed, she waded into the water and swam for the ship.

On March 14 Admiral Nimitz declared victory. But the last pocket of enemy resistance was not eliminated until March 26—36 days after the marines first landed. The fighting had lasted longer than any military official had predicted. So bloody was the campaign that only 1,083 of the 20,000 Japanese defenders survived to be taken prisoner, and by one calculation approximately 700 Americans lost their lives for every square mile of Iwo taken. More than 6,000 Americans lay dead, almost 18,000 more wounded. Some 2,000 others succumbed to "combat fatigue," their sanity brutalized by all they had endured.

Victory on Iwo Jima had come at an enormous price, but it had been essential. For the flight crews of the B-29s that by the completion of the war would make a total of 2,400 emergency landings en route to or from Tokyo, Iwo Jima meant the difference between life and death. "Whenever I land on this island," one pilot said fervently, "I thank God for the men who fought for it."

Marine private Ira H. Hayes stepped out of a landing vehicle on March 27 to grasp the cargo net hanging from the troop transport ship USS *Winged Arrow.* Slowly he pulled himself upward. Spent, Hayes hung motionless at the top of the net for a few moments until someone reached out and helped him onto the ship's deck. After five weeks of fighting on Iwo Jima, Hayes had been one of the lucky ones: He had survived. But when his ship arrived in Hawaii, Hayes found his way to his company's first sergeant, John Daskalakis, to make a full confession.

"First Sergeant," said the soft-spoken Pima Indian from Arizona, "I'm the one they're looking for in the flag-raising picture."

A startled Daskalakis snapped into action. The marines had indeed been searching for Ira Hayes.

Within the last month Joe Rosenthal's photo of the flag-raising on Mount Suribachi had been reprinted again and again in American newspapers and magazines, been the subject of a congressional bill to authorize a monument based on the image, and stirred poets to write tributes to the men and the sacrifice it represented. Men on Iwo received clippings of the photo from hometown newspapers and national magazines, and one Seabee carved a simplified version of the image in high relief on a sandstone bluff at the island's north end. Amateur and professional artists at home were reproducing the flag-raising in various media, children reenacted the scene on neighborhood hills, and the U.S. government was making preparations to issue a postage stamp of it.

Rosenthal, who had returned to the States, was being toasted and feted by officials throughout the

> *"Few of us would have admitted we were bound by the old-fashioned principle of death before dishonor, but it was probably this, above all else, that kept us pressing forward."*
>
> UNITED STATES MARINE, AFTER THE BATTLE OF IWO JIMA

country. But not even the photographer himself could answer the one question people kept asking about the picture: Who were the men in it?

Within days of the photograph's initial publication, the marines set out to discover the identities of the anonymous flag-raisers, and on March 24 President Roosevelt himself issued a special order: Find those men and bring them home. The ailing commander in chief wanted them to help with the latest bond drive.

As the fighting on Iwo continued, five of the six men were named. Hayes, meanwhile, kept his head down and his mouth shut. He was no hero. If anyone deserved credit, he felt, it was the men who had secured Suribachi and raised the first flag.

When the six men, five marines and one sailor, all were identified eventually, people found that they represented a geographic cross section of America: Private Ira Hayes, the Pima Indian from Arizona; Pharmacist's Mate John Bradley, a midwestern navy corpsman; Private Rene Gagnon, a New Englander

John Bradley *(far left)*, Rene Gagnon *(pointing)*,
and Ira Hayes—the three surviving men of the six
in Joe Rosenthal's immortal flag-raising photo—
flank President Harry Truman and Secretary of
the Treasury Henry Morgenthau at the kickoff of
the Seventh War Loan Drive on April 20, 1945.
"The bond tour was really lots of fun for
a while," Hayes wrote his mother in June. But
after a week of doing "the same old stuff," he
added, "it got so boring and tiresome."

of French Canadian descent; Private Franklin Sousley, a Kentucky mountain boy, who lost his life on Iwo Jima; Sergeant Michael Strank of Pennsylvania, the son of Czechoslovakian immigrants, who also died on the island; and Corporal Harlon Block, from a small town in Texas. Block had been misidentified initially as Sergeant Henry O. Hansen, who had actually helped raise the first flag, a mistake not immediately discovered because neither man survived the battle.

So it happened that on April 20 a reluctant Hayes joined Gagnon and Bradley in Washington, D.C., to kick off the tour. Posing for publicity shots, Hayes was troubled by thoughts of "those guys who were better men than me not coming back at all, much less to the White House." Lost in his own concerns, the unhappy private was unaware that another man standing near him was also reluctant to have been called to his present position.

Harry S. Truman, the new president of the United States, had been in office only eight days. Just after 5:00 on the evening of April 12, Truman had hurried to the White House after receiving an urgent call. He thought the president wanted to see him. Upon his arrival, however, he was ushered into Eleanor Roosevelt's private quarters. She put her arm around his shoulders.

"Harry, the president is dead," she said.

For a long moment Truman could not speak, feeling the weight of enormous responsibility descend upon him. Collecting himself, he asked Mrs. Roosevelt, "Is there anything I can do for you?"

"Is there anything *we* can do for you?" inquired the woman whose husband had died of a cerebral hemorrhage less than an hour before. "For you are the one in trouble now."

Truman felt that to his bones. Once, soon after becoming the party's vice presidential candidate, he had awakened from a nightmare in which Roosevelt had died, leaving him to shoulder the burden of wartime leadership. The nightmare had just become reality. "Boys, if you ever pray, pray for me now," he instructed a group of reporters on April 13. "I don't know whether you fellows ever had a load of hay fall on you, but when they told me yesterday what had happened, I felt like the moon, the stars, and all the planets had fallen on me."

The former haberdasher from Missouri had not wanted to succeed Roosevelt as president; as a matter of fact, he had not even wanted to be his vice president. Roosevelt, however, needed a new running mate in 1944. His third-term vice president, Henry Wallace, was unpopular with southern voters because of his views on racial equality, and at the last minute Democrats decided to drop him from the ticket. Some key players suggested substituting the less controversial Truman. For his part, then-senator Truman regarded the vice presidency as little more than "a very high office which consists entirely of honor and I don't have any ambition to hold an office like that." But when Roosevelt accused the obstinate Missourian of wanting "to break up the Democratic party in the middle of the war," Truman finally capitulated.

Truman had always believed in doing what was right. Born on a farm in Lamar, Missouri, on May 8, 1884, he grew up in the town of Independence, a studious, responsible boy with a cheerful disposition. When World War I broke out he shipped out to France as an artillery officer. Upon his return he married childhood sweetheart Bess Wallace, whom he had first seen at the age of six in the First Presbyterian Church of Independence. Then and for the rest of Harry's life, Bess was "the most beautiful and the sweetest person on earth."

To support his new family, Truman opened a men's clothing store in Kansas City with an old army friend, Eddie Jacobson. But by 1922 Truman and Jacobson, purveyors of gentlemen's furnishings, had gone under. Later his critics would ask how a man who "couldn't even sell shirts" could ever succeed in high office. Succeed he did, however, first as a Missouri county judge, then as a prominent junior senator in Washington, and then as Roosevelt's vice president—for 82 days.

Now Truman needed to succeed as president, a task made more difficult as the country measured him against his much beloved and respected predecessor. After more than 12 years under the blue-blooded and velvet-voiced Roosevelt, Americans suddenly had a man in the White House who spoke with a twang, played poker weekly, and had never owned a house. Some Americans loved homespun Harry, "the amiable Missourian with the touch of country in his voice and manner," as one reporter put it. He epitomized the ideal of the straightforward and trustworthy midwesterner for many. Others, such as a writer for *Time* magazine, cringed at the thought of "the mousy little man from Missouri" leading the nation. Citizens shook their heads, repeating, "If Harry Truman can be president, so can my next-door neighbor."

At least one cabinet member shared their doubts. Henry Stimson, the 77-year-old secretary of war, belonged to Roosevelt's world of cultured gentlemen. A graduate of Yale and of Harvard Law School, he was a veteran diplomat who spent his free time on his Long Island estate fox hunting and playing deck tennis. But Stimson's concerns about the new president arose not so much from a difference in background as from interactions with Truman when he was chairman of the Special Committee to Investigate the National Defense Program.

In 1941 Senator Truman, with the tenacity of a bloodhound, had begun sniffing out waste and corruption among war contractors. Two years later one of his investigations had led to a mysterious, costly military program known as the Manhattan Project.

Determined to get to the bottom of it, Truman called the secretary of war. Stimson informed him that it was an essential but deeply confidential enterprise, and Truman agreed to drop his inquiry. But the project kept popping up, and Truman investigated again in 1944. Angered, the secretary warned Truman off once more and wrote in his diary, "Truman is a nuisance and a pretty untrustworthy man. He talks smoothly but he acts meanly."

But on April 12, as Stimson watched the new president take the oath of office and conduct an impromptu cabinet meeting, his opinion was already undergoing a change. He admired the way the plainspoken Missourian handled himself in the face of the shock of Roosevelt's death and his own sudden assumption of leadership. Truman indicated to the cabinet members that he would continue Roosevelt's

er, has such a bearing on our present foreign relations and has such an important effect upon all my thinking in this field that I think you ought to know about it without much further delay."

Promptly at noon the next day Stimson appeared at the Oval Office. He opened his briefcase and removed a typewritten memo, finished just that morning. "Within four months," it began, "we shall in all probability have completed the most terrible weapon ever known in human history, one bomb of which could destroy a whole city." Stimson went on to discuss the postwar ramifications of the bomb. Only the United States had the technology and resources to build an atomic bomb at this time, but others would gain both sooner or later. "The world in its present state of moral advancement compared with its technical development would be eventually

"Boys, if you ever pray, pray for me now. I don't know whether you fellows ever had a load of hay fall on you, but when they told me yesterday what had happened, I felt like the moon, the stars, and all the planets had fallen on me."

HARRY S. TRUMAN, THE DAY AFTER FRANKLIN ROOSEVELT'S DEATH

foreign and domestic programs. But, he told them, he would also be "president in my own right."

Stimson knew that President Truman, unlike Senator Truman, could be kept in the dark no longer about the Manhattan Project. As the cabinet meeting ended, Stimson approached him, asking for a private word. Truman listened as the secretary spoke obliquely about "an immense project underway—a project looking to the development of a new explosive of almost unbelievable destructive power." Stimson declined to elaborate at that moment, however, and made no mention of the Manhattan Project by name, leaving the new president more puzzled than informed. Then, on April 24, Truman received a note from Stimson requesting a meeting "as soon as possible on a highly secret matter"— namely, the project Stimson had mentioned two weeks earlier but had held off on because of the extreme pressure Truman had been under. "It, howev-

at the mercy of such a weapon," the secretary stated. His intense blue gray eyes fixed on Truman across the desk, Stimson delivered a succinct warning: "In other words, modern civilization might be completely destroyed."

Just then, General Leslie L. Groves entered from an outer office, joining the meeting. To avoid arousing the curiosity of newspaper reporters, the burly head of the Manhattan Project had slipped into the White House through a side door and traveled through a ground-floor passageway. The general handed the president a 24-page report, filled with scientific data on the more technical aspects of the project. When Truman indicated that he preferred to discuss the long report rather than read it, the exasperated Groves insisted, "Well, we can't tell you this in any more concise language. This is a big project."

Truman began reading, frequently stopping to ask Groves and Stimson questions. After going over the report, the three men discussed further action. Stimson admitted that, despite all his concerns for the future, he still favored using the bomb against Japan since, if it worked, it would "in all probability shorten the war." Truman agreed to the creation of a special panel, to be called the Interim Committee, that would advise him on the ramifications of atomic energy for the present and the future. Stimson consented to serve as chairman.

Over the next several weeks, as Truman adjusted to his new burdens and responsibilities, the loneliness of leadership was compounded by personal loneliness. At the end of May, the first lady and her daughter had packed up their bags and boarded a train for Independence. In truth, the Truman women had found it difficult to move into the White House, where they discovered rats, decrepit furniture in the private rooms, and a housekeeper whose response to every instruction was, "Mrs. Roosevelt never did things that way." Twenty-one-year-old Margaret wrote in her diary, "The White House is a mess." In addition, Bess Truman abhorred the glare of publicity surrounding the first lady. Summer in Missouri looked like a refuge.

Truman missed them greatly. "I have no one to raise a fuss over my neckties and my haircuts, my shoes and my clothes generally. I usually put on a terrible tie . . . ," he confessed in his diary, "just to get a loud protest from Bess and Margie. When they are gone I have to put on the right ones and it's no fun." He sorely needed the comfort of his wife's presence as he sat up into the wee hours reading reports, memos, and cables, and learning how to be president in a time of war.

On the morning of June 18, Truman rose at 6:30 and headed straight for the private presidential refrigerator he had ordered installed outside his bedroom. After a glass of orange juice, he prepared for

Head bowed, the recently inaugurated Harry Truman, with wife Bess and daughter Margaret, attends Franklin Roosevelt's funeral in Hyde Park, New York, on April 15, 1945. In his diary two days earlier, Truman had written: "Signed Proclamation for Pres. R's funeral & holiday. First official Act."

On May 11, 1945, a kamikaze bomber plummets toward the USS *Bunker Hill,* already aflame from a similar attack just seconds earlier. The ship, whose planes were preparing for air strikes on Okinawa, was engulfed by fire on three top decks. After a six-hour battle the crew was able to extinguish the fire, but hundreds of men were killed by flames or smoke inhalation *(below).* American sailors dreaded the suicidal Japanese fliers. As one correspondent noted, "The strain of waiting, the anticipated terror, made vivid from past experience, sent some men into hysteria, insanity, breakdown."

his daily prebreakfast stroll. With perhaps a momentary pang of regret, he selected a proper blue bow tie to go with the double-breasted suit, crisp pocket handkerchief, and fresh white shirt that were his usual Washington uniform. Though he may have teased his wife and daughter about neckties, Truman was actually quite particular about his appearance, seldom going without a straw or fedora hat over his neatly styled gray hair.

Despite Bess and Margaret's continued absence, Harry's mood was good. A pack of reporters joined him on his morning constitutional and, as always, were curious about his schedule. Would anything important break today? Truman breezily answered this routine query with his stock answer, "Wait and see."

The president had spent the previous day boating down the Potomac with several close advisers, discussing relations with postwar Europe and the progress of the Pacific war. Germany had surrendered unconditionally on May 7, but Truman was all too aware of how the war with Japan raged on, exacting huge casualty tolls on both sides. "We have another war to win and people must realize it," Truman had written to his mother the day before the Germans surrendered. "I hope they will anyway." In the month following V-E Day, he continued to dwell on his options in the Pacific theater. "I have to decide Japanese strategy—shall we invade Japan proper or shall we bomb and blockade?" he asked himself in his diary. "That is my hardest decision to date." So secret was the atomic bomb project, referred to by Stimson and others as S-1, that Truman did not mention it even in the privacy of his own journal.

The president also refrained initially from discussing the bomb at a conference on the afternoon of June 18 to plan the invasion of Japan. Army Chief of Staff General George C. Marshall opened the briefing by outlining Operation *Downfall,* the Joint Chiefs' two-phase design for the final defeat of Hirohito. Part One, code-named Olympic, would begin on November 1 with a force of 815,548 American troops invading Kyushu, the southernmost of the Japanese islands. Operation *Coronet,* the plan for the

larger invasion of Honshu, would begin the following March. What price, Truman wanted to know, would Americans pay for this invasion? He deeply hoped "there was a possibility of preventing an Okinawa from one end of Japan to the other."

Okinawa, 350 miles from Kyushu and less than 1,000 from Tokyo, was meant to be the last island the Americans seized before Operation *Downfall* began. As the men in the room knew, however, after two and a half months the battle for Okinawa was still raging, and already the casualty rate had far surpassed the 24,000 of Iwo Jima. As at Iwo, Americans had stormed ashore to find Japanese forces dug firmly into caves and other defensive structures, ready to give their lives and determined to take as many Americans with them into death as possible. That determination was terrifyingly clear in the hundreds of sudden and unpredictable strikes by Japanese suicide planes, or kamikazes, that plunged into the American armada. Thousands of naval personnel had already been killed or wounded in those attacks, and many others, suffering severe combat fatigue, were unfit for battle.

But Marshall refused to predict casualty numbers for the proposed invasion of Kyushu other than to say losses in the first 30 days should not exceed 31,000 men. But the battles in the Pacific had each been so different from one another, he explained, "it is considered wrong" to give estimates. And in any event, he reminded the group, "It is a grim fact that there is not an easy, bloodless way to victory in war." Others around the table insisted that casualties would be much greater, based on the horror of Okinawa. General Douglas MacArthur's staff estimated initial losses might total 50,000, although MacArthur himself, eager for a D-day invasion in the Pacific to rival Eisenhower's at Normandy, dismissed that calculation as too high. Despite serious misgivings about the loss of American lives, Truman approved the Joint Chiefs' plan for a November 1 invasion.

The meeting's participants had begun gathering up their papers when Truman turned to his respected assistant secretary of war, John J. McCloy.

"McCloy, you haven't said anything. What is your view?" the president asked.

McCloy looked at his boss, who knew his opinion on the matter. "Go ahead," Stimson said. "We should have our heads examined," McCloy told the president, "if we don't consider a political solution."

Contact the Japanese, warn them of the powerful new weapon, and negotiate a surrender, McCloy suggested, as others had before him. Furthermore, rather than insisting on "unconditional surrender," as the United States had been doing, McCloy said, tell the Japanese they could keep their emperor as a constitutional monarch. If the warning failed to have an effect, the atomic bomb, he suggested, might offer a way to terminate the war without a costly conventional attack and landing. Immediately the room fell silent, as if McCloy had breached decorum with the mere mention of the secret weapon. Nevertheless he pressed on. Even if the enemy did not agree, "our moral position would be better if we gave them specific warning of the bomb."

Those around the table immediately voiced their dissent: "Suppose it doesn't go off," someone replied. "Our prestige will be greatly marred," added another. One admiral present was concerned that the "longhairs" on the Manhattan Project were wasting billions of dollars to create a product no better than cordite, the explosive that powered battleship weapons.

The meeting had proceeded as if the atomic option did not exist because, in some sense, it would not exist as a feasible option until it had been tested. After listening to all the reactions, Truman, not ready to commit himself, asked McCloy to prepare a memo with his recommendations for the State Department and promised to seriously consider it.

Meanwhile, plans for a November invasion would proceed. The Joint Chiefs of Staff began staging mil-

lions of troops, many of them from Europe, for the final attacks on Japan. In addition, intelligence experts initiated an elaborate deception plan, code-named PASTEL-TWO, to confuse the Japanese about just where and when the Americans would land. MacArthur's staff planned to broadcast fictitious radio reports, arrange misleading news stories, and drop psychological-warfare pamphlets on the coast of China and later the Japanese island of Shikoku. This false information would suggest that the United States, rather than immediately invading Kyushu or Honshu, was pursuing a strategy of encirclement, blockade, and bombardment of the enemy homeland by capturing and setting up bases on the China coast and Shikoku. There were plans made for a sham airborne corps on Okinawa; men on the island would build dozens of dummy gliders to trick the

> "I am getting ready to go see Stalin and Churchill, and it is a chore. I have to take my tuxedo, tails,…high hat, low hat, and hard hat, as well as sundry other things."
>
> HARRY S. TRUMAN, SHORTLY BEFORE THE BIG THREE CONFERENCE IN POTSDAM, GERMANY

Japanese into expecting a full-scale airborne attack.

The Japanese, however, would not be fooled. By June 1945 they had accurately predicted that the United States would invade Kyushu, although they were not certain when. In preparation for the expected onslaught they dug in ever deeper, training special suicide attack forces, including kamikaze aircraft, manned torpedoes launched by a submarine but controlled by their occupants for greater maneuverability, and suicide frogmen, who would swim up to a landing craft and detonate it with a stickbomb. Local men, women, and children were organized into a civilian home defense force and told to fight out the invasion and even work as guerrilla fighters if necessary. They were trained to attack soldiers with bamboo spears, swords, and hand grenades, to rush tanks with explosives or roll rocks down on them, to kick a man in his testicles or stab him in the pit of the stomach. One 15-year-old Japanese girl was told, "If you don't kill at least one enemy soldier, you don't deserve to die!"

By this point Japan realized that it was doomed to be defeated militarily. Knowing it could not drive the Americans from the beaches, it hoped to inflict such high casualties in the first few days that the invaders would settle for a negotiated peace rather than an unconditional surrender.

I am getting ready to go see Stalin and Churchill, and it is a chore," Truman wrote his mother on July 3. "I have to take my tuxedo, tails, . . . high hat, low hat, and hard hat, as well as sundry other things." The Big Three—the United States, Great Britain, and the Soviet Union—were meeting in Potsdam, Germany, to discuss the fate of postwar Europe, including what would prove to be contentious territorial disputes and the continuing war with the Japanese. Truman did not look forward to going. The whole conference would be a disaster, he knew, if he let Stalin—or Churchill, for that matter—outnegotiate him. Congress was suspicious that President Truman, like his predecessor, would make international deals that he would reveal to the Hill only when and as it suited him. Moreover, Truman believed that the average American did not like to see the president "cavorting abroad, at state dinners in royal palaces," as his daughter, Margaret, phrased it. But it was his job, and on July 7, he boarded the cruiser USS *Augusta* for the eight-day passage to Europe.

Truman found little to lift his mood upon his arrival in Berlin. The bombed-out city was a haunting reminder of the devastation wrought by weapons of war. He had never seen such utter ruin. The women, children, and old men scavenging in the rubble, carting about their few remaining possessions, depressed him the most. "Wish you and Margie were here," he wrote his wife. "But it is a forlorn place and would only make you sad."

The Truman women probably would have been disheartened by the quarters the president and his entourage were assigned. Number 2 Kaiserstrasse, a three-story, turn-of-the-century stucco villa in Babelsberg, a Berlin suburb near Potsdam, was built near a lovely lake, but that was its only redeeming fea-

Corporal Henry Bahe Jr. *(left)* and Private First Class George H. Kirk, both Navajos from Arizona, operate a portable radio in a jungle clearing on Bougainville in December 1943.

TALK SILENT, SPEAK SWIFT, STAY ALIVE

Pacific commanders realized early in the war that the Japanese had broken or stolen U.S. secret codes and were easily deciphering vital military communications. A new, foolproof system was needed. But instead of turning to experts in cryptography, the marines placed their faith in a people whose language few others understood: the Navajo.

The first Navajo marine recruits were suspicious when ordered to develop a Navajo code. After all, as children they had been punished for speaking their native tongue in government schools. Assured the war need was real, however, they set to work. The system they created was not a simple translation but a code based on their native vocabulary, using words they could easily associate with military terms. Thus, a bomber plane became *jay-sho,* or "buzzard," and a battleship *lo-tso,* or "whale." To supplement the code they came up with an alphabet, to be employed when parts of a message had to be spelled out. Navajo words designated the first letter in their English counterparts: *woll-a-chee,* Navajo for "ant," stood for the letter *a,* and *shush,* or "bear," the letter *b.*

The Navajo code talkers hit beaches from Guadalcanal to Okinawa, sending messages with amazing speed and accuracy. And the enemy could not translate or easily stop them. "Sometimes we had to crawl, had to run, had to lie partly submerged in a swamp . . . pinned under fire," said one code talker. "We transmitted our messages under any and all conditions." Because their work was veiled in secrecy, the Navajo received little recognition. Their task, said one marine officer, was to "talk silent, speak swift, stay alive."

ture. The official White House log condemned the bathroom facilities as "wholly inadequate," and guests fought losing battles with the swarms of mosquitoes that flew into the house through screenless windows. The general ambiance of the house itself was, as one reporter noted, "oppressive and awesome in its gloom." Unbeknown to the president, in the weeks before his arrival Russian soldiers had repeatedly terrorized the owner and his family and then given them scarcely an hour to pack up and get out. The Russians had then stripped the villa of all its priceless objects and replaced them with a hodgepodge of heavy furnishings and somber art collected from neighboring homes. Truman, who thought the Germans had ruined the architecture of what was basically a French chateau, described the interior as a "nightmare."

Still, the Little White House, as it came to be called, served its purpose. On July 16, the day after his arrival, Harry Truman met Winston Churchill for the first time. Churchill wanted to be at the top of the new president's agenda, so Truman suggested meeting at 11:00 a.m. Mary Churchill, acting as the prime minister's chauffeur, noted wryly that her father had not been up that early in a decade.

Churchill, who had been so close to Franklin Roosevelt and had come from a similarly privileged background, was pleased to find himself favorably impressed by the new president. "He says he is sure he can work with him," Mary Churchill gushed in a letter to her mother. "I nearly wept with joy and thankfulness, it seemed like divine providence. Perhaps it is FDR's legacy. I can see Papa is relieved and confident." Churchill's own brief record confirms his daughter's glowing account. "He seems," Churchill wrote of Truman, "a man of exceptional character."

For his part, the more reserved midwesterner characterized Churchill's effusive comments during their meeting as "a lot of hooey about how great my country is and how he loved Roosevelt and how he intended to love me, etc., etc." Almost in spite of himself, though, Truman was somewhat charmed by Churchill and judged that they could "get along if he doesn't try to give me too much soft soap."

Late that evening, Truman was resting at the Babelsberg house when an excited Henry Stimson hurried in with a top-secret cable from George Harrison, a special assistant in Washington, D.C. "Operated on this morning," the cable read. "Diagnosis not complete but results seem satisfactory and already exceed expectations." Before taking the telegram to the president, the secretary of war had joked to an aide that he no longer feared imprisonment for the misuse of the billions of dollars that Senator Truman had been upset about a few years earlier.

Harrison's cryptic message, decoded, meant: The atomic bomb worked; the Manhattan Project had succeeded. But Truman would have to wait for a follow-up report to learn further details.

Just before noon the next day, as Truman sat writing at a desk in his second-floor suite, he glanced up from his papers and was surprised to see standing in the doorway a graying, mustached man who was dressed in army khakis with red seams running down the legs of the trousers. Generalissimo Joseph Stalin had delayed his arrival in Potsdam—in order to emphasize his own importance, some said—but was now slightly early for his meeting with the president. Truman immediately rose and crossed to shake his visitor's hand, noting with interest that the Soviet leader was "a little bit of a squirt," about four inches shorter than Truman's own modest height of five feet nine inches.

With their interpreters hovering, the American president offered the Soviet leader a seat in an overstuffed chair, then seated himself. After some attempts at small talk failed to break the ice, Truman declared that he hoped to deal with Stalin as a friend. "I am no diplomat," he told his guest, indi-

In Potsdam's vast Cecilienhof Palace in late July 1945, Harry Truman *(bottom center)*, Winston Churchill *(far left)*, and Joseph Stalin *(far right)* attempt to hammer out agreements on the fate of postwar Europe. Before the conference ended, Churchill's party would lose an election, stripping him of the prime ministership, and Clement R. Attlee would replace him at Potsdam. Truman was not happy with this turn of events. "If Stalin should suddenly cash in," he wrote in his diary, "it would end the original Big Three."

cating he usually gave a straight yes-or-no answer to questions rather than beating around the bush. Stalin, who was still recovering from a mild heart attack and appeared stiff and tired, looked pleased for the first time during their conversation. Truman in turn was pleased with the Soviet leader, whom he assessed to be "honest—but as smart as hell" and was certain he could work with. Before his departure, Stalin repeatedly emphasized that Russia would enter the Pacific war by mid-August.

But Soviet help, which Truman had once sought, now appeared superfluous. On the morning of July 18 Truman was still at breakfast when Stimson arrived with a second cable from Harrison:

"Doctor has just returned most enthusiastic and confident that the little boy is as husky as his big brother. The light in his eyes discernible from here

sure they will when Manhattan appears over their homeland." Until receiving word of the successful test, Truman had been able to discuss the weapon only in hypothetical terms. Even now it was difficult for him or anyone else to grasp the full magnitude of this new destructive force. Dwelling uneasily among the remnants of a bombed-out Berlin, he considered the chilling implications. "We have discovered the most terrible bomb in the history of the world," he wrote in his diary. But the fast-mounting toll of casualties in the Pacific—in the last three months they had reached almost half the number of casualties in that theater for the previous three years combined—pressed him to decide quickly whether to use this awful weapon.

After receiving Harrison's second cable, Truman went to deliver the news to Winston Churchill.

"Doctor has just returned most enthusiastic and confident that the little boy is as husky as his big brother. The light in his eyes discernible from here to Highhold and I could have heard his screams from here to my farm."

GEORGE HARRISON, IN A CODED CABLE TO HENRY STIMSON FOLLOWING THE TRINITY TEST

to Highhold and I could have heard his screams from here to my farm."

Transmitted during the night, the cable had shocked the decoding officer at the army message center. Had the aged Stimson become a father? In fact, the wire did contain news of a birth—the birth of the atomic age. Harrison's message told Truman that the light from the July 16 test had been visible for 250 miles, the distance from Washington to Highhold, Stimson's Long Island estate. The sound had carried some 50 miles, the distance from the capital to Harrison's farm in Upperville, Virginia. The attending "doctor" was General Leslie Groves. Furthermore, the physicists were certain that the second atomic bomb, code-named Little Boy, would be just as deadly as its predecessor. And this was the bomb that would be dropped on Japan.

Truman confided to his diary that evening, "Believe Japs will fold up before Russia comes in. I am

Over lunch, the two agreed that Stalin ought to be told about the bomb, but Churchill insisted that Truman should reveal none of the "particulars." The prime minister suggested relaying the news in a timely fashion—but how should it be conveyed? In writing or face to face? At a formal meeting or in a casual discussion? Truman allowed as how he would just wait for an appropriate moment after one of the scheduled meetings.

As the Potsdam Conference dragged into its second week, the participants actively sparring over the final disposition of European territories, Truman held behind-the-scenes meetings with his advisers about the atomic bomb. General Groves had proposed three possible target cities: Kyoto, Hiroshima, and Nagasaki. But Stimson urged that Kyoto, Japan's religious and cultural capital, be spared. Destroying this city would mean eliminating hundreds of Buddhist and Shinto temples and shrines as well as

"DEATH, THE DESTROYER OF WORLDS"

Standing in a bunker in New Mexico, on July 16, 1945, a tense Robert Oppenheimer heard the countdown begin. It was 5:10 a.m., and in 20 minutes the world's first atomic bomb would drop from a 100-foot tower five and a half miles away. In Potsdam, Germany, President Harry Truman waited for news of the test. Oppenheimer, physicist and civilian head of the Manhattan Project, hoped that, after an investment of three years and two billion dollars, the bomb would not fail.

Earlier in the project, a more horrifying concern had haunted Oppenheimer and his team of physicists. Could the detonation of a nuclear bomb, they wondered, create enough heat to ignite the atmosphere and destroy the planet? Early calculations suggested it might. But as work proceeded on the bomb, relieved physicists finally determined that neither the extreme pressures nor the temperature would be high enough to trigger annihilation.

In 1944 Oppenheimer and his team explored possible test sites, settling on a desolate New Mexico area named Jornada del Muerto—Journey of Death. Construction on the site, which came to be called Trinity, began in November. Eight months later both site and bomb were ready. The test was scheduled for July 16, only to be threatened by a violent thunderstorm. But pressure against any delay forced the scientists to give the go-ahead, and the bomb's timing mechanism was set.

At 5:29:45 a.m. the atomic explosion gouged a crater a half-mile wide and killed every living thing within a one-mile radius. With a payload of a mere 12 pounds of plutonium, the bomb had released as much energy as 18,500 tons of TNT. Watching his creation explode in the predawn sky, Robert Oppenheimer remembered a line from the Bhagavad-Gita: "I am become Death, the destroyer of worlds."

Following the July 16, 1945, atomic test, physicist Robert Oppenheimer and General Leslie Groves *(right)* examine the remains of the site, known as Trinity. The blast produced a massive cloud *(above)* that rose 38,000 feet in seven minutes and a flash of light seen in three states. "One felt as though he had been privileged to witness the Birth of the World," wrote *New York Times* journalist William Laurence, "—to be present at the moment of Creation when the Lord said: 'Let there be Light.' "

other landmarks dating back to the city's founding in 793. Stimson was concerned about more than just Kyoto, however. He had earlier argued that the United States should warn the Japanese about the bomb and negotiate a surrender that would allow them to keep their emperor. Other top officials rejected both the warning and the retention of Hirohito. Truman listened, and although he would agree not to drop the bomb on Kyoto or Tokyo, he sided with those who argued that negotiating with the Japanese over terms would be a waste of time.

On the morning of July 24, Truman, Churchill, and their respective military advisers sat around the dining table in the Little White House and formalized the decision that seemed to have been settled tacitly already: The bomb would be used, and sometime in the next few weeks. Late that afternoon all three Allied leaders met in the huge, dimly lit reception hall of the forbidding Cecilienhof Palace, former summer residence of Crown Prince Wilhelm of Prussia. As the conversation turned to operations against Japan, Truman knew the time had come to reveal his secret to Stalin. At the close of the meeting he gathered his papers and walked around the enormous table to face the Soviet leader.

"I casually mentioned to Stalin that we had a new weapon of unusual destructive force," Truman recorded. "The Russian Premier showed no special interest. All he said was that he was glad to hear it and he hoped we would make 'good use of it against the Japanese.' "

When Truman walked outside to wait for his car, an anxious Churchill asked, "How did it go?"

"He never asked a question," shrugged Truman.

What neither man realized was that Stalin did not need to ask any questions. For some time a German-born spy at the Manhattan Project's headquarters at Los Alamos, Klaus Fuchs, had been feeding Stalin information about the atomic bomb, thus greatly accelerating Russia's own nuclear-development project.

On July 26 the United States, Britain, and China (the Soviet Union had not yet officially entered the war against Japan) issued the Potsdam Declaration.

Based on the memo Truman had asked John McCloy to prepare for the State Department back in June, it assured the Japanese people that they would not be "enslaved as a race or destroyed as a nation." Although the document promised the Japanese they would "be given an opportunity to lead a peaceful and productive life," it left the fate of Emperor Hirohito deliberately unclear. The only alternative to accepting these terms was to face "prompt and utter destruction." The declaration remained silent, however, as to what form this "utter destruction" might take.

While American planes dropped millions of pamphlets with a translation of the declaration over Tokyo and other Japanese cities, the Japanese prime minister and his cabinet gathered for an all-day meeting. In the end, the government found the terms unacceptable. The prime minister delivered a brief statement to the press explaining that as the government did not find "any important value" in the Potsdam Declaration, they had chosen to "ignore it entirely."

Now it was time for Truman, the inveterate poker player, to show his ace, releasing his order to drop the bomb. On the morning of July 31 he handed an aide a message for transmission to Washington. The president had it penciled on the back of a pink message slip, and the aide took no particular notice of it except to note that Truman obviously did not want anything happening until he was well away from Potsdam. Addressed to Stimson, the cable read simply, "Release when ready but not sooner than August 2. HST."

A horrified William "Deak" Parsons watched on the night of August 4 as an overloaded B-29 crashed just after takeoff, lighting up the night sky in an explosion of bombs, torpedoes, and incendiaries that killed everyone aboard. It was one of several B-29 crashes the 44-year-old navy captain had witnessed since arriving on the Pacific island of Tinian in the Marianas only a few days before. In his mind's eye, Parsons could envision yet another heavily laden B-29 straining to break free of gravity and failing. But when this one crashed, it would destroy half the island and its inhabitants.

The tall and lean chief of the Ordnance Division of the Manhattan Project could vividly imagine such an explosion because he had witnessed one only 19 days earlier in the New Mexico desert. And just that afternoon at a 3:00 briefing he had described the results to a specially trained group of experienced airmen gathered in a Quonset hut. Standing at the front of the meeting, a tense-looking Parsons began by saying, "The bomb you are going to drop is something new in the history of warfare. It is the most destructive weapon ever produced. We think it will knock out almost everything in a three-mile area." A collective gasp rose from his audience.

The captain then motioned to a waiting projectionist. "The film you are about to see—" he began. A clattering noise sounded through the room, and Parsons turned to find the celluloid film hopelessly tan-

must remain ignorant of the full import of Special Bombing Mission 13 for one more day. Standing at Parsons's side, however, was a man fully aware of the mission's nature, Lieutenant Colonel Paul Tibbets.

Eleven months earlier, in September 1944, Tibbets had sat in a Colorado Springs office being interviewed by Parsons for command of a unit specifically formed to wage atomic war. Parsons and his colleagues selected Tibbets for the job despite the fact that the wavy-haired officer was only 29—on the face of it too young to command such an important mission. But the man exuded an air of cool confidence, efficiency, and reliability and had proved himself to be one of the air force's best pilots. He had conducted the first B-17 bombing sortie from England to Europe, had flown Eisenhower to Gibraltar before the North Africa invasion, and had led the first bombing mission of that

"I casually mentioned to Stalin that we had a new weapon of unusual destructive force. The Russian Premier showed no special interest. All he said was that he was glad to hear it and he hoped we would make 'good use of it against the Japanese.'"

HARRY S. TRUMAN, AFTER THE BIG THREE CONFERENCE IN POTSDAM, GERMANY

gled in the sprockets of the machine. "The film you are *not* about to see," he continued wryly, earning a shout of nervous laughter, "was made of the only test we have performed." The laughter died as Parsons described the explosive fireball and its effects. "A soldier 10,000 feet away was knocked off his feet. Another soldier more than five miles away was temporarily blinded. A girl in a town many miles away who had been blind all her life saw a flash of light."

Reaching into a cardboard box, he pulled out a pair of tinted goggles that looked like welder's safety glasses. Every man aboard a plane anywhere near the explosion must wear these, he cautioned. "No one knows exactly what will happen when the bomb is dropped from the air. That has never been done before," he warned.

Although he explained the effects of the weapon in vivid detail, Parsons nonetheless refrained from using the word *atomic*. The men making the strike

invasion. In addition, he had been test-piloting the B-29 for more than a year and knew all the idiosyncrasies of the new bomber.

While Parsons returned to Los Alamos to continue work on the bomb, Colonel Tibbets established a training camp for the members of his new 509th Composite Group at an airfield in Wendover, Utah. So remote that comedian Bob Hope had dubbed it Leftover Field in a USO show, this outpost was isolated enough to ensure maximum security. Everyone received strict orders not to discuss this top-secret mission although all the majority of them had been told was that it could end the war. But every detail of the operation, no matter how small, was fiercely guarded. Unknown to the members of the 509th, Wendover authorities routinely monitored telephone calls, private conversations, and mail. When surveillance measures caught a few soldiers who could not keep their mouths shut, they

Captain William "Deak" Parsons, chief of the Manhattan Project's Ordnance Division *(standing, left),* and Colonel Paul Tibbets *(standing, right)* brief crewmen in August 1945 about their secret mission to Japan. On August 6 Tibbets, Parsons, and the crew took off in the *Enola Gay (below),* carrying a bomb called Little Boy.

were summarily packed up and shipped off to Alaska for the war's duration.

In May 1945 the unit left for Tinian to spend three months flying training missions. Other units stationed there grew suspicious of the 509th, questioning why other men risked their lives daily in Japanese skies while this "bunch of pampered dandies" flew only training runs with occasional flights over enemy territory. Resentful airmen hurled insults at Tibbets's men and tossed rocks on the tin roofs of their private Quonset huts in the middle of the night. Angered, the "dandies" evidently indicated they were there to win the war for America. A sarcastic poem soon circled the island, the final verse ending, "We should have been home a month or more, / For the 509th is winning the war." Tibbets's fuming fliers could only bite their tongues and wait it out.

By the day of Parsons's briefing in August their wait was almost over. Word came down that the mission would leave on August 6. On the morning of August 5, with the memory of four B-29 crashes from the night before still vivid in his mind, Parsons walked into a meeting with General Thomas Farrell, Admiral William Purnell, Tibbets, and several others.

"If we crack up and the plane catches fire," Parsons said emphatically, "there is danger of an atomic explosion that could wipe out half of this island."

Grimacing, Farrell replied, "We will just have to pray that doesn't happen."

But Parsons did not plan to depend solely on spiritual help. "If I made the final assembly of the bomb after we left the island, it couldn't happen."

"Are you sure you can do it?" asked the general.

"No," Deak Parsons admitted to him, "but I've got all day to learn."

Farrell hesitated. He and the others worried about Parsons working on an extremely sensitive mechanism in a cramped bomb bay while the B-29 rode out whatever the elements might throw its way. In the end, though, Farrell gave his consent; how could he argue with a man who wanted to safeguard lives? What Parsons had not told Farrell was that he had waited until the last minute to mention the change in plans so General Groves, back in the States, could not countermand the decision. Two months before, Groves had specifically shot down the idea of arming the bomb in flight, considering it too dangerous.

It was up to Parsons now to minimize that risk. The ordnance chief had earned a reputation for meticulous dedication to any given task, analyzing and testing until he had solved the problem. Carrying two compact containers, one holding tools and the other a detonator and the bomb's propellant

charge, he climbed aboard B-29 number 82. There he lowered himself into the dark, stifling bomb bay where Little Boy awaited him. Belying its name, Little Boy measured 10 feet long and 20 inches in diameter and crushed the scales at 9,000 pounds. Engineers had expanded the airplane's bomb bay to accommodate the dull gunmetal gray behemoth, which hung from a hook in the ceiling. Over the next several hours Parsons repeatedly went through the numerous steps necessary to arm the atomic bomb. When he finally emerged, his hands were cut and bleeding from handling sharp metal edges. Farrell, waiting on the tarmac outside, took one look at the captain's hands and offered to loan him a pair of pigskin gloves, adding, "They're thin ones."

"I wouldn't dare," Parsons replied. "I've got to feel the touch."

Just after 1:00 a.m. on August 6, Parsons and Tibbets drove to the Tinian runway to prepare for takeoff. The navy captain and air force colonel were shocked by what they saw. There sat their B-29, about to carry out the highest-security mission of the entire war, surrounded by cameramen and floodlights. Tibbets almost expected "to see MGM's lion walk on to the apron or Warner's logo light up the sky." General Groves had said that there would be "a little publicity." This was nothing short of a Hollywood premiere.

"What's going on?" Parsons demanded. A photographer rudely shoved the captain against one of the airplane's wheels.

"Smile!" he said. "You're going to be famous."

Parsons turned angrily away and walked toward the plane's nose ladder to get aboard. He was stopped by Farrell, who noticed the captain had forgotten his side arm. No one flew over enemy territory, where his plane might be shot down, without a personal weapon. An MP offered his pistol, and Parsons strapped it on.

Another precaution had been taken for this special mission. In his pocket Paul Tibbets carried a small pillbox filled with cyanide capsules, one for each member of the crew except Parsons, who carried his own in a matchbox. The crew had not been informed about the capsules. They would be told only if they were forced to land in or bail out over Japan. Then the men on board could choose to commit suicide, by capsule or pistol, rather than face possible torture and reveal their secrets to Japanese interrogators.

But Japan was still hours away. First they had to get the B-29, dangerously overloaded, safely off the runway and airborne. Its crew had only to look at the four charred skeletons of the B-29s that had crashed less than 36 hours earlier to be reminded of what might go wrong.

Observers watching from the control tower grew nervous as Tibbets sped down the airfield without lifting off. Farrell was certain he had never seen a plane "use that much runway." Even Tibbets's co-pilot, Bob Lewis, hands tensing, was worried; he knew the runway ended in a cliff, with only the ocean below. With barely 100 feet to spare, Tibbets finally eased back on the yoke, lifting the plane easily into a steady climb. He had deliberately held the overloaded airplane down until the last moment, milking every possible bit of speed from its straining engines to ensure that they would not become the newest corpse in the B-29 graveyard.

Just before 3:00 a.m., only minutes after taking off, Deak Parsons lowered himself into the plane's unheated, unpressurized bomb bay. His ordnance assistant, Lieutenant Morris Jeppson, followed behind with a flashlight. Parsons knelt to unscrew the rear plate of Little Boy and gingerly inserted a charge of gunpowder. When detonated, this charge would send a six-inch slug of uranium shaped like a can of soup flying through a larger uranium ring, setting off the chain reaction to cause the biggest explosion the world had ever seen.

With the plane's engines thundering in his ears and Jeppson handing him tools, Parsons worked carefully and silently, concentrating completely on his task. Little Boy had more built-in safety devices than any weapon ever produced, but this was the first time he had ever assembled the fusing mechanism at a cruising altitude of 4,700 feet.

Sailors, reporters, and officers from all the Allied countries crowd the deck of the USS *Missouri* during Japan's formal surrender on September 2, 1945, in Tokyo Bay. Two Japanese representatives signed the surrender documents, followed by MacArthur, Nimitz, and other Allied officers. "The morning had dawned with a gray overcast . . . ," wrote one correspondent. "But as the last name was written, the sun burned through brilliantly."

Parsons completed his part of the assembly in about 20 minutes; the final touches would fall to Jeppson in a few hours. As they had been the day before, Parsons's hands were cut up and covered with the graphite used to lubricate the movable parts of the weapon. That day he had joked, perhaps with a twinge of guilt, that he would just have to bomb Japan with "dirty hands." He had no jokes this time.

Parsons had devoted more than two years to the project, and he harbored serious doubts about what he was undertaking. He abhorred the idea of playing Dr. Frankenstein, of creating a monster that might someday destroy the world. But he realized as he sped toward Japan that there was no turning back now.

Three B-29s were flying ahead to serve as weather scouts; their reports on cloud cover would determine where the bomb would drop. In addition, two more B-29s carrying photographic and laboratory equipment were accompanying Tibbets's plane to the target site to record the event. A seventh B-29 was waiting on Iwo Jima, to serve as an alternate; if the original strike plane developed a problem, the bomb would be switched to the backup craft.

Among Tibbets's crew, the atmosphere seemed relaxed. Once safely aloft there was little for most of them to do but sit and wait. The monotonous drone of the engines put Tibbets to sleep soon after he had handed the controls to his copilot. However, in the cockpit was the crew's collection of good-luck charms from Wendover Field: three pairs of silk panties with a pamphlet on VD; a pinup photo of the scantily clad "Wendover Mary," who had befriended several members of the 509th in Utah; six prophylactic kits; and one lucky ski cap purchased in Salt Lake City. Even Tibbets had added his own charm the day before. The usually reserved pilot had been thinking of his red-haired mother, whose quiet confidence had always been a source of strength for him. And he remembered what she had said when he decided to become a pilot. "I know you will be all right, son." So on the nose of his plane, Tibbets put her name: Enola Gay.

About an hour after waking up Tibbets circled over Iwo and looked down to see the imposing Mount Suribachi. As the *Enola Gay* rendezvoused here with the photographic and laboratory planes, the crew still remained officially ignorant of the secret they carried. The three B-29s fell into a V formation just before 6:00 a.m. as a red sun appeared over the island.

The planes roared north. Jeppson slipped back into the bomb bay to finish the delicate operation Parsons had initiated a few hours earlier. A reserved and religious young officer on his first combat mission, Jeppson shared some of his superior's ambivalence about the bomb. He had studied enough science at Harvard, Yale, and MIT not only to have penetrated early the secrecy shrouding it but also to fear the long-term consequences of radiation exposure.

But now, as he inched along the bomb bay catwalk to the middle of Little Boy, he could afford no uncertainty. With infinite care he unscrewed three green safety plugs from the weapon and replaced them with three red ones. As he secured the last plug firmly in its casing, he reflected that "this *was* a moment." The electrical circuit to the bomb's fusing chain was now activated.

Parsons went to tell Tibbets and found the pilot, feet propped up in the cockpit, calmly smoking a pipe of his favorite English tobacco. Upon hearing that Little Boy was fully armed, Tibbets turned on the intercom to make his announcement to the crew. Finally, after months of evasion, he could say the words: "We are carrying the world's first atomic bomb."

A few men let out exclamations of surprise. Warning them that their conversations from then on would be recorded, Tibbets cautioned, "This is for history, so watch your language."

The crew spent the next hour in suspense as they waited for the weather reports that would determine their target city. Even before their destination was confirmed, the *Enola Gay* and her two companions began climbing to a bombing height of six miles. At 7:25 a.m. a coded message from one of the weather planes finally came crackling over the radio.

For once even the imperturbable Tibbets sounded excited as he switched on the intercom and reported: "It's Hiroshima!" ◆

VICTORY IN EUROPE, VICTORY OVER JAPAN

*"The news came this afternoon out at camp, came with a shouting and hailing but without surprise.
There's not the celebrating in the streets tonight...just happy relief, and that's even better."*

PRIVATE BARRIE GREENBIE WRITING FROM THE PHILIPPINES TO HIS WIFE, AUGUST 14, 1945

For many Americans in 1945 the idea of a world at peace seemed almost as incomprehensible as the concept of total war had been before the attack on Pearl Harbor. After years of rationing, training, fighting, and dying, V-J—Victory over Japan—Day had at last arrived. "This is the great day," declared Harry Truman on the evening of August 14. "This is the day we have been looking for since December 7, 1941. This is the day when fascism and police government ceases in the world. This is the day for the democracies." The president's announcement of the Japanese surrender was greeted with relief, thanksgiving, and nationwide celebration.

Just three months earlier Berlin had fallen to the Allies and the Nazis had surrendered. But except in New York City, Victory in Europe Day had been celebrated with restraint, and in Washington, D.C., government offices remained open. The war, most realized, was only half finished. Many of the troops leaving Europe following Germany's collapse were scheduled to be redeployed for a massive invasion of Japan; as many as five million soldiers, sailors, and airmen were slated for the invasion of the island nation, and casualty estimates were fearfully high.

Invasion had proved unnecessary, however, and when the Japanese capitulated after the United States dropped a second atomic bomb, on the city of Nagasaki, soldiers' thoughts quickly turned to home. Those thoughts were perhaps the sweetest for men who had been prisoners of war. For most, like the airman above shown kissing the ground upon his arrival back in the States, war's end meant reunion with friends and family—and a chance to relax and savor the idea of peace.

After the euphoria of V-J Day had died down, thousands of smaller, more intimate thanksgivings took place in homes across the country, as the boys returned from Europe and Asia. Here and on the pages that follow is a look back on that great time of celebration through the letters and remembrances of the people who lived it.

FREEDOM AT LAST

*"The only thing you talked about is, What're ya gonna do?
Where you gonna eat as soon as you get back? Everybody was goin' to Frisco.
They wanted to go to Fisherman's Wharf. Everybody wanted to get
some fried oysters or a big steak."*

ANTON BILEK, FORMER POW IN THE PACIFIC THEATER

NEAR FRANKFURT, GERMANY, an American GI who had been liberated from a Nazi prison camp joyfully begins to do the paperwork that was the first step in the processing of ex-prisoners.

MARCHING OUT OF A JAPANESE PRISON, American POWs begin the first leg of their long journey home, some shouldering precious food rations. "We hovered on the brink of tears and laughter," recalled one man, "not daring to give way to either for fear we could not stop."

NEW YORKERS THRONG WALL STREET under a storm of ticker tape on V-E Day, their spirits undampened by President Truman's caution that victory was "but half won."

THE HOME FRONT REJOICES

"In New York, half-a-million people flooded into Times Square to celebrate. In Washington, the streets were quiet. V-E Day was not even a holiday. Government employees were ordered to report to work as usual."

NEWSMAN DAVID BRINKLEY REMEMBERING V-E DAY

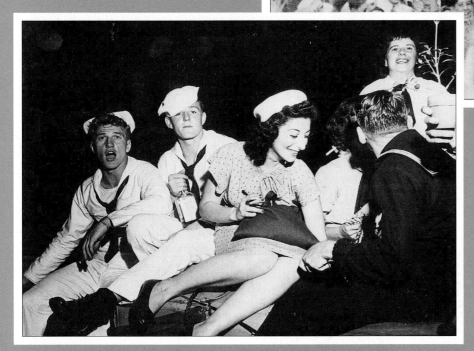

"The streets filled with people shouting, singing, running about not certain what to do but looking frantically for ways to express their relief and their joy. A crowd on F Street spontaneously sang "The Star-Spangled Banner." ...Young servicemen embraced and kissed women they passed by in the streets."

BRINKLEY ON V-J DAY IN WASHINGTON

ON F STREET in Washington, D.C. *(above, right)*, pandemonium breaks out following the announcement of V-J Day, and a group of celebrators still going strong that night hitch a ride on top of a car.

THE VOYAGE STATESIDE

"I hope to be on a boat by the 25th at least....don't tell anybody, but I am sorta scared of that boat ride.
You know to tell you the truth, I never did like big boats and transocean trips, 'cause I am a landlubber, I guess!
Anything though, I'll ride a bathtub home if I could, I've just got to get there."

LIEUTENANT CHARLES TAYLOR IN A LETTER TO HIS WIFE, OCTOBER 1, 1945

AS THEIR SHIP MOVES UP THE HUDSON RIVER to its dock, the skyline of midtown Manhattan greets soldiers who were maimed in the war.

EAGER TO GLIMPSE THE NEW YORK SKYLINE, returning servicemen cover every square inch of deck space on the *Queen Mary*. The use of the English luxury liner to transport Americans back to the States caused resentment overseas among British troops, many of whom had a long wait for transport home.

A DISABLED SOLDIER RETURNS to his old neighborhood and the proud embrace of his family. Nearly 700,000 American men and women were wounded in action.

HOME AT LAST

"There are so many little things I want to do—smell the lake at night, feel the air, drink in just lots of sun, be on the beach and feel the sand between my toes, get all burned and feel the sting of the sheet on my back, or sit in church and hear the preacher with my ears, and think about where I'll be hunting the next day."

LIEUTENANT CHARLES TAYLOR IN A LETTER TO HIS WIFE, OCTOBER 7, 1945

IN HAWAII, Sergeant Howard Kiyama is tearfully welcomed home by his father after the close of the war. Kiyama served in the 442d Division, a much decorated Japanese American unit that fought in Europe.

A RETURNING SERVICEMAN lucky enough to catch a rare plane ride home leaps from the stairway into the arms of his waiting family.

"Mother and Dad had a huge party to celebrate their twenty-fifth anniversary, and my homecoming. There were hundreds of people at our home...and as we greeted our friends, I remembered the little things of the homecoming...the warm light in Mother's eyes, the proudness that shone in Dad's face—I was home at last, I was home to stay."

SERGEANT NEWTON MINOW, PACIFIC THEATER VETERAN, JUNE 12, 1946

AGAINST A NIGHT SKY, navy rockets, flares, and searchlights announce V-J Day in Pearl Harbor, marking the end of fighting for Americans in the place where the war began.

CELEBRATION AT PEARL HARBOR

"To see fascism defeated, nothing better could have happened to a human being. You felt you were doing something worthwhile. You felt you were an actor in a tremendous drama that was unfolding. It was the most important moment in my life. I always felt lucky to have been part of it."

WALTER ROSENBLUM, VETERAN OF D-DAY

THE LEGACY OF WAR

Anna Roosevelt Boettiger threw a surprise sixty-third birthday party for her father, Franklin, aboard the USS *Quincy* on the evening of January 30, 1945. Instead of one cake, there were five, four representing his past and present terms as president, and the fifth decorated with a question mark. Though clearly tired and worn, Roosevelt seemed delighted with everything, including his gift: a map tracing his present journey from the United States to the Crimean town of Yalta.

The trip to this remote port on the Black Sea for a Big Three conference was a strenuous undertaking for the ailing Roosevelt. But Joseph Stalin had refused to meet the American president and Winston Churchill anywhere else. And Roosevelt had three important goals to accomplish face to face with the Soviet leader: securing the future of the United Na-

tions for the sake of world peace; persuading the Soviet Union to enter the Pacific war so it could be brought to an early end; and restoring the independence of Poland, which had been invaded by Germany in 1939 and was now occupied by Soviet troops, along with the rest of Eastern Europe.

Stalin came to Yalta demanding not one vote in the fledgling United Nations but 17—one for the USSR as a whole, and one for each of the 16 Soviet republics. Roosevelt knew that the U.S. Senate would never vote to join the organization under those circumstances, but to his surprise Stalin compromised, agreeing to accept only two extra votes, for the Ukraine and Belorussia.

Stalin promised to wage war with the Allies against Japan. But Soviet participation would cost dearly: America and Britain must sanction Russian expansion into Japanese and Chinese territory. With the atomic bomb untested and its potential for cutting the war short an open question, Roosevelt felt compelled to agree, and Churchill gave his consent as well.

The prime minister's major concern was not the Far East but postwar Europe. Churchill had asked before Yalta, "What are we going to have between the white snows of Russia and the white cliffs of Dover?" It became increasingly clear as the conference proceeded that England would not be buffered by an independent Poland. Although Stalin promised free Polish elections, he would not bind himself to a timetable. Roosevelt, chided later by his military aide for allowing this ominous loophole, replied, "It's the best I can do for Poland at this time." With Poland's future in question, Churchill sought to strengthen France. At his insistence, the French would be given a zone of occupation along with the United States, Britain, and the USSR when a defeated Germany was partitioned.

"We have wound up the Conference—successfully I think," the president reported to his wife, Eleanor, after the week-long meeting had ended on February 11. "I am a bit exhausted but really all right." Many analysts would soon disagree strenuously with FDR's assessment of Yalta, claiming he had conceded far too much to Stalin. And his reassuring words about his own condition proved wrong. Within two months, Roosevelt was dead.

When the war ended, the Allies sought retribution for what they called crimes against peace and humanity. Benito Mussolini had been executed by Italian partisans on April 28 and Adolf Hitler had committed suicide two days later, but other military and civilian leaders of the Axis nations could, and would, be tried. In November 1945, 21 defendants went on trial in Nuremberg, Germany, before a military tribunal formed by the United States, the Soviet Union, Britain, and France. The evidence gathered from eyewitnesses, captured documents, photographs, and newsreels revealed the sadistic medical experiments, torture, murder, and systematic extermination visited upon millions of Jews, Gypsies, Slavs, homosexuals, and other victims by the defendants. Eleven of them were con-

demned to death, seven received prison terms, and three were acquitted. Twelve subsequent trials took place at Nuremberg, while elsewhere in Europe, hundreds of thousands of Nazi collaborators were tried, convicted, and sentenced to death or prison. In Tokyo, 11 nations formed another court, which tried 28 defendants over a period of 30 months, sentencing seven to death by hanging and 18 others to prison. Thousands of other Japanese throughout Asia received similar penalties for their actions during the war.

Yet even as Americans and Russians sat side by side in judgment of those who had committed crimes against peace and humanity, their own countries, now the world's most powerful, were bracing for a new struggle. By 1946 Stalin had crushed any hopes for democracy in Poland and the rest of Eastern Europe. "From Stettin in the Baltic to Trieste in the Adriatic, an iron curtain has descended across the Continent," Winston Churchill observed. Alarmed by the USSR's hard-line policies, America geared up for battle.

"I believe that it must be the policy of the United States to support free peoples who are resisting attempted subversion by armed minorities or by outside pressures," President Truman told a special joint session of Congress on March 12, 1947. Though specifically requesting money to help Greece and Turkey fight Communist domination, he was also declaring a new worldwide policy of Communist containment, known as the Truman Doctrine. Effective containment would depend greatly on a strong European economy, so the United States proposed a system of financial aid, commonly called the Marshall Plan, to help European nations recover from the war.

Then, in 1949, the United States, Canada, and most of Europe's non-Communist countries gave their common anti-Communist policy teeth by forming the military organization known as the North Atlantic Treaty Organization (NATO). In response, the USSR and its satellites signed bilateral defense agreements, replaced later by the Warsaw Pact.

Foreshadowed by Yalta, the Cold War was now full blown. For decades to come, the United States would remain locked in conflict with the USSR.

A GALLERY OF HEROES

For an entire generation of Americans, World War II was the defining experience of their lives. Whatever their backgrounds or the military ranks they achieved, whether they volunteered or were drafted, the millions of men and women who took part in the fight against fascism and imperialism were bound together by what they had seen, done, and endured. Their acts of courage and sacrifice were countless, and some who participated in the war gained the luster of fame for their great heroism. Others, already famous, only enhanced their reputations during their service in the military.

At right is a selection of prominent Americans from that war generation: two Hollywood movie stars, a record-breaking baseball player, the world heavyweight boxing champion, two future presidents, and a future U.S. senator. They were called on to serve their country in distinct ways and in different parts of the world. Their stories embody seven variations of American heroism.

GEORGE BUSH

From an early age, George Herbert Walker Bush had been taught the virtues of sacrifice. So great was his reputation for sharing snacks and treats with other children that he was nicknamed Have Half. And when war came in 1941, the 18-year-old showed the same sense of obligation to others: Fresh from prep school he enlisted in the navy and a year later earned his wings as the navy's youngest aviator.

"I got the impression that my instructor thought I was still too fuzz-faced to trust with an expensive piece of equipment," Bush said. But in the fall of 1943 he shipped out to the Pacific, where he flew 58 torpedo bombing missions, many in a plane he named *Barbie* after then fiancée Barbara Pierce. Years later, as the nation's commander in chief, President Bush would often refer to his wartime experiences, for which he received four medals, including the Distinguished Flying Cross: They were, he said, "good mental seat belts against future hawkishness."

JOE DiMAGGIO

When the famous New York Yankees hitter joined the Army Air Force in February 1943, his orders were clear: Hit home runs for God and country. And while other cadets competed for slots as bombardiers and pilots, Staff Sergeant Joe DiMaggio shipped out to Honolulu—and the starting lineup of the Seventh Air Force baseball team.

DiMaggio's commanding officer was just one of many U.S. generals and admirals who personally picked the ball teams that were such morale boosters for the other troops: When DiMaggio's air force team played the navy in June 1944, 20,000 fans cheered him on. The baseball star responded by hitting a home run that many in the crowd swore traveled 450 feet.

Playing for the air force was not like playing in Yankee Stadium, but DiMaggio still felt pressure. The stomach ulcers that had plagued him continued. He spent the last stretch of his service in and out of army hospitals.

CLARK GABLE

Before she died in a plane crash on a war bond tour, actress Carole Lombard told her husband, Clark Gable, to "get in this man's army." Grief-stricken, Gable decided to comply. "I'm going in," he told a friend after the accident. "And," he added, "I don't expect to come back."

In the summer of 1942, just three years after his performance as Rhett Butler in *Gone with the Wind*, a middle-aged Gable enlisted as a private in the Army Air Force, went through officer candidate school, and was sent to an air base in England. There he insisted on going on bombing missions over Europe, and displayed a worrisome recklessness. "The guy's crazy," despaired Gable's commanding officer. "He's trying to get himself killed."

Gable survived the war; and in June 1944, too old for combat, he was removed from active duty. He left the service with the rank of major and with an Air Medal "for superior performance of duty"—none of which, Gable insisted, made him a hero.

DANIEL INOUYE

America "has been good to us," Dan Inouye's father told him on the day the 18-year-old left to join the army. "And now it is you who must try to return the goodness." The young Hawaiian, who had worked with a first-aid team in Honolulu on the day Pearl Harbor had been bombed, vowed to follow his father's instructions. Posted to the European theater, he saw bitter fighting in Italy and France before losing his right arm. He spent nearly two years recuperating in military hospitals and returned to Hawaii a decorated hero.

Inouye would serve his country again, as a congressman—the first of Japanese descent in U.S. history—and as a senator. When his turn came at the swearing-in ceremony for new congressmen, he stepped before House Speaker Sam Rayburn. "Raise your right hand and repeat after me," said the Speaker. A hush fell over the House as the new arrival raised not his right hand but his left and repeated the oath of office.

JOHN F. KENNEDY

When 25-year-old Jack Kennedy joined the navy in 1942, he wanted the command of a torpedo boat and the chance to get in close combat with the enemy. Within a year Lieutenant Kennedy got both.

In the early hours of August 1, 1943, a Japanese destroyer off the Solomon Islands emerged out of the darkness and sliced Kennedy's torpedo boat, *PT-109*, in half. Kennedy and his 12-man crew were flung into the water, clinging to the wreckage, and drifted for more than 11 hours. They came close to a Japanese-held island before a sudden shift in current took them on to the safety of a tiny coral island the enemy had not occupied. Kennedy and another officer met two Solomon Islanders in a canoe. Kennedy handed them an SOS scratched on a coconut, and they took it to the closest U.S. torpedo boat base. Five days later, the crew of *PT-109* were rescued. For leadership and courage Kennedy received the Navy and Marine Corps Medal.

JOE LOUIS

Joe Louis was at the peak of his boxing career when he was called up for military service. The only recent defeat the Brown Bomber had suffered was to Germany's Max Schmeling. Louis had secured his revenge over the German boxer in 1938—in a fight referred to as the U.S.A. versus the Nazis—and when he entered the U.S. Army in January 1942 he thought he would get to fight the Nazis for real.

Louis, however, was too great a celebrity to be given a rifle and sent to the front. He was also a black man in an army that was segregated, and few blacks at that time were assigned to combat duty. Louis was assigned to a special-services unit and told to do what he did best—box.

During 46 months of duty, Louis put on 96 boxing exhibitions and entertained more than two million soldiers in England, Italy, and the U.S. For his "incalculable contribution to the general morale," the army gave Louis the Legion of Merit.

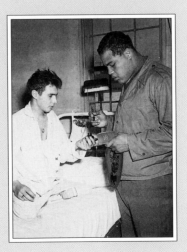

JIMMY STEWART

Before leaving for duty in Europe in the fall of 1943, Army Air Force captain Jimmy Stewart asked his father, a veteran of World War I, if he'd ever been afraid in combat. "Every man is, son," replied the elder Stewart. "But just remember you can't handle fear all by yourself. Give it to God. He'll carry it for you." Then he gave his movie star offspring a letter and told him not to open it until he was in transit.

Less than two weeks after arriving at his new post in England, Stewart was on his first bombing mission, over the port of Kiel, Germany. He would fly 20 combat missions in all during the war, for which he received an Air Medal, an Oak Leaf Cluster, and the Distinguished Flying Cross. Back safely on the ground after these hazardous flights over the Continent, Stewart would pull out his father's letter for comfort. It contained a copy of the 91st Psalm: "I will say of the Lord, He is my refuge and my fortress," it read. "His truth shall be thy shield and buckler."

U.S. STATISTICS

POPULATION

1941	133,402,000
1945	139,928,000

GROSS NATIONAL PRODUCT

1941	$124 billion
1945	$211 billion

NATIONAL DEBT

1941	$ 49 billion
1945	$258 billion

AVERAGE ANNUAL EARNINGS

1941	$1,443
1945	$2,190

TAX FILERS

1941	18 million
1945	43 million

AVERAGE RETAIL PRICES

	1941	1945
5 lb. flour	.22	.32
1 lb. bread	.08	.09
1 doz. eggs	.40	.58
1 lb. coffee	.23	.31

ON THE HOME FRONT

ACADEMY AWARD-WINNING MOVIES

1941	*How Green Was My Valley*
1942	*Mrs. Miniver*
1943	*Casablanca*
1944	*Going My Way*
1945	*The Lost Weekend*

HIT SONGS OF THE WAR

"White Christmas"

"I Left My Heart at the Stage Door Canteen"

"As Time Goes By"

"Comin' In on a Wing and a Prayer"

"I'll Be Seeing You"

"Don't Fence Me In"

WORLD SERIES WINNERS

1941	New York Yankees beat Brooklyn Dodgers
1942	St. Louis Cardinals beat New York Yankees
1943	New York Yankees beat St. Louis Cardinals
1944	St. Louis Cardinals beat St. Louis Browns
1945	Detroit Tigers beat Chicago Cubs

• Nearly 15.5 million Americans migrated to industrial centers during WWII, more than at any other time in history.

• Consumer prices rose 9 percent from 1942 through 1945.

• Agricultural production rose by 45 percent during the war, while farmers' incomes rose by 250 percent.

• Rationing became a way of life for Americans. Twenty "essential" food items such as sugar, meat, coffee, and butter were allotted through a stamp and point system. Gas rationing began in early 1942 and limited personal cars to three gallons per week.

• The labor force increased 22 percent during the war years. By 1945 more than 18 million women and more than three million teenagers joined the work force. Two million black Americans went to work in the defense industry.

• Rubber shortages were so severe that in addition to instituting scrap collecting and rationing, the government spent $700 million to build 51 synthetic-rubber factories. By 1944 production grew to 800,000 tons of rubber per year, equal to the amount from 180 million rubber trees.

• Federal scientific research and development spending increased from $74 million in 1940 to $1.6 billion in 1945.

• Victory gardens were planted all over the country, and by 1943 more than 20 million gardens produced 40 percent of all vegetables consumed on the home front.

• Federal government employees increased threefold during the war.

D-DAY: the code designation for the beginning of a military operation, just as D-1 stands for the day before the operation and D+3 stands for three days after. Although first coined in World War I, the term was used widely in World War II and is most often associated with June 6, 1944, the day of the Allied invasion of France.

GI: originally meant government issue; the clothing and equipment issued to personnel of the armed forces during the war. As the war progressed, the term came to mean an enlisted man in the army.

GISMO: probably derives from the Arabic phrase *shu ismo,* meaning "handy gadget"; first used by American soldiers in the North Africa campaign.

JEEP: the nickname for the versatile army vehicle used in WWII. The word may be a corruption of the official designation of the vehicle, GP, for "general purpose."

KAPUT: broken down, no longer functional; from the German word *kaputt,* used by American soldiers serving in Europe.

"KILROY WAS HERE": phrase spread by GIs during WWII. Kilroy represented the common soldier during the war.

"PRAISE THE LORD AND PASS THE AMMUNITION": phrase coined by a chaplain during the attack on Pearl Harbor to keep up the sailors' morale.

SNAFU: situation normal—all fouled up; used by the armed forces during WWII.

ARMED FORCES

	Army	Navy	Marines
1941	1,462,315	284,427	54,359
1945	8,267,958	3,380,817	474,680

Total Killed/Missing	292,000
Total Wounded	675,000

PRISONERS OF WAR

Held by Germany	90,000
Held by Japan	15,000

PROFILE OF U.S. SERVICE PERSONNEL

- More than 200,000 women served in the armed forces.
- More than one million black Americans were drafted into military service: approximately 700,000 in the army, 17,000 in the marines, and 100,000 in the navy.
- 39 percent of U.S. service personnel were volunteers.
- Average duration of service was 33 months.
- Average monthly base pay was $71.33 for enlisted personnel and $203.50 for officers.
- 73 percent of U.S. military personnel served overseas.

WAR PRODUCTION: July 1, 1940, to July 31, 1945

296,429	Combat aircraft
71,062	Naval ships
5,425	Cargo ships
372,431	Artillery
20,086,061	Small arms
41,585,000,000	Ammunition rounds
5,822,000	Aircraft bombs
102,351	Tanks and self-propelled guns
2,455,064	Trucks

COST OF WAR: Total federal outlay on national defense

1941	$6 billion	1945	$82 billion

NAMING OF WARSHIPS

During World War II the U.S. Navy used the following convention when naming warships: Battleships were named after states, carriers after famous early ships or battles of the Revolutionary War, cruisers after cities, destroyers after distinguished U.S. naval personnel, and submarines after types of fish.

1941	1942

MILITARY MILESTONES IN AMERICA'S WORLD WAR

The United States officially entered the Second World War two and a half years after Germany's 1939 invasion of Poland. Although America had supported the European allies politically and financially prior to its military involvement, the country—fearful of international entanglements—was reluctant to join the global conflict. The declaration of war, however, became a mere formality following Japan's attack on U.S. naval forces in Hawaii.

MARCH 1 U.S. Navy forms a convoy protection force for the Atlantic Fleet.

MAY 21 American cargo ship *Robin Moor* sunk by a U-boat in the North Atlantic.

JUNE 22 Germany invades the Soviet Union.

OCTOBER 31 USS *Reuben James* is the first American warship sunk by a U-boat; 100 sailors lost.

DECEMBER 7 Japanese attack Pearl Harbor.

DECEMBER 8 United States declares war on Japan.

DECEMBER 11 Germany and Italy declare war on the United States.

FEBRUARY 27 Battle of the Java Sea.

MARCH 11 MacArthur escapes from the Philippines.

MARCH 17 MacArthur appointed commander of the Southwest Pacific area.

APRIL 9 U.S. troops surrender in Bataan Peninsula.

MAY 7 Battle of the Coral Sea.

JUNE 4-6 Battle of Midway.

AUGUST 7 U.S. Marines land in the Solomon Islands.

NOVEMBER 8 Allied landings in North Africa.

NOVEMBER 12-15 Naval Battle of Guadalcanal.

NAVY DOG TAGS

THE POLITICS OF GLOBAL WAR

Japan's attack on Pearl Harbor changed America's position in World War II from one of helpmate to that of participant. During the United States' 45-month involvement in the war, life on the domestic front was transformed: Millions entered military service; rationing became a way of life; and American industry became the "Arsenal of Democracy." Public opinion concerning foreign policy also changed: U.S. entry into the war ended two decades of American isolationism and signaled the country's emergence as a world leader.

JANUARY 6 Roosevelt's State of the Union address outlines a global reduction in armaments.

MARCH 11 Lend-Lease Act signed into law by Roosevelt.

APRIL 13 Japan and USSR sign neutrality pact.

JULY 26 Roosevelt freezes all Japanese assets in the United States, halts oil shipments to Japan.

AUGUST 9-12 Roosevelt and Churchill agree to sign the Atlantic Charter.

NOVEMBER 6 United States extends a one-billion-dollar lend-lease credit to the USSR.

SWEETHEART PIN

PROPAGANDA POSTER

JANUARY 1 United Nations Declaration signed by China, Great Britain, the Soviet Union, the United States, and 24 other Allied nations.

JANUARY 13 War Production Board formed.

FEBRUARY 19 Executive Order 9066 signed by Roosevelt removed Japanese Americans from homes to internment camps.

ARMY OFFICER'S CAP

MAY 11 United States recaptures Attu Island in the Aleutians.

MAY 13 Axis forces capitulate in North Africa.

JULY 10 Allies land in Sicily.

SEPTEMBER 3 Allies land on Italian mainland.

SEPTEMBER 8 Surrender of Italy is announced.

DECEMBER 24 Eisenhower named Supreme Commander Allied Expeditionary Force.

FEBRUARY 22 United States invades the Marshall Islands.

JUNE 4 Allies enter Rome.

JUNE 6 Allied invasion of Normandy.

JUNE 15 United States begins strategic air offensive against Japan.

JUNE 19-20 Battle of the Philippine Sea.

JULY 19 Island of Saipan falls to U.S. forces.

AUGUST 25 Germans abandon Paris.

OCTOBER 24 Battle of Leyte Gulf begins.

DECEMBER 16 Battle of the Bulge begins.

JANUARY 9 U.S. forces land on Luzon, the Philippines.

FEBRUARY 19 U.S. forces land on Iwo Jima.

APRIL 1 U.S. forces land on Okinawa.

MAY 7 Germany surrenders.

AUGUST 6 United States drops atomic bomb on Hiroshima.

AUGUST 9 United States drops atomic bomb on Nagasaki.

AUGUST 14 Hirohito announces Japanese surrender.

AUGUST 30 U.S. occupation of Japan begins.

SEPTEMBER 2 Formal Japanese surrender takes place on USS *Missouri* in Tokyo harbor.

MACARTHUR'S CORNCOB PIPE

JANUARY 14-24 Roosevelt and Churchill meet at the Casablanca Conference.

FEBRUARY 9 Roosevelt orders 48-hour workweek in war-related industries.

MAY 27 U.S. Office of War Mobilization established in Washington, D.C.

JULY 25 Mussolini resigns and is arrested.

NOVEMBER 9 United Nations Relief and Rehabilitation Administration established in Washington, D.C.

NOVEMBER 28-DECEMBER 1 Teheran Conference takes place, attended by Roosevelt, Churchill, and Stalin.

AUGUST 21 Dumbarton Oaks Conference in Washington, D.C., attended by delegates from 39 nations to set guidelines for the formation of a United Nations organization.

SEPTEMBER 12-16 Churchill and Roosevelt meet in Quebec to discuss future Allied strategy.

NOVEMBER 7 Roosevelt wins fourth presidential term.

ROOSEVELT/TRUMAN CAMPAIGN POSTER

FEBRUARY 4-11 Roosevelt, Churchill, and Stalin meet at the Yalta Conference.

APRIL 12 Roosevelt dies; Truman sworn in as 33d U.S. president.

APRIL 25-26 Delegates from 50 nations gather in San Francisco for the inaugural meeting of the United Nations.

APRIL 28 Mussolini is killed by Italian partisans.

APRIL 30 Hitler commits suicide.

JULY 16 First atomic bomb tested in New Mexico.

JULY 17-AUGUST 2 Truman, Churchill, and Stalin meet at the Potsdam Conference.

NOVEMBER 20 War crimes trials begin in Nuremberg, Germany.

ACKNOWLEDGMENTS

The editors wish to thank the following individuals and institutions for their valuable assistance in the preparation of this volume:
Raymond Barton, Augusta, Ga.; Donald J. Blakeslee, Miami, Fla.; Terese M. Buckley, American Airpower Heritage Museum, Midland, Tex.; Joseph Dawson, Corpus Christi, Tex.; Cyndy Gilley, Woodbine, Md.; Judy Litoff, Bryant College, Smithfield, R.I.; F. Bradley Peyton III, Greenwood, Va.; Mark Renovitch, Franklin D. Roosevelt Library, Hyde Park, N.Y.; J. Robert Slaughter, Roanoke, Va.

PICTURE CREDITS

The sources for the illustrations are listed below. Credits from left to right are separated by semicolons, from top to bottom by dashes.
Cover: AP/Wide World Photos, New York.

6, 7: Map by Maryland CartoGraphics, Inc. 8: UPI/Corbis-Bettmann, New York. 10, 11: National Archives; U.S. Navy —U.S. Navy; Admiral Furlong Collection/Hawaii State Archives; National Archives. 12, 14: Courtesy Franklin D. Roosevelt Library, Hyde Park, N.Y. 16, 17: National Archives, neg. no. 080-G-71198; inset from *New York Herald Tribune Front Page History of the Second World War,* New York Tribune Inc., New York, 1946. 18: National Archives/copied by Larry Sherer. 21: Melville Jacoby. 23: AP/Wide World Photos, New York. 24: MacArthur Memorial Archive, Norfolk, Va. 25: UPI/Corbis-Bettmann, New York. 26, 27: National Archives, neg. no. 999-W & C-1145—National Archives, neg. no. 999-W & C-1144. 29: *Seattle Post Intelligencer* Collection/Museum of History and Industry, Seattle. 30: Map by Maryland CartoGraphics, Inc. 33-35: U.S. Navy. 36: Courtesy Yoshimasa Yamamoto. 37: Imperial War Museum, London. 39, 40: National Archives. 41: Dmitri Kessel for LIFE—National Archives; Oklahoma Historical Society (2). 42: National Archives. 43: AP/Wide World Photos, New York; courtesy Kathleen Krull—AP/Wide World Photos, New York; UPI/Corbis-Bettmann, New York. 44: National Archives. 45: Edmund B. Gerard; courtesy Trudy Pearson—Elizabeth Timberman for LIFE; *New York Daily News.* 46: Copied by Lee Boltin/courtesy Billy Rose Theater Collection, New York Public Library for the Performing Arts, Astor, Lenox and Tilden Foundation. 47: Library of Congress; courtesy Kathleen Krull—AP/Wide World Photos, New York; International News Photo. 48: Map by Maryland CartoGraphics, Inc. 49: National Archives—U.S. Army. 50: U.S. Army. 51: National Archives, neg. no. 111-SC-186517. 52: National Archives, neg. no. 111-SC-184386. 53: National Archives, neg. no. 999-W & C-1033—National Archives, neg. no. 111-SC-181320. 54: Imperial War Museum, London. 57: Courtesy Jane Coughran. 58, 59: AP/Wide World Photos, New York. 60: U.S. Army; Hulton Getty Picture Collection, London. 62: Map by Maryland CartoGraphics, Inc. 64: U.S. Army/courtesy Dwight D. Eisenhower Library, Abilene, Kans. 65: U.S. Army. 66: Courtesy Higgins Family and Jerry Strahan—Eisenhower Center for American Studies, New Orleans. 68: National Archives, neg. no. 999-W & C-1042. 69: R. O. Barton Jr. 72: National Archives, neg. no. 111-c-741/courtesy Salamander Books, London—D-Day Museum, Southsea, Hampshire, England. 73: UPI/Corbis-Bettmann, New York. 74, 75: U.S. Coast Guard. 76, 77: © Robert Capa/Magnum Photos, New York. 78: Courtesy J. Robert Slaughter. 80: © Robert Capa/Magnum Photos, New York. 81: From *D-Day: Operation Overlord,* foreword by Winston S. Churchill, Salamander Books, London, 1993—John Frost Historical Newspaper Service, London. 83: National Archives, neg. no. 999-W & C-1059—courtesy Jeffrey L. Ethell. 85: Courtesy American Airpower Heritage Museum, Midland, Tex. 86: Library of Congress, neg. no. F9-02-4501-050-6/photograph by Toni Frissell—National Air and Space Museum/Smithsonian Institution. 87: Dennis Wrynn Collection. 88, 89: National Air and Space Museum/Smithsonian Institution (3); courtesy Jeffrey L. Ethell; courtesy Colonel Donald J. Blakeslee. 90: Courtesy American Airpower Heritage Museum, Midland, Tex.—Philip Kaplan, Glasbury-on-Wye, Herefordshire, England. 91: U.S. Air Force. 92: Smithsonian Institution—courtesy F. Bradley Peyton III. 93: U.S. Air Force. 94: From *Round the Clock,* by Philip Kaplan, Random House, New York, 1993 —Library of Congress, neg. no. F9-02-4501-012-10/photograph by Toni Frissell. 95: U.S. Air Force. 96, 99: Patton Museum of Cavalry and Armor, Fort Knox, Ky. 100: From *Life Goes to War: A Picture History of World War II,* Little, Brown, Boston, 1977. 101: Map by Maryland CartoGraphics, Inc. 103: Suddeutscher Verlag, Munich. 104: AP/Wide World Photos, New York. 105: Imperial War Museum, London. 106: National Archives, neg. no. 111-SC-198241. 109: National Archives. 112-115: U.S. Army. 116: National Archives, neg. no. 999-W & C-1086. 117: U.S. Army. 120: UPI/Corbis-Bettmann, New York. 121: Margaret Bourke-White for LIFE. 122: National Archives. 124: National Archives, neg. no. 111-SC-223848-S. 125: National Archives, neg. no. 999-W & C-754. 127: UPI/Corbis-Bettmann, New York—from *Headline History of World War II,* St. Joseph News Press/St. Joseph Gazette, Missouri, 1945. 128: From *Extra, Extra, Read All About: Headlines of History,* by Bona Ventura and Vecchi, Stockton Trade Press, Santa Fe Springs, N.Mex., 1974; UPI/Corbis-Bettmann, New York. 129: UPI/Corbis-Bettmann, New York—U.S. Navy. 130: Courtesy Franklin D. Roosevelt Library, Hyde Park, N.Y.—British Library, London. 131: Courtesy Franklin D. Roosevelt Library, Hyde Park, N.Y. 132: From *New York Herald Tribune Front Page History of the Second World War,* New York Tribune Inc., New York, 1946—National Archives, #080-G-35190; courtesy Franklin D. Roosevelt Library, Hyde Park, N.Y. 133: Studio Sun, Ltd. 134: Courtesy Franklin D. Roosevelt Library, Hyde Park, N.Y.—International News Photos. 135: AP/Wide World Photos, New York—from *The Stars and Stripes: World War II Front Pages,* Hugh Lautner Levin Associates, New York, 1985. 136: From *Extra, Extra, Read All About: Headlines of History,* by Bona Ventura and Vecchi, Stockton Trade Press, Santa Fe Springs, N.Mex. 1974—Edward Clarke for LIFE. 137: Thomas D. McAvoy for LIFE. 138: National Archives, neg. no. 999-W & C-1221. 140: Map by Maryland CartoGraphics, Inc. 141: Defense Intelligence Agency. 142, 143: U.S. Marine Corps. 144: W. Eugene Smith for LIFE. 146: National Archives. 148: Courtesy Harry S. Truman Library, Independence, Mo. 151: UPI/Corbis-Bettmann, New York. 152: U.S. Navy/National Archives. 155: National Archives, neg. no. 127-GR-137-69889-13. 156, 157: National Archives, neg. no. 111-SC-209239. 159: Jack W. Aeby for LIFE—UPI/Corbis-Bettmann, New York. 162, 163: U.S. Air Force. 165: National Archives. 167: *Boston Globe.* 168, 169: U.S. Army. 170: Press Association/Topham Picture Source, Edenbridge, Kent, England. 171: Public Library of the District of Columbia, Washingtoniana Collection—National Archives. 172: National Archives. 173: From *Life Goes to War: A Picture History of World War II,* Little, Brown, Boston, 1977. 174: National Archives. 175: National Archives; *Honolulu Star Bulletin.* 176, 177: National Archives, neg. no. 80-G-495604. 178: National Archives. 180: Courtesy Bush Presidential Library; Kobal Collection—National Baseball Library and Archive, Cooperstown, N.Y. 181: John F. Kennedy Library, no. PC101; National Archives—courtesy Senator Daniel K. Inouye; U.S. Army. 184: Courtesy Ellen Pattisall/photographed by Mike Pattisall —Courtesy Mike Pattisall; Library of Congress. 185: Courtesy Jane Coughran/photographed by Jeff Watts; courtesy MacArthur Memorial Archive, Norfolk, Va.—courtesy Franklin D. Roosevelt Library, Hyde Park, N.Y.

BOOKS

Aaseng, Nathan. *Navajo Code Talkers*. New York: Walker, 1992.

Alexander, Joseph H. *Closing In: Marines in the Seizure of Iwo Jima* (Marines in World War II commemorative series). Washington, D.C.: Marine Corps Historical Center, 1994.

Allen, Thomas B., and Norman Polmar. *Code-Name Downfall: The Secret Plan to Invade Japan and Why Truman Dropped the Bomb*. New York: Simon & Schuster, 1995.

Ambrose, Stephen E. :
Eisenhower: Soldier, General of the Army, President-Elect, 1890-1952. New York: Simon & Schuster, 1983.
The Supreme Commander: The War Years of General Dwight D. Eisenhower. Garden City, N.Y.: Doubleday, 1970.

Argyle, Christopher. *Chronology of World War II*. New York: Exeter Books, 1980.

Armor, John, and Peter Wright. *Manzanar*. New York: Times Books, 1988.

Astor, Gerald. *June 6, 1944: The Voices of D-Day*. New York: St. Martin's Press, 1994.

Ayers, Eben A. *Truman in the White House: The Diary of Eben A. Ayers*. Edited by Robert H. Ferrell. Columbia: University of Missouri Press, 1991.

Badsey, Stephen. *D-Day: From Normandy Beaches to the Liberation of France*. Godalming, England: Colour Library Books, 1993.

Balkoski, Joseph. *Beyond the Beachhead: The 29th Infantry Division in Normandy*. New York: Dell, 1989.

Bartley, Whitman S. *Iwo Jima: Amphibious Epic*. Washington, D.C.: U.S. Marine Corps, 1954.

The Battle of Midway: 4-6 June 1942. Missoula, Mont.: Pictorial Histories, 1990.

Blair, Joan, and Clay Blair Jr. *The Search for JFK*. New York: G. P. Putnam's Sons, 1976.

Blassingame, Wyatt. *Combat Nurses of World War II*. New York: Random House, 1967.

Bliss, Edward, Jr. (ed.). *In Search of Light: The Broadcasts of Edward R. Murrow, 1938-1961*. New York: Alfred A. Knopf, 1967.

Bradley, Omar N. *A Soldier's Story* (The Great Commanders series). New York: Henry Holt, 1994.

Brinkley, David. *Washington Goes to War*. New York: Alfred A. Knopf, 1988.

Buell, Thomas B. *The Quiet Warrior: A Biography of Admiral Raymond A. Spruance*. Boston: Little, Brown, 1974.

Burns, James MacGregor. *Roosevelt: The Soldier of Freedom*. New York: Harcourt Brace Jovanovich, 1970.

Butcher, Harry C. *My Three Years with Eisenhower*. New York: Simon & Schuster, 1946

Callahan, Sean (ed.). *The Photographs of Margaret Bourke-White*. New York: New York Graphic Society, 1972.

Casdorph, Paul D. *Let the Good Times Roll: Life at Home in*

BIBLIOGRAPHY

America during World War II. New York: Paragon House, 1989.

Chadakoff, Rochelle (ed.). *Eleanor Roosevelt's My Day: Her Acclaimed Columns, 1936-1945*. New York: Pharos Books, 1989.

Coffey, Frank. *Always Home: 50 Years of the USO*. McLean, Va.: Brassey's (US), 1991.

Cole, Hugh M. *The Ardennes: Battle of the Bulge* (United States Army in World War II series). Washington, D.C.: Office of the Chief of Military History, United States Army, 1965.

Collins, James L. (ed.). *The Marshall Cavendish Illustrated Encyclopedia of World War II* (Vols. 6 and 8). New York: Orbis, 1972.

Conrat, Maisie, and Richard Conrat. *Executive Order 9066: The Internment of 110,000 Japanese Americans*. Los Angeles: California Historical Society, 1972.

Cooper, Page. *Navy Nurse*. New York: McGraw-Hill, 1946.

Craven, Wesley Frank, and James Lea Cate (eds.). *Europe: Argument to V-E Day* (Vol. 3 of *The Army Air Forces in World War II*). Washington, D.C.: Office of Air Force History, 1983.

Cross, Robin. *VE Day: Victory in Europe, 1945*. London: Sidgwick & Jackson, 1985.

D-Day: Operation Overlord, From Its Planning to the Liberation of Paris. New York: Salamander Books, 1993.

Dear, I. C. B. (ed.). *The Oxford Companion to World War II*. New York: Oxford University Press, 1995.

Descent into Nightmare (The Third Reich series). Alexandria, Va.: Time-Life Books, 1992.

D'Este, Carlo. *Patton: A Genius for War*. New York: HarperCollins, 1995.

Dolan, Edward F. *America in World War II: 1943*. Brookfield, Conn.: The Millbrook Press, 1992.

Drez, Ronald J. (ed.). *Voices of D-Day: The Story of the Allied Invasion, Told by Those Who Were There*. Baton Rouge: Louisiana State University Press, 1994.

Durson, Joseph. *DiMaggio: The Last American Knight*. Boston: Little, Brown, 1995.

Eisenhower, Dwight D. *Crusade in Europe*. New York: Doubleday, 1948.

Eisenhower, John S. D. *The Bitter Woods*. New York: G. P. Putnam's Sons, 1969.

Essame, H. *Patton: A Study in Command*. New York: Charles Scribner's Sons, 1974.

Farago, Ladislas. *The Last Days of Patton*. New York: McGraw-Hill, 1981.

Ferrell, Robert H.:
Harry S. Truman : A Life. Columbia: University of Missouri

Press, 1994.
Truman: A Centenary Remembrance. New York: Viking Press, 1984.

Ferrell, Robert H. (ed.). *Off the Record: The Private Papers of Harry S. Truman*. New York: Harper & Row, 1980.

Forrestel, E. P. *Admiral Raymond A. Spruance, USN*. Washington, D.C.: U.S. Government Printing Office, 1966.

Freeman, Roger A.:
The Mighty Eighth: Units, Men and Machines. Garden City, N.Y.: Doubleday, 1970.
Mustang at War. Garden City, N.Y.: Doubleday, 1974.

Freidel, Frank. *Franklin D. Roosevelt: A Rendezvous with Destiny*. Boston: Little, Brown, 1990.

Gelb, Norman. *Desperate Venture: The Story of Operation Torch, the Allied Invasion of North Africa*. New York, William Morrow, 1992.

Goldstein, Donald M., Katherine V. Dillon, and J. Michael Wenger. *Nuts! The Battle of the Bulge*. Washington, D.C.: Brassey's, 1994.

Goodwin, Doris Kearns. *No Ordinary Time, Franklin and Eleanor Roosevelt: The Home Front in World War II*. New York: Simon & Schuster, 1994.

Green, Fitzhugh. *George Bush: An Intimate Portrait*. New York: Hippocrene Books, 1989.

Hastings, Max. *Overlord: D-Day and the Battle for Normandy*. New York: Simon & Schuster, 1985.

Hatch, Alden. *George Patton: General in Spurs*. New York: Julian Messner (Pocket Books), 1965.

Hemingway, Albert. *Ira Hayes: Pima Marine*. Lanham, Md.: University Press of America, 1988.

Historical Statistics of the United States: Colonial Times to 1970. (Vols. 1 and 2). Washington D.C.: U.S. Department of Commerce, U.S. Bureau of the Census, 1975.

Hodgson, Godfrey. *The Colonel: The Life and Wars of Henry Stimson, 1867-1950*. New York: Alfred A. Knopf, 1990.

Hoopes, Roy:
Americans Remember the Home Front. New York: Hawthorn Books, 1977.
When the Stars Went to War: Hollywood and World War II. New York: Random House, 1994.

Hoyle, Martha Byrd. *A World in Flames: A History of World War II*. New York: Atheneum, 1970.

Hoyt, Edwin P. *The GI's War: The Story of American Soldiers in Europe in World War II*. New York: McGraw-Hill, 1991.

Illustrated Story of World War II. Pleasantville, N.Y.: Reader's Digest, 1969.

Inouye, Daniel K. *Go for Broke*. Englewood Cliffs, N.J.: Prentice-Hall, 1967.

Irving, David. *The War between the Generals*. New York: Congdon & Lattès, 1981.

Jablonski, Edward, and the Editors of Time-Life Books.

America in the Air War (The Epic of Flight series). Alexandria, Va.: Time-Life Books, 1982.

James, D. Clayton. *The Years of MacArthur: 1941-1945* (Vol. 2). Boston: Houghton Mifflin, 1975.

Jeansonne, Glen. *Transformation and Reaction: America 1921-1945*. New York: HarperCollins, 1994.

Kaplan, Philip, and Jack Currie. *Round the Clock: The Experience of the Allied Bomber Crews Who Flew by Day and by Night from England in the Second World War*. New York: Random House, 1993.

Kawano, Kenji. *Warriors: Navajo Code Talkers*. Flagstaff, Ariz.: Northland, 1990.

Keegan, John:
The Second World War. New York: Penguin Books, 1989.
Six Armies in Normandy. New York: Viking Press, 1982.

Krull, Kathleen. *V Is for Victory: America Remembers World War II*. New York: Alfred A. Knopf, 1995.

Kurzman, Dan. *Day of the Bomb: Countdown to Hiroshima*. New York: McGraw-Hill, 1986.

Lash, Joseph P. *Eleanor and Franklin*. New York: W. W. Norton, 1971.

Leuchtenburg, William E., and the Editors of *Life*. *New Deal and Global War* (The *Life* History of the United States series). New York: Time, 1964.

Life Goes to War: A Picture History of World War II. Boston: Little, Brown, 1977.

Litoff, Judy Barrett, and David C. Smith (eds.). *Since You Went Away: World War II Letters from American Women on the Home Front*. New York: Oxford University Press, 1991.

Lord, Walter. *Incredible Victory*. New York: HarperPerennial, 1993.

MacArthur, Douglas. *Reminiscences*. New York: McGraw-Hill, 1964.

McClain, S. *Navajo Weapon*. Boulder: Books Beyond Borders, 1994.

McCullough, David. *Truman*. New York: Simon & Schuster, 1992.

Macdonald, Charles B. *A Time for Trumpets: The Untold Story of the Battle of the Bulge*. New York: Bantam Books, 1984.

Macdonald, John. *Great Battles of World War II*. New York: Macmillan, 1986.

Maddox, Robert James. *Weapons for Victory: The Hiroshima Decision Fifty Years Later*. Columbia: University of Missouri Press, 1995.

Manchester, William. *American Caesar: Douglas MacArthur, 1880-1964*. Boston: Little, Brown, 1978.

Marling, Karal Ann, and John Wetenhall. *Iwo Jima: Monuments, Memories, and the American Hero*. Cambridge: Harvard University Press, 1991.

Mead, Chris. *Champion Joe Louis: Black Hero in White America*. New York: Charles Scribner's Sons, 1985.

Miller, Merle. *Plain Speaking: An Oral Biography of Harry S. Truman*. New York, G. P. Putnam's Sons, 1974.

Miller, Nathan. *FDR: An Intimate History*. Garden City, N.Y.: Doubleday, 1983.

Miller, Russell. *Nothing Less Than Victory*. New York: William Morrow, 1993.

Moeller, Susan D. *Shooting War: Photography and the American Experience of Combat*. New York: Basic Books, 1989.

Morehouse, Clifford P. *The Iwo Jima Operation*. Washington, D.C.: U.S. Marine Corps, 1946.

Morison, Samuel Eliot. *The Invasion of France and Germany: 1944-1945* (Vol. 11 of History of United States Naval Operations in World War II). Boston: Little, Brown, 1957.

Mulvey, Deb (ed.). *We Pulled Together . . . and Won!* Greendale, Wis.: Reminisce Books, 1993.

Natkiel, Richard. *Atlas of World War II*. Greenwich, Conn.: Bison Books, 1985.

Newcomb, Ellsworth. *Brave Nurse: True Stories of Heroism*. New York: D. Appleton-Century, 1945.

Newcomb, Richard F. *Iwo Jima*. New York: Bantam Books, 1965.

Omaha Beachhead: 6 June-13 June 1944 (American Forces in Action series). Washington, D.C.: Center of Military History, United States Army, 1984.

O'Neill, Brian D. *Half a Wing, Three Engines, and a Prayer: B-17s over Germany*. Blue Ridge Summit, Pa.: Tab Books, 1989.

Patton, George S. *War As I Knew It*. Boston: Houghton Mifflin, 1975.

Paul, Doris A. *The Navajo Code Talkers*. Philadelphia: Dorrance, 1973.

Perret, Geoffrey. *Old Soldiers Never Die: The Life of Douglas MacArthur*. New York: Random House, 1996.

Perseverance (African Americans Voices of Triumph series). Alexandria, Va.: Time-Life Books, 1993.

Persico, Joseph E. *Edward R. Murrow: An American Original*. New York: McGraw-Hill, 1988.

Phillips, Cabell. *The 1940s: Decade of Triumph and Trouble* (The New York Times Chronicle of American Life). New York: Macmillan, 1975.

Potter, Lou, William Miles, and Nina Rosenblum. *Liberators: Fighting on Two Fronts in World War II*. New York: Harcourt Brace Jovanovich, 1992.

Prange, Gordon W.:
At Dawn We Slept: The Untold Story of Pearl Harbor. New York: McGraw-Hill, 1981.
Miracle at Midway. New York: McGraw-Hill, 1982.

Rhodes, Richard. *The Making of the Atomic Bomb*. New York: Touchstone (Simon & Schuster), 1988.

Ross, Bill D. *Iwo Jima: Legacy of Valor*. New York: Vanguard Press, 1985.

Rummel, Jack. *Robert Oppenheimer: Dark Prince* (Makers of Modern Science series). New York: Facts On File, 1992.

Ryan, Cornelius. *The Longest Day: June 6, 1944*. New York: Simon & Schuster, 1959.

Schaller, Michael. *Douglas MacArthur: The Far Eastern General*. New York: Oxford University Press, 1989.

Shadow of the Dictators: TimeFrame AD 1925-1950. Alexandria, Va.: Time-Life Books, 1989.

Sherrod, Robert. *On to Westward: War in the Central Pacific*. New York: Duell, Sloan and Pearce, 1945.

Skarmeas, Nancy J. *Victory*. Nashville: Ideals Publications, 1995.

Skates, John Ray. *The Invasion of Japan: Alternative to the Bomb*. Columbia: University of South Carolina Press, 1994.

Slaughter, J. Robert. *Wartime Memories of J. Robert Slaughter and Selected Men of the 116th Infantry, 29th Division 1941-1945*. In press.

Smith, William Ward. *Midway: Turning Point of the Pacific*. New York: Thomas Y. Crowell, 1966.

Stein, R. Conrad. *World at War: The Home Front*. Chicago: Childrens Press, 1986.

Strawson, John. *The Italian Campaign*. New York: Carroll & Graf, 1988.

Sulzberger, C. L. *World War II*. New York: American Heritage, 1966.

Szasz, Ferenc Morton. *The Day the Sun Rose Twice: The Story of the Trinity Site Nuclear Explosion, July 16, 1945*. Albuquerque: University of New Mexico Press, 1984.

Tapert, Annette. *Lines of Battle*. New York: Times Books (Random House), 1987.

Tateishi, John. *And Justice for All: An Oral History of the Japanese American Detention Camps*. New York: Random House, 1984.

Taylor, Barbara Wooddall. *Miss You: The World War II Letters of Barbara Wooddall Taylor and Charles E. Taylor*. Athens: University of Georgia Press, 1990.

Terkel, Studs. *"The Good War": An Oral History of World War II*. New York: Pantheon Books, 1984.

This Fabulous Century. New York: Time-Life Books, 1969.

Thomas, Gordon, and Max Morgan Witts. *Ruin from the Air: The Enola Gay's Atomic Mission to Hiroshima*. Chelsea, Mich.: Scarborough House, 1990.

Tibbets, Paul W., Jr. *The Tibbets Story*. New York: Stein and Day, 1978.

Toland, John. *The Rising Sun: The Decline and Fall of the Japanese Empire, 1936-1945*. New York: Bantam Books (Random House), 1970.

Truman, Margaret:
Bess W. Truman. New York: MacMillan, 1986.
Harry S. Truman. New York: William Morrow, 1973.

Voss, Frederick S. *Reporting the War: The Journalistic Coverage of World War II*. Washington, D.C.: Smithsonian Institution Press, 1994.

The War against Germany: Europe and Adjacent Areas (United

States Army in World War II series). Washington, D.C.: Office of the Chief of Military History, United States Army, 1951.

The War against Germany and Italy: Mediterranean and Adjacent Areas (United States States Army in World War II series). Washington, D.C.: Office of the Chief of Military History, United States Army, 1951.

Weigley, Russell F. *Eisenhower's Lieutenants: The Campaign of France and Germany, 1944-1945*. Bloomington: Indiana University Press, 1981.

Weintraub, Stanley. *The Last Great Victory: The End of World War II, July/August 1945*. New York: Turman Talley Books (Dutton), 1995.

Wentworth, Harold, and Stuart Berg Flexner (comps. and eds.). *Dictionary of American Slang*. New York: Thomas Y. Crowell, 1975.

Wheeler, Richard. *Iwo*. Annapolis, Md.: Naval Institute Press, 1980.

Whelan, James R. *Hunters in the Sky: Fighter Aces of WWII*. Washington, D.C.: Regnery Gateway, 1991.

Whittemore, Katharine (ed.). *The World War Two Era* (The American Retrospective series). New York: Franklin Square Press, 1994.

Willmott, H. P. *June 1944*. Dorset, England: Blandford Press, 1984.

Wilmot, Chester. *The Struggle for Europe*. New York: Harper & Brothers, 1952.

Wise, Nancy Baker, and Christy Wise. *A Mouthful of Rivets: Women at Work in World War II*. San Francisco: Jossey-Bass, 1994.

The World at Arms: The Reader's Digest Illustrated History of World War II. London: Reader's Digest, 1989.

World War II (39 vols.). Alexandria, Va.: Time-Life Books, 1976-1983.

Yarrington, Gary A. (ed.). *World War II: Personal Accounts, Pearl Harbor to V-J Day*. Austin, Tex.: Lyndon Baines Johnson Foundation, 1992.

Young, Peter. *The World Almanac of World War II*. New York: Bison Books, 1981.

PERIODICALS

Alexander, Joseph H.:
"The Americans Will Surely Come." *Naval History,* January/February 1995.
"Combat Leadership at Iwo Jima." *Marine Corps Gazette,* February 1995.

Bradley, Henry D. "Headline History of World War II." *St. Joseph News-Press and Gazette,* December 1, 1945.

"D-Day: Eyewitness to the Invasion." *Newsweek,* May 23, 1994.

Fort, Cornelia. "At the Twilight's Last Gleaming." *Woman's Home Companion,* July 1943.

Mydans, Shelley. "Flight Nurse." *Life,* February 12, 1945.

"Pearl Harbor: December 7, 1941-December 7, 1991." *Life,* Fall 1991.

Phinney, Susan. "Seattle Woman's Saga Captured in Photo." *Seattle Post-Intelligencer,* September 20, 1994.

"Prisoners of Japan." *Life,* February 7, 1944.

Rosenthal, Joe, and W. C. Heinz. "The Picture That Will Live Forever." *Collier's,* February 18, 1955.

OTHER SOURCES

"A Brief History of the U.S. Army in World War II." Pamphlet. Washington, D.C.: Center of Military History, United States Army, 1992.

Cirillo, Roger. "Ardennes-Alsace: 16 December 1944-25 January 1945." The U.S. Army Campaigns of World War II. Brochure. Washington, D.C.: U.S. Army Center of Military History.

Dillahunty, Albert. "Shiloh: National Military Park, Tennessee." Handbook. Washington, D.C.: National Park Service, 1955.

Hammond, William M. "Normandy." The U.S. Army Campaigns of World War II. Brochure. Washington, D.C.: U.S. Army Center of Military History.

Nalty, Bernard C. "The United States Marines on Iwo Jima: The Battle and the Flag Raising." Pamphlet. Washington, D.C.: U.S. Marine Corps, 1962.

INDEX

TIME LIFE® BOOKS   Time-Life Books is a
division of Time Life Inc.

TIME LIFE INC.

PRESIDENT and CEO: George Artandi

TIME-LIFE BOOKS

PRESIDENT: John D. Hall
PUBLISHER/MANAGING EDITOR: Neil Kagan

THE AMERICAN STORY

WORLD WAR II

EDITOR: Sarah Brash
DIRECTOR, NEW PRODUCT DEVELOPMENT:
Curtis Kopf
MARKETING DIRECTOR: Pamela R. Farrell

Deputy Editor: Mary Grace Mayberry
Text Editors: Robin Currie (principal), Denise Dersin,
James Lynch
Design Director: Dale Pollekoff
Art Director: Ellen L. Pattisall
Associate Editors/Research and Writing: Robert Speziale,
Jarelle Stein
Copyeditor: Judith Klein
Picture Coordinator: Catherine Parrott
Editorial Assistant: Patricia D. Whiteford

Special Contributors: Ronald H. Bailey, Maggie Debelius,
Thomas A. Lewis, John K. Newton, John Sullivan (text);
Roberta Conlan (editing); Steve Hirsch, Katya Sharpe,
Mary Davis Suro, Marilyn Murphy Terrell, Elizabeth
Thompson, Robert Wooldridge Jr. (research and writing);
Magdalena Anders, Megan Barnett, Patti Cass, Jane
Coughran, Stacy W. Hoffhaus, Barbara L. Klein
(research); Jennifer Rushing-Schurr (index).

Correspondents: Christine Hinze (London), Christina
Lieberman (New York), Maria Vincenza Aloisi (Paris).
Valuable assistance was also provided by Dick Berry
(Tokyo), Angelika Lemmer (Wachtberg), Carolyn L.
Sackett (Seattle).

Vice President, Director of Finance: Christopher Hearing
Vice President, Book Production: Marjann Caldwell
Director of Operations: Eileen Bradley
Director of Photography and Research: John Conrad Weiser
Director of Editorial Administration (Acting): Barbara Levitt
Production Manager: Marlene Zack
Quality Assurance Manager: James King
Library: Louise D. Forstall

The Consultants
Colonel Joseph Hammond Alexander (Ret.) served more
than 28 years in the United States Marine Corps. He
acted as chief of staff of the 3d Marine Division, completed two combat tours in Vietnam, and directed the
Marine Corps Development Center. Colonel Alexander is
the author of *Utmost Savagery: Three Days of Tarawa, Storm
Landings: Forcible Amphibious Epics of the Central Pacific,*
and three World War II 50th anniversary commemorative
histories. He is a consultant and on-screen authority for
the History Channel and for Arts and Entertainment's
Biography series. Colonel Alexander is a life member of
the U.S. Naval Institute, the Marine Corps Historical
Foundation, and the Society for Military History.

Lieutenant Colonel Roger Cirillo (Ret.) served in United
States Army armored cavalry units in the United States,
Korea, and Germany, as a staff officer in infantry and
armored brigades, as special assistant to the commander
in chief in Europe, and as a war plans officer in NATO's
Central Army Group. He was recalled to active duty in
1992 to advise on World War II combat operations for the
50th anniversary commemorations. Lieutenant Colonel
Cirillo is the author of books and articles on military
strategy and history, including *The Ardennes-Alsace Campaign,* and is a coauthor of *March to Victory.* He also contributed to *D-Day: Operation Overlord.*

© 1997 Time Life Inc. All rights reserved. No part of
this book may be reproduced in any form or by any
electronic or mechanical means, including information
storage and retrieval devices or systems, without prior
written permission from the publisher, except that brief
passages may be quoted for reviews.

First printing. Printed in U.S.A.
School and library distribution by Time-Life Education,
P.O. Box 85026, Richmond, Virginia 23285-5026.

TIME-LIFE is a trademark of Time Warner Inc. U.S.A.

Library of Congress Cataloging-in-Publication Data
World War II / by the editors of Time-Life Books.
    p.   cm.—(American story)
    Includes bibliographical references and index.
    ISBN 0-7835-6253-5
    1. World War, 1939-1945—United States. 2. United
States—History—1939-1945. I. Time-Life Books. II. Series.
D769.W67 1997
940.53'73—dc20   96-43987
                                                         CIP

For information on and a full description of any
of the Time-Life Books series listed above, please
call 1-800-621-7026 or write:

Reader Information
Time-Life Customer Service
P.O. Box C-32068
Richmond, Virginia 23261-2068

On the cover: U.S. soldiers prepare to wade ashore
from a landing barge on a beach west of Oran,
Algeria, on November 26, 1942. Code-named Operation *Torch,* the amphibious invasion of German-
occupied North Africa was the first major Allied
operation of the war.